JOHN KNOX:
PORTRAIT OF A CALVINIST

JOHN KNOX
From a posthumous portrait in Beza's 'Icones,' 1580.

EDWIN MUIR

JOHN KNOX:
PORTRAIT OF A CALVINIST

With four illustrations

BOOKS FOR LIBRARIES PRESS
FREEPORT, NEW YORK

First Published 1929
Reprinted 1971

INTERNATIONAL STANDARD BOOK NUMBER:
0-8369-5656-7

LIBRARY OF CONGRESS CATALOG CARD NUMBER:
76-148892

PRINTED IN THE UNITED STATES OF AMERICA

TO
HUGH M'DIARMID
IN ADMIRATION

Orthodox! orthodox, wha believe in John Knox,
Let me sound an alarm to your conscience.

BURNS

CONTENTS

ILLUSTRATIONS

PREFACE

For this biography I have gone chiefly to the writings of Knox himself, and to the usual contemporary records. The Reverend Dr. M'Crie's and Professor Hume Brown's Lives have also been of help, but my particular gratitude is due to Andrew Lang's *John Knox and the Reformation*, the one biography I have found which attempts to be critical.

My reading of Knox's life disagrees with that of most of his other biographers since M'Crie. It is on the whole supported, however, by the eighteenth century estimate represented by David Hume and Burns. If I show bias it is not, at any rate, theological bias.

The object of this book is somewhat different from that of the biographies which I have mentioned: it is to give a critical account of a representative Calvinist and Puritan. The temper in which I have attempted this may perhaps best be described as realistic; I assume, for example, that terms such as predestination and election do not actually describe for the present age the change which took place in Knox's life, and I assume equally that his firm conviction of his prophetic powers was a delusion. In other words I have attempted to tell in contemporary terms how a typical Calvinist and Puritan lived, felt and thought,

and thus to convey as vivid a notion as possible of
two things which have deeply influenced our ancestry
and ourselves. With the historical figure I am not
particularly concerned, and I have filled in only such
a rough sketch of the sixteenth century Scottish background as I thought necessary to make the Calvinist
comprehensible.

CHAPTER I

THE RIDDLE

THE life of Knox is broken in two. For the first forty years we can vaguely discern a devout Catholic; for the next twenty-seven we see another character, with the same name, the same appearance, and probably the same affections and passions, but with entirely different opinions. This new figure is born at the age of forty, and seems to have no ancestry. For Knox left no record either of his early life or of his conversion: the one is like an absolute event which had existed from eternity, the other is as if it had never been.

History, however, has discovered that Knox was a Roman Catholic priest, and that he remained one long after the new truths were widely disseminated in Scotland. When the future reformer was twenty-two, young Patrick Hamilton had begun the preaching campaign which was to conduct him presently to the stake. Twelve years later five more Protestants were burned, nine recanted, and a great number were sent into exile. Next year the Reformation had reached the recognized stage of image-breaking, and three years afterwards the Protestants were so powerful that the Government did not know what to do with them. Yet strangely enough, amid all the national quickening,

Knox still continued to live the life of an obscure Catholic priest. Had the hour of election appointed by God not yet struck? Or was the priest as obstinate as the reformer was to be?

At any rate all that the first forty years of the reformer's life disclose are a few conflicting dates and facts. He was born, most authorities agree, in 1505, and in or near the town of Haddington. His father, William Knox, was probably a small farmer. His mother seems to have died some time after his birth, and his father to have married again.

Haddington, where he received his schooling, was one of the strongest centres of Catholicism in Scotland. From there he presently went to Glasgow, a town equally Catholic, to study divinity at the University. Next he seems to have proceeded to St. Andrews, and finally, perhaps about 1531-2, he entered the Roman Church as a priest. Between 1540 and 1543 we find him engaged as an ecclesiastical notary, and up to March of 1543 he was certainly in the Catholic Church. Of the life he led during this time his fellow reformers tell us not a word, but the Catholics maintain that it was notorious for its immorality, and even assert that he was guilty of committing adultery with his step-mother. Such is the early Knox as history and scandal disclose him. When we next hear of him he is a reformer.

The youth and early manhood of Knox, then, present a blank from which it is hard to deduce the figure who later emerged. But a hint here and there faintly prefigures him. In Haddington he would see enough of the Roman priesthood to impress and to shock. Then at Glasgow and St. Andrews he sat for some time under John Major. Major was an old-fashioned Catholic theologian who was tireless in his denunciation of the lives of the clergy, and held the surprising view that the people might legitimately depose a bad prince. Knox was deeply impressed by those opinions, but something else impressed him even more. He has told us what passage in the Scriptures led him to embrace the new faith; it was the seventeenth chapter of the Gospel of St. John.

This chapter contains the last prayer of Jesus with His disciples before His betrayal: 'I have manifested Thy name unto the men which Thou gavest me out of the world; Thine they were, and Thou gavest them Me; and they have kept Thy Word. . . . I pray for them; I pray not for the world, but for them which Thou hast given Me; for they are Thine. And all Mine are Thine, and Thine are Mine; and I am glorified in them. . . . Neither pray I for these alone, but for them also which shall believe on Me through Thy Word; that they all may be one; as Thou, Father, art in Me, and I in Thee, that they may also be one in us.'

This chapter is of crucial importance for the understanding of Knox. It led logically to Calvinism. In the most absolute terms it stated the doctrines of election, of special grace, and of assured salvation. It welded the invisible Church into a firm and everlasting body; it welded that Church to Christ and through Christ to God; and it welded Knox, at the moment

when he made his decision, indissolubly and forever
to that mystical corporation. At the same time it
separated the elect from all the rest of the world. 'I
pray not for the world,' Christ was made to say, 'but
for them which Thou hast given Me.' Thus mankind
were divided into two hosts: the elect and the reprobate. In a moment of illumination, in a confused
ecstasy of awe, terror, relief and self-gratulation such
as it is almost impossible to imagine now, Knox recognized that he had received the incredible assurance.
Awe at his election would predominate at first, but
as time went on and he grew familiar with his fate,
other emotions would inevitably tend to rise up. Very
soon they did rise up.

Knox was now a member of the elect, but he did not
yet know how a member of the elect comported himself: he had not yet met a genuine reformer. He was to
do so presently. With all the prestige of a sojourn in
Germany young George Wishart returned to his
native country and began to spread the Lutheran
faith. He had great successes at first, in Dundee and
Ayr; and at the end of 1545 he came to Leith: his objective was Edinburgh itself. Knox was at the time
humbly tutoring the sons of Douglas of Langniddry
and Cockburn of Ormiston in the neighbourhood.
He went to hear the famous reformer, so much
younger and so much more brilliant than himself; he
found a tall man with a long black beard, whose
eloquence seemed to echo the mystical thunders of
the Hebrew prophets. A legend had gathered round
Wishart. He loved, it was said, to sleep between

coarse canvas sheets; he fasted, denied himself the simplest superfluities, and was extravagantly lavish in his charity to the poor. Not long before, while he was preaching in Dundee during the plague, a Catholic priest had tried to assassinate him, and ever since then a long two-handed sword had been carried before him wherever he went by one of his disciples. He had been at Cambridge; he had travelled in France and Germany and had spoken face to face with the great continental figures on the Protestant side; he belonged to a good family, and he was young. Knox put himself entirely at the service of this brilliant figure, and presently, as a supreme token of favour, was entrusted with the sword.

In the few weeks that they were to be together Knox, as his later writings show, studied religiously the demeanour of his master. He noted that Wishart had the power of prophecy. Did that power belong of right, perhaps, to every true servant of the Almighty? Might he not even possess it himself, although it had not yet manifested itself? Wishart had foretold his own death, and it came true! Prophecy, then, was obviously one of the gifts of a Protestant. He observed next that Wishart knew Greek; he, too, would learn Greek.

Wishart had come to Midlothian relying on the protection of a few lairds in the neighbourhood, and on an armed body of Protestants who had promised to come in from the West. They did not arrive, and Cardinal Beaton, the powerful prelate, was awaiting an opportunity to secure him. The Midlothian lairds

were in the pay of the English Government, and
one of them had taken a leading part in a plot
against Beaton's life. Their protection, therefore,
was worse than none, but now Wishart could not
turn back. A few weeks after his first meeting with
Knox, he preached at Haddington. His first sermon
drew a large audience. He preached again, but
influences had been at work, and the attendance
was small: he decided to preach a third time. But by
now it was clear that he could not escape much longer,
and in his agitation he walked for an hour and a half
up and down before he could muster courage to
ascend the pulpit. His worst fears were justified, the
audience was smaller than ever. The great hopes with
which he had come to Scotland, the successes he had
won at first, in Dundee and Ayr, the helplessness of his
present position, the power of the Cardinal: all rushed
into his mind, and he burst into an extraordinary
prophecy which was to be a model for so many of his
successors during the next hundred years: 'O Lord,
how long shall it be that Thy holy Word shall be
despised, and men shall not regard their own salvation?
Sore and painful, Haddington, shall the plagues be
that shall ensue, because of this thy contempt. Yea,
thou Haddington in special, strangers shall possess
thee, and you, the present inhabitants, shall either in
bondage serve your enemies or else ye shall be chased
from your own habitations; and that because ye have
not known, nor will not now know the time of God's
merciful visitation.' He gave a short sermon on the
second commandment and shook the dust of

Haddington from his feet. 'In such vehemency and threatening,' wrote Knox, still in his capacity as diligent learner, 'continued that servant of God, near an hour and a half; in the which he declared all the plagues that ensued, as plainly as after our eyes saw them performed.'

Late that afternoon Wishart said good-bye to his disciple, and the sword was given back. Knox begged to be allowed to stay. 'No, no,' replied Wishart, 'return to your bairns, and God bless you. One is enough for a sacrifice.' Darkness was falling and the countryside lay under a heavy frost when Knox went back in dejection to Langniddry. Next night Wishart was seized, and a little over a month later his dead, strangled body was burned in front of the Castle of St. Andrews before the eyes of Beaton.

Such was the figure whom Knox met at the beginning of his long reforming career. Coming when he did, Wishart probably completed what the seventeenth chapter of St. John had begun. Of no other man, at any rate, did Knox ever speak again with greater affection and reverence. Wishart, he said many years later, was 'a man of such graces as before him were never heard within this realm, yea, and are rare to be found yet in any man, notwithstanding this great light of God that since his days has shined unto us.' From now on accordingly Knox is distinguished by his championship of the poor, his prophesying of plagues on such as would not listen to him, his claim to a special revelation, his aspirations, never quite realized, to learn Greek, the severity of his demeanour, and the increasing length of his beard. The temper of his prophecies, it is true, came to be all his own, and he never imitated his master in the matter of asceticism; but from St. John and Wishart he emerged complete and set, as if newly cleared for action against the Roman Catholic Church.

CHAPTER II

ST. ANDREWS AND THE GALLEYS

THREE months after Wishart's death Cardinal
Beaton was murdered in the Castle of St. Andrews by
a party of Fifeshire Protestants. Having shown the
Cardinal's dead body from a window, they prepared to
hold the Castle.

Vengeance had been done and Knox was exultant.
It was a 'godly act' he was to hold still, when twenty
years afterwards he was transcribing his witty account
of Beaton's last hours. But for the moment he had to
think of himself; the murder had roused the Catholics,
and Archbishop Hamilton, Beaton's successor, was on
the new reformer's heels. Knox, moving about from
house to house, lived in constant apprehension. At
one time he thought of fleeing to Germany; but a tutor
is not his own master, and the fathers of his pupils
wanted them to benefit further by his instruction. At
last they persuaded him to continue it in the comparative safety of the Castle of St. Andrews. Knox, with
his three pupils, entered the Castle during the Easter
of 1547, almost a year after the murder of the
Cardinal.

The assassins of Beaton had for some time been besieged by the Regent Arran, at the moment a Catholic,

but when Knox joined them a truce had been concluded, both parties were busily intriguing for aid, the one side with France, the other with England, and there was free intercourse between the Castle and the town. The party in the Castle had grown alarmingly since the murder. Those who were enthusiastic for the new religion or flying from the law flocked there; the courts and rooms were filled with a strange rabble; and distinguished visitors like Sir David Lyndsay of the Mount came and went. The 'Castilians' alternated between wild licence and earnest repentance, between enthusiastic brawling and fervent participation in the Lord's Supper. Among them were women, assassins, theologians, professional soldiers, and preachers. The most godly of these were at the time the chief vindicators of the Protestant cause in Scotland.

In these surroundings Knox settled down to his work of tuition. Deaf to the tumults around him he doggedly instructed his pupils in grammar, Latin, and the catechism, and publicly examined them in the Parish Kirk of St. Andrews. At the same time he was expounding the Gospel of St. John in the chapel of the Castle, taking it up where he had left it in the quiet house of Langniddry. Presently he was drawing large and enthusiastic audiences, and everybody urged him to become a regular preacher. But now began the long series of hesitations which were to disturb the rest of his life. For a time he stedfastly refused; he would not run, he said, where God had not called him. It was pointed out that Rough, the Castle preacher, was no match for the Catholic theologians of the town, and

finally even Rough himself added his persuasions.
But Knox still held out, and the faithful in despair
contrived a pious plot. Rough preached a sermon on
the election of ministers, and indicated the dreadful
perils which might follow the refusal of a genuine call.
Then addressing Knox directly he charged him in
the name of Jesus Christ and those present not to
refuse. Knox burst into tears and left the church.
'His countenance and behaviour,' he wrote many
years later, 'from that day till the day that he was
compelled to present himself in the public place of
preaching, did sufficiently declare the grief and
trouble of his heart; for no man saw any sign of
mirth from him, neither had he pleasure to
accompany any man for many days together.'

The decision he was called to make was indeed
fearful enough to have daunted anybody. From the
windows of the Castle he could see the place where
Wishart had been burned only a year before. And the
novelty of his new vocation in itself filled him with
apprehension. Would he be able to give a true account
of his stewardship to God? Could he nerve himself to
speak 'the whole counsel of God, keeping nothing
back?' Would his feeble constitution stand the strain
of the persecution, imprisonment and exile which
were the common lot of a reformer's life? Had God
really called him this time? Was the Castle a safe
place? Would the English help arrive before the
French? These were important questions; and if he
accepted the call now he could never turn back. He
hesitated, therefore, as he had probably done before

he embraced Protestantism, and as he was to do again, in a crisis important for him and for Scotland. When he appeared at last in the pulpit every trace of hesitation had vanished.

With what care, in these circumstances, must he have chosen his first text! Yet it was an inexplicably obscure one: 'And another king shall rise after them, and he shall be unlike the first, and he shall subdue three kings, and shall speak against the Most High, and shall consume the saints of the Most High, and think that he may change times and laws, and they shall be given into his hands, until a time, and times, and dividing of times.' Never again was Knox to choose such an incoherent rigmarole as a text, and his choice was perhaps a betrayal of some lingering vestiges of doubt in his mind. He attacked it confidently, however. From this passage he demonstrated that the Pope was the Man of Sin and that the Roman Church was variously the Synagogue of Satan, the Last Beast, and the Whore of Babylon. The leading churchmen of the town and university were present; accordingly he exposed the vices of popes and shavelings, and the fraud of pardons and pilgrimages. He drew a distinction between the true and the false Church; the first was founded on the Word of God, the second on men's vain imaginations. Such logic as this had never before been encountered by the delighted Protestants. 'Others lopped the branches of the Papistry,' they exclaimed, 'but he strikes at the root to destroy the whole.'

Knox's preaching now became so powerful that the Catholics took alarm. They decided on an unprecedented action; they resolved to preach themselves. The Abbey and the University between them, it was hoped, would prove equal to the strain of filling the Parish Kirk pulpit for two or three hours every Sunday, and of keeping Knox out. But Knox began to preach on the week-days, and the Church retired in despair. Soon a great number of the townspeople were openly professing.

For some time the Castle party had been getting money and provisions from England; they were now hanging on in expectation of an armed force. They had twice promised England that they would not surrender without her consent; they had also promised Arran, however, that they would surrender on the arrival of a free absolution from the Pope. The absolution had arrived, and the besieged were in an embarrassing position. Fortunately the pardon contained an ambiguous phrase: 'We remit the crime that cannot be remitted,' and the Protestants caught at this and stuck to the Castle. But all was in vain, for in the middle of July about a score of French galleys appeared and summoned them to surrender. The galleys shot at them for two days, but only knocked a few slates off the roofs. The Castle's fire was more effective, killing four or five rowers and soldiers, and the French retired to Dundee for repairs.

For a moment the Castilians were elated by their success, but meantime plague had broken out, and Knox was behaving in a very strange manner. Only appointed a few weeks ago, he was already beginning to prophesy, and he prophesied defeat. His position indeed was unenviable. He saw that the Castilians were in a trap, yet they were still talking confidently of beating the French, and he grew impatient. Remembering Wishart he told them that God would punish them for their corrupt lives, that their walls were but eggshells, and that they would be delivered into their enemies' hands. Discouraged by the plague and Knox's extraordinary predictions, the garrison surrendered as soon as the Regent began to bombard them from the land. It was on the 29th of July 1547.

Yet all did not seem to be lost. The terms secured that the Castilians should be spared their lives, that they should be transported to France, and that if they did not wish to remain there they should be conveyed, at the French king's expense, to whatever country they desired. The terms were not kept. On the 7th of August, loaded with spoil and a hundred and twenty prisoners, the galleys sailed away. When they touched France the prisoners of birth were confined in fortresses, the commoners sent to row in the galleys. Among these was Knox. His career as a preacher had lasted for a few weeks; he was now to pass nineteen months among criminals, in feeble health, exposed to the weather, and cut off from all but one or two of his brethren.

For nineteen months again, therefore, we almost lose sight of Knox. Hardly anything is known of his life in the galleys, and very little is known about the galleys themselves, except that they were inhuman.

24

The slaves were chained side by side to benches which ran crossways from the bow to the stern of the ship. Above them was a raised platform where an officer walked with a whip, scourging the backs of the lazy or the exhausted. The insubordinate were chained face downwards on a bench and flogged until they lost consciousness. At night, winter and summer, the slaves slept under their benches without cover. But the horror of the galleys is perhaps best conveyed by one fact: after nightfall the slaves were left to themselves because the officers and crew dared not go down among them in the dark.

Once more, then, Knox's life shows us a blank, shot through only by a few irrelevant and confusing flashes. For the first winter his galley lay at Nantes, then we find it at Rouen, then twice in sight of the coast of Scotland. On the second occasion Knox, lying very ill, saw across the water the spire of the Parish Kirk in St. Andrews, and prophesied that he would preach there again. But even this incident is shrouded in mystery. According to his own account, Knox uttered this prophecy to James Balfour, who was sitting beside him. Later asked to recollect it, Balfour denied that he had been in the same galley at all, but Balfour, Knox assures us, was a notoriously unreliable man as well as a renegade.

While he was in Rouen, 'lying in irons, and sore troubled by corporal infirmity,' Knox received a treatise on Justification written by Henry Balnaves, one of the old Castilians. Coming when it did that dry and correct summary of what a good Protestant should

25

believe seemed to Knox an inspired work; and during his illness he fondly divided it into chapters and wrote a digest and a letter recommending it to the scattered congregation in St. Andrews. The letter breathes a spirit superior to its surroundings. 'I beseech you, beloved brethren,' he called them to witness, 'earnestly to consider, if we deny anything presently (or yet conceal or hide) which any time before we professed. . . . And now we have not the Castle of St. Andrews to be our defence, as some of our enemies falsely accused us, saying, "If we wanted our walls, we should not speak so boldly." . . . But we pray the Eternal God that the same affection, which now and then remained in us, remain with you eternally. The Lord shall judge if all which we spake was not of pure heart, having no respect either to love or hatred of any person, but only to the Word of God, and verity of His Scriptures, as we must answer on the great day of the Lord, where no man shall have place to dissemble. But blessed be the Lord, Whose infinite goodness and wisdom hath taken from us the occasion of that slander, and hath shown unto us that the serpent hath power only to stang the heel; that is, to molest and trouble the flesh, but not to move the spirit from constant adhering to Jesus Christ, nor public professing of His true Word.' 'I pray you pardon me, beloved brethren,' he concluded, 'that in this manner I digress; vehemency of spirit (the Lord knoweth I lie not) compelleth me thereto.' The same largeness of spirit animated his exposition of the true doctrine. Writing among outlaws and criminals he said: 'In Adam, after his transgression, remained a little of that knowledge and power, with the which he was endued by God; and from him it descended on his posterity.' Writing later at the command of the Scottish Protestant nobles, as their friend, and backed by their power, he was to affirm that no virtue whatever resided in men; that they were entirely corrupt. 'God loveth us because we are His own handiwork,' he wrote now, but when he sat down with full power to dictate the faith of Scotland, he set up a God of wrath. Adversity, in fact, improved him. In prosperity he hardened, in success he became intolerable, in the changing gamble for success he became monstrous. On the galleys he was still young in spirit, still generous; his qualities were soon to change.

For his confinement ended as abruptly as it had begun. The new king of England, Edward VI, was a Protestant, representations were made to the Government of France, and Knox, along with the rest of the Castilians, was released. His sufferings had been dreadful, but only by a word or two did he refer to them afterwards. 'What torment I sustained in the galleys, and what were the sobs of my heart,' he said nobly, 'is now no time to recite.'

He arrived in England, a Protestant country, in the spring of 1549.

CHAPTER III

KNOX HARDENS

When Knox arrived in England, Cranmer was already beginning to have the situation in hand. About three-quarters of the population were Catholic, it was true, but London and several of the more powerful towns were on his side, and he could count on the King, Somerset the Protector, and the noble families who had been enriched by the dissolution of the monasteries. One of his first measures was to compile a book of homilies and order it to be read every Sunday in all churches. The bishops and lower clergy were restive, however, and Cranmer invited foreign reformers over to help him. The illustrious divines Ochino, Peter Martyr, Utenhovius, John à Lasco, Martin Bucer and others obeyed the call. Presently, as Cranmer felt himself more secure, bishops and priests were forbidden to preach beyond their cures; then they were forbidden to preach at all, unless they possessed a licence from the King, Somerset or himself. By these means the Church was muzzled while the great mass of the people remained Catholic. Preachers, as many and as powerful as possible, were urgently needed. The zeal of Knox was known, and by the 7th of April, a few weeks after his arrival, he was in possession of a licence, and preaching the reformed faith under the orders of the Government.

The situation for him was completely changed; he was now in a position of power, and he had greater power at his back. Immediately, with the exact force of a mathematical law, his detestation of the priesthood was changed into contempt. He was not only right now as a matter of personal conviction; he was right objectively and manifestly, for the elect of God were also the elect of England. He had been the instrument of that invisible Church which had existed since the creation of Adam; which had perpetuated itself in the Jewish patriarchs and prophets, in Abraham, Noah, David, Isaiah, Jeremiah, and all their compeers; which had been glorified in Christ Jesus, had been carried onward by the apostles and the early fathers, had subsisted in secret under the tyranny of the Roman Antichrist, and had been recently persecuted and defeated in Scotland. Now he was the instrument of the visible Church on earth, a Church with all the resources of political power, and all the sanctions of legal right. In the galleys he had felt he was right: in England, with a powerful Protestant Government at his back, he felt that he could never be wrong. As a human being suffering under the curse of Adam, he had still cause for reproaching himself, it was true, but as an instrument he was already justified by his very function. But human affairs are more complicated than this; even a reformation cannot be carried out without some help from forces which are ambiguous; and in future Knox was to find it difficult sometimes to distinguish between the voice of the man, full of human error, and the voice of the instrument, speaking with divine certitude.

Meantime, however, his course was clear, and the instrument was called into ceaseless employment. It never tired, even when his 'miserable carcase' was sick. The Government sent him to Berwick at first. The North was the headquarters of the Roman heresy, and Berwick, even more than other garrison towns, was notorious for its violence and profligacy. Knox had been in the Castle of St. Andrews among Scottish Protestants, and in the galleys among thieves and murderers; obviously he was the man for the post.

When he arrived the town was in a deplorable state. Soldiers returned from the war with Scotland roamed the streets and starved in the gutter; law was in abeyance; violent assault and murder were common occurrences; and the streets were so filthy that when an alarm was sounded the soldiers could hardly make their way to the walls. Yet under the ministrations of Knox the town was soon reduced to order, and presently communion was being celebrated as it had been in St. Andrews, according to the severe model of scriptural truth. Berwick, almost incredibly, became as law-abiding as an ordinary town.

It was a triumph for Knox's personal force, yet already, after this initial success, his conviction that he could not be wrong was beginning to show itself. As a licensed preacher of the Government he was obliged to observe the forms of the 'First Book of Common Prayer,' which enjoined that communicants should kneel when they received the bread and wine. He did not observe them. Whatever the Government might think to himself kneeling before the sacrament savoured obviously of superstition, and pandered to the abominable error of Transubstantiation. He bade his congregation sit, therefore, for that, he conjectured, was the attitude in which the disciples had received the bread and wine. Cranmer presently denied it; the disciples, he held, had reclined in a recumbent position. Berwick decided not to recline in a recumbent position; it sat; the rest of England knelt. The question was to come up again.

At Berwick, too, one of those friendships with women began, which were to play such a great part in Knox's life. In his congregation was a certain Mrs. Bowes, the wife of Richard Bowes of Norham Castle, a fort about six miles up the Tweed. She was the mother of five sons and ten daughters, and she was anxious about her soul. Her husband was not in favour of the new doctrines; her family, too, were in the main cold. Naturally, therefore, she was assaulted by doubts and temptations. She feared that she would succumb to the pressure of her family or the fascinations of idolatry; she could never feel for long that she was one of the elect. Darker doubts still assailed her; she revelled in the thought of her own depravity, and innocently imputed to herself sins of which she only knew the names. She was probably about fifty when Knox became intimate with her; he was forty-five or six. Her fifth daughter, Marjory, came with her to hear the sermon, and presently the preacher and the young girl became engaged. But it was to Mrs. Bowes that he poured out his confidences. In the letters which were always passing between them when presently, as he did, he left Berwick to go to Newcastle, he addressed her most often as 'Dearly beloved mother.' They had opened their hearts to each other on one dramatic occasion, 'standing at the cupboard at Alnwick.' Till then Knox had thought that no creature had ever been as tempted as he; now he found that the enemy troubled Mrs. Bowes with the very words which he knew so well himself. Encouraged by the sympathy and confidence of such a remarkable man, the beloved mother pursued him wherever he went with vivid descriptions of her fleshly weaknesses and spiritual struggles. Knox never grew weary of those pious begging letters: in answering the doubts in them he helped to soothe his own.

The letters, indeed, gradually became a necessity to him. When he was deprived of the comfort of her 'corporal presence,' he wrote, he would call to mind 'how that oft-times when, with dolorous hearts, we have begun our talking, God hath sent great comfort unto both, which now for my own part I commonly want.' As a relief from the knocks of a reformer's life, amid which he had to be perpetually the stern, objective instrument, he needed a feminine intimacy, an intimacy on the one side almost maternal, on the other almost filial, in which the instrument could with a good conscience be laid aside, and the man with all his weaknesses might appear. Mrs. Bowes fulfilled the conditions to perfection. She was older than he, she was already his prospective mother-in-law, she was a religious woman, and she was so weak in the faith that while being comforted by her he could still appear to be the comforter. His pride would have recoiled from an intimacy in which he received reassurance and gave none. Here, however, he found himself so much the stronger that he could afford to be yielding; he could luxuriate in the voluptuous relief which her weakness provided because he felt that he was, in the circumstances, a prop and stay. Mrs. Bowes' correspondence fulfilled yet another office for him. 'The exposition of your troubles,' he wrote after several months of listening to her doubts, 'and acknowledging of your infirmity, were first unto me a very mirror and glass wherein I beheld myself so rightly painted forth, that nothing could be more evident to my own eyes. And then,' he added in a tone very unusual in him, 'the searching of the Scriptures for God's sweet promises, and for His mercies freely given unto miserable offenders, were unto me as the breaking and handling with my own hands of the most sweet and delectable unguents whereof I could not but receive some comfort by their natural sweet odours.' Even when he was sick her complaints never irritated him. 'Your messenger,' he wrote, 'found me in bed, after a sore trouble and most dolorous night, and so dolour may complain with dolour when we two meet.'

In the midst of incessant work, of trouble, sickness and danger, he was always reassuring her. 'The remembrance of your continual battle is dolorous unto me,' he wrote one week, 'yet fear I nothing less than your victory by Him who even hath vanquished when Satan appeared to have possessed all.' 'In my conscience I judge,' he wrote again somewhat desperately, 'and by the Holy Spirit of my God am fully certified, that ye are a member of Christ's body.' 'The manifold and continual assaults of the devil,' he wrote yet again, 'raging against you, and troubling your rest, while ye thirst, and most earnestly desire to remain in Christ, doth certify unto me your very election, which the devil envies in all the chosen of God.' But her hunger for comfort was inappeasable, and she invented new difficulties, which she fondly thought were insuperable, or would draw forth, at any rate, a longer reply. The devil had tried to persuade her that 'God's Word is of no effect, but that it is a vain tale invented by man, and so all that is spoken of Jesus the Son of God is but a vain fable.' Knox amicably chided her for this foolish imagination, one of the commonplaces with which the devil assaulted the elect: 'Why do ye not here laugh him to scorn,' he asked, 'and mock him in your heart?' 'The devil is so subtle,' he added astutely, 'that he can cause his temptations to appear to be the cogitations of our own hearts. But so be they or not, ye hate them, lament and mourn for them, which is the testimony of your faith.' Her temptation, he said to clinch the matter, was but a trite one. The devil had more subtle snares than this; for instance, he had made certain philosophers to affirm that the world never had a beginning. This strange error Knox disproved by

34

reminding her that God predicted the pains of child-bearing. She knew something of these, but she was not comforted.

Once he showed some natural impatience. Mrs. Bowes had sent a very strange letter indeed, and it troubled him, he complained, 'not a little.' 'Alas!' she had written, 'wicked woman that I am, my body is far wrong, for the selfsame sins that reigned in Sodom and Gomorrha, wherefore they perished, reigns in me, and I have small power or none to resist.' Knox expostulated. 'Mother,' he wrote, 'my duty compels me to advertize you, that in comparing your sins with the sins of Sodom and Gomorrha ye do not well. As the man offends that excuses his offence, so he that confesses crime where none is committed is injurious to the power and operation of God.' But she did not know what she was saying. 'The cause of this your unthankfulness I take to be ignorance in you, that you know not what were the sins of Sodom and Gomorrha.' He told her discreetly what these were. She was not troubled by them again.

Sometimes, to convince her that she was not singular in impiety, he would go the length of complaisantly blackening himself. A pious competition in wickedness began. 'No,' he maintained, 'I am worse than pen can express. In body ye think I am no adulterer; let so be, but the heart is infected with foul lusts, and will lust, albeit I lament never so much. Externally I commit no adultery; but my wicked heart loveth the self, and cannot refrain from vain imaginations. I am no mankiller with my hands; but I help not my needy

brother so liberally as I may or might. I steal not
horse, money, nor clothes from my neighbour; but
that small portion of my worldly substance I bestow
not so rightly as His holy law requireth. I bear no
false witness against my neighbour in judgment, or
otherwise before men; but I speak not the truth of God
so boldly as it becometh the true messenger to do.
And thus, in conclusion, there is no vice repugnant to
God's holy will, expressed in His law, wherewith my
heart is not infected.'

In such ways for several years Knox found relief
from the insupportable fatigue of being an instrument,
and brought relief to a fellow-Christian and a woman.
He had a sincere affection both for the Christian and
the woman; but in his heart did he wish his consola-
tions to console her? Did he hope for a cessation of the
temptations which made her correspondence so inter-
esting? But the more she harped on her secret sins,
the more perfect their intimacy became. The acknowledging of her infirmity, moreover, he had confessed,
had given him for the first time 'a very mirror and glass'
in which he saw himself 'so rightly painted forth that
nothing could be more evident.' But that was what,
as a man, he needed most. To see himself rightly
painted forth might have been disquieting to the
instrument, but to the man it could not but have given
a warming glow. Writing to Mrs. Bowes that his
heart was 'infected with foul lusts' and could not
'refrain from vain imaginations,' he was administering
an indirect consolation to her, but he was also giving
relief to himself; he was reinstating the natural man

without disguise, and making the prophet more inter-esting. In a man who imposes on himself an exalted task, and compels himself to live up to it, the need to be 'human' becomes urgent, and if nothing else will serve, he will make himself out to be worse or more weak than he is. Mrs. Bowes, beset by the recondite sins of Sodom and Gomorrha, was a strange repository for Knox's imperative confessions. Yet to confess to a woman younger than himself would have offended his pride; to confess to one less weak and complaisant would have invited admonition, and admonition he could never endure. In his letters to Marjory Bowes, the daughter, he was brief and dignified. 'Dearly Beloved Sister in the common faith of Jesus our Saviour,' he began his first letter to her. 'The place of John, forbidding us to salute such as bringeth not the wholesome doctrine. . . .' He develops the text, and then tells her what arguments she should use to allay her mother's doubts. He ends abruptly: 'I think this be the first letter that ever I wrote to you. In great haste, your brother, John Knox.' What would Mrs. Bowes have thought had she received such a letter?

While the man was dallying with his penitent confessor, however, the instrument was fully occupied. Somerset, the Protector, had fallen, Northumberland, a man still more corrupt, though a Protestant, was in his place, and Knox could not remain silent. It was true, he complained, that Somerset had become so cold to the exhortations of God's preachers that while they were speaking he would walk away to oversee his masons. Yet Northumberland was, if anything, worse, and Knox's conscience told him that if the one had been made away with, the other should be too. The execution of one Protestant protector by another, however, had been a difficult matter for the instrument to explain. He was finally convinced that in some inexplicable way it was the work of 'the devil and his members, the pestilent Papists,' devised by them to impede the work of Christ's disciples. God, he said later, compelled his tongue to express those opinions in more places than one; but meantime he remained in the pay of the Government, of which Northumberland was the head.

While he was denouncing those political crimes, the question of kneeling or sitting came up again. Early in 1551 he had been removed from Berwick to Newcastle. From there or from London he wrote to his old congregation. As for the chief points of his religion, he said, he would 'give place to neither man nor angel.' But he would have no objection to kneeling now, if magistrates made known that it was not retained for maintenance of any superstition, or interpreted as adoration of the elements. With this for the time he would be pleased, 'daily thirsting and calling on God for reformation of that and other things.'

Some time before this he had preached a sermon against the Mass before the Council of the North. He had stated the truth in two syllogisms. 'All worshipping, honouring, or service invented by the brain of man in the religion of God, without His own express commandment, is idolatry: The Mass is

invented by the brain of man, without any commandment of God: Therefore it is idolatry. . . . All
honouring or service of God, whereunto is added
a wicked opinion, is abomination. Unto the Mass
is added a wicked opinion: Therefore it is
abomination.' God, he declared, was offended by
any zeal which exceeded that which He prescribed
Himself. 'Disobedience to God's voice is not only
when man doth wickedly contrary to the precepts of
God, but also when of good zeal, or good intent, as we
commonly speak, man doth anything to the honour or
service of God not commanded by the express Word of
God.' Saul had had good reason to admit the truth
of this. He had been commanded to slaughter the
Amalekites, with all their oxen, cattle, camels and
asses. Moved by foolish pity he had saved one man,
Agag the king; moved by injudicious gratitude he had
set aside some of the fatter beasts to make a sacrifice
to God. But God had been angry, and had rebuked
him sharply through the mouth of Samuel. 'God
loveth us because we are His own handiwork,' Knox
had written a few years before, lying sick among
murderers. Now, with success, he had changed his
opinion.

For now he was acquiring more power, and simul-
taneously, by a convenient evolution, God was beginning to acquire more power too. The more absolute
the divine power could be made, however, the more
absolute would become the demands which Knox
could impose upon the people in his charge; but if that
power was to become great enough to satisfy him, God

had to be feared, not merely worshipped. Accordingly from now on Knox's thirst for power slowly and inexorably altered the image of the great Means by which he alone could hope to acquire it. Himself of an anxious temper, easily accessible to fear, henceforth he was to strike fear into the hearts of multitudes. Fear was to become an instrument in his hands, an instrument which he rarely laid aside, and which sometimes got beyond his control. He threatened when he could make good his threats; he threatened still more wildly when he could not. He threatened his friends when they disagreed with him; he threatened his enemies when they could afford to laugh at him. He threatened Mary of England when he was flying from her; he threatened Elizabeth when he hoped to get a favour out of her. Where insensibility was shown to his threatenings, he took refuge in hatred. Three women, Mary of England, Mary of Guise, and Mary Stuart, were unimpressed by his lightnings; he revenged himself by slander and prophecies of plagues where he could not by civil wars. The desire to see the palpable proof of his power in the trembling dismay of his enemies had not grown yet, however, to great proportions. During his stay in England it was shown only in his attitude to the idolaters, from now on his name for those who believed in the Catholic religion. He did not try to convert them: he consigned them laconically to the wrath of God. He was more concerned that they should tremble than that they should be saved.

Now, therefore, writing to his old Berwick flock, he

could easily afford to stretch a point on a mere ceremony. And perhaps he already knew that the same
point was to be raised by far more powerful interests,
and that in sight of all England there might be an
opportunity to prevail. He had written the letter to
his Berwick congregation during his ministry in
Newcastle. While he was still there, he had been
made one of the King's chaplains, and had gone to
London to preach before the court. At that time,
about the end of September 1552, the Second Prayer
Book seemed to have taken its definitive form, for it had
already been ordered to be used in all churches from
the 1st of November, and it contained a command to
kneel at the Lord's Supper. In his sermon before the
King, Knox 'freely inveighed against the Anglican
custom of kneeling at the Lord's Supper.' His protest
came, it almost seemed, too late, yet it proved successful. Cranmer had to write to the Privy Council on the
7th of October. The book as it was, he complained,
had the sanction of King and Parliament; now, it
seemed, without that sanction, it was to be altered. He
warned them against arrogant and unruly spirits
'which can like nothing but that is after their own
fancy, and cease not to make trouble and disquietude
when things be most quiet and in good order.' At
the end his anger boiled over; obviously meaning
Knox, he wrote: 'I will set my foot by his to be tried
in the fire, that his doctrine is untrue, and not only
untrue but seditious, and perilous to be heard of any
subjects, as a thing breaking the bridle of obedience
and loosing them from the bond of all princes' laws.'

What Knox's reply was to this outburst we do not know, but a 'Confession' was drawn up by him and his friends, and that passage was inserted into the Prayer Book which not long ago produced such an astounding flow of religious eloquence in the House of Commons. This important passage read: 'For as concerning the sacramental bread and wine, they remain still in their very natural substances, and therefore may not be adored, for that were idolatry to be abhorred of all faithful Christians. And as concerning the natural body and blood of our Saviour Christ, they are in heaven and not here. For it is against the truth of Christ's true natural body to be in more places than in one at one time.' This passage was inserted on the 27th of October, five days before the book was to come into general use. Berwick had triumphed.

In the dispute over the Prayer Book, Knox had found a party on his side. His power obviously was growing, and back now in Newcastle he was proving a very uncomfortable neighbour for the Duke of Northumberland. 'I would to God,' the Duke wrote Cecil on the 28th of October, 'it might please the King's Majesty to appoint Mr. Knox to the office of Rochester bishopric.' Indeed, Northumberland was growing sick of him. 'Master Knox's being here to speak with me,' he wrote Cecil on the 7th of December, 'saying that he was so willed by you, I do return him again, because I love not to have to do with men which be neither grateful nor pleasable. I assure you I mind to have no more to do with him, but to wish him well.'

But Northumberland did not get rid of him. The

bishopric of Rochester was offered and refused. Knox
had no conscientious objections to bishoprics at that
time, but it was clear that Edward VI could not live
long, and Mary, the heir to the throne, was a firm
Catholic. Knox was next offered the vicarage of
Allhallows in Bread Street, but the objections to that
were equally valid and he refused again.

Yet soon, in spite of this, he was in trouble over a
sermon which he preached on Christmas Day in
Newcastle. The King was now very ill; he could not
last much longer; Knox, therefore, accused the
Catholics of thirsting for his death, 'which their
iniquity would procure.' To accuse the Catholics of
a thing which was bound to happen was both good
policy and adroit prophecy, but it seems to have
aroused some indignation. Knox was indicted of
treason by the mayor of Newcastle; he immediately
cast himself on the mercy of Northumberland.
Already engaged in a plot to supplant Mary, and
unwilling to alienate an instrument who might prove
useful for more than God's purposes, Northumberland
came to the reformer's aid. On the 9th of January
he sent Cecil a letter 'from poor Knox, by the which
you may perceive what perplexity the poor soul re-
maineth in at present; the which in my poor opinion,
should not do amiss to be remembered to the rest of
my lords, that some order might be taken by their
wisdoms for his recomfort.' He did not, indeed, go
the length of wishing that Knox's 'abode should be of
great continuance in those parts'; but would the King
and his councillors allow the preacher to come and go

as he pleased, and make known that he was in good favour with them? Otherwise the cause of the new religion might suffer a set-back, for the people were by nature inconstant. Would it please the King and Council, also, to administer a rebuke to the mayor of Newcastle for accusing poor Knox? Northumberland's letter seems to have been attended to; for no further proceedings were taken.

Yet very soon Knox was in trouble again. In the spring of 1553 he wrote in great agitation to Mrs. Bowes. 'Rejoice now and be glad from the heart, for that which long the prophets of God hath cried, appeareth now shortly to come to pass: the elect of God to suffer as they have done from the beginning.' He wrote with conviction. 'My Lord of Westmoreland has written unto me this Wednesday, at six of the clock at night, immediately thereafter to repair unto him, as I will answer at my peril.' The summons awoke mingled exultation and diffidence in him. 'And why,' he very naturally asked Mrs. Bowes, 'should ye rejoice? Because,' he answered, 'it is a sure seal and testimony of that word, which we profess to be the very true and infallible word of God, to the which who adheres shall not be confounded; and also, because our glory cannot be perfect till first we taste of that cup, which albeit it be unpleasing to the flesh, yet it is most wholesome and profitable.' Still, when he thought of Westmoreland waiting for him, he became less confident. 'As for myself, albeit the extremity should now apprehend me, it is not come unlooked for. But, alas! I fear that yet I be not ripe, nor able to glorify Christ by my death, but

what lacketh now God shall perform in His own time.'
In this state, expecting imminent martyrdom, or at
least not knowing what to expect, he still found time to
answer Mrs. Bowes' doubts and to reassure her. It was
as if he clung to this as a comfort on the verge of
unknown terrors.

The danger was smaller than he had imagined, but
he was ill at the time, troubled by pains in his head
and stomach, and a hallucination that his brain was
decaying. He was in London on the 1st of March,
apparently to answer the accusations of Westmoreland.
'Heinous were the delations laid against me,' he wrote
Mrs. Bowes, 'and many are the lies that are made to
the Council.' But 'this assault of Satan has been to his
confusion, and to the glory of God. And therefore,
sister, cease not to praise God and to call for my comfort; for great is the multitude of enemies, whom every
one the Lord shall confound.'

While he was asking for comfort in Berwick, he was
not entirely without it in London. 'The very instant,'
he wrote Mrs. Bowes, 'that your letters were presented
unto me, was I talking of you, by reason that three
honest, poor women were come to me, and was complaining their great infirmity, and was showing unto
me the great assaults of the enemy, and I was opening
the cause and commodities thereof, whereby all our
eyes weeped at once, and I was praying unto God that
ye and some others had been there with me for the
space of two hours, and even at that instant came your
letters to my hands; whereof a part I read unto them,
and one of them said, "Oh, would to God I might

speak with that person, for I perceive that there be more tempted than I." '

In a few weeks Knox, unripe as he was, had to appear yet again before the Council. This time he had to answer three questions: Why he had refused Allhallows? Whether he thought it was impossible for a Christian to administer the rites according to the Church of England? And whether he did not think kneeling at the Sacrament a matter which might be left to people's individual judgment? His answer to the first question was confused. He replied that his services were more valuable outside London, and therefore he did not feel inclined to accept the charge, and that he might have accepted it, but Northumberland had ordered him not to. His answer to the second question was extremely politic. Many things in England needed reforming; without their reformation no minister could fully discharge his conscience; yet he himself did not reject any minor office in which he might disseminate the Gospel. He justified, in short, his adherence to the Church, while evading any post of responsibility within it. His answer to the third question was simple and direct. Christ's attitude ·at the Last Supper was the most perfect, and He had supped sitting, and not kneeling.

A few weeks later Knox gave Mrs. Bowes his real reason for refusing Allhallows; he refused it, he said frankly, 'from the foresight of troubles to come.' His answers, however, extricated him from the snare spread by the enemy; he retained his licence;

and at Easter he was preaching again before the King.

Everybody was now expecting the early death of Edward, and the preachers were wrought up to desperation, for with Edward's death the Protestants' rule would be over. They could not trust Northumberland, even if his plot to seat Lady Jane Grey on the throne were to succeed; they had nothing to hope from Mary but a Catholic reaction. Grindal, Lever, Bradford and Haddon, the court preachers, did not know where to turn. They prophesied against Northumberland, and Northumberland had to listen to them, for he needed their help to secure the success of his plots. The court chapel, where the dying young King sat, was a bear-garden. Knox was the most violent of the lot. 'Was David and Ezechias,' he shouted, while the King and courtiers sat by 'was David and Ezechias, princes of great and godly gifts and experience, abused by crafty councillors and dissembling hypocrites? What wonder is it, then, that a young and innocent king be deceived by crafty, covetous, wicked and ungodly counsellors? I am greatly afraid that Achitophel be counsellor, that Judas bear the purse, and that Shebna be scribe, comptroller, and treasurer.' The outburst was unreasonable. Northumberland had helped Knox when he was in danger. The Protector was not a pattern of virtue, but neither was he a wizard who could prolong the King's life, and meantime he was doing all in his power to supplant Mary and provide a Protestant successor for the throne. Only the survival of Edward or the success of that plot

could have satisfied the preachers. Their denunciations were the outcome of panic.

Soon afterwards Knox was sent to preach in
Buckinghamshire. While he was there the King
died, and the preaching licence expired on the same
day; it was in the first week of July. While the short
struggle between Northumberland and Mary was
going on, Knox was in the pretty country town of
Amersham.

Presently Mary triumphed and Knox instituted a
public prayer for her. 'Illuminate the heart of our
Sovereign Lady, Queen Mary, with pregnant gifts
of the Holy Ghost. . . . Repress Thou the pride of
those that would rebel. . . . Mitigate the hearts of
those that persecute us.' But his mind was divided;
he went up to London to see the coronation, he beheld
the senseless joy of the people, he rebuked one or two
of them, and went back to Mrs. Locke's house near
Bow Church, and his circle of admiring women. But
he could not relax himself for long in their society. He
was preaching in Carlisle by the end of July. On the
16th of August Mary showed her hand; she forbade
her Protestant and Catholic subjects to interrupt each
other's services and prohibited all preaching on either
side not licensed by herself. Knox nevertheless continued to preach in various parts of the country, in the
North, in Kent, even in London itself. He was in
London on the 22nd of September; he was still there
in the beginning of November. Cranmer and Latimer
were by that time in the Tower and people were
speaking of the Queen's marriage with Philip of Spain.

Catholicism was fully restored, and Knox's own affairs were not going well.

This of all moments he chose to ask the Catholic Bowes for the hand of Marjory. He wrote almost tearfully to his 'mother.' He had spoken, he said, to her brother-in-law, Sir Robert, of 'the matter ye know, according to your request: whose disdainful, yea, despiteful words hath so pierced my heart that my life is bitter unto me. I bear a good countenance with a sore troubled heart, while that he that ought to consider matters with a deep judgment is become not only a despiser, but also a taunter of God's messengers.' 'God be merciful unto him,' he continued. 'Among others his most unpleasing words, while that I was about to have declared my heart in the whole matter, he said, "Away with your rhetorical reasons, for I will not be persuaded by them." God knows, I did use no rhetoric nor coloured speech; but would have spoken the truth, and that in most simple manner. I am not a good orator in my own cause,' he added, forgetting his masterly replies to the Council, 'but what he would not be content to hear of me' – that is, the proposal for Marjory's hand – 'God shall declare to him a day to his displeasure, unless he repent. It is supposed that all the matter comes by you and me. I pray God,' he concluded despairingly, 'that your conscience were quiet and at peace, and I regard not what country consume this my wicked carcase; and were it not that no man's unthankfulness shall move me (God supporting my infirmity) to cease to do profit to God's congregation, that days would be brief that

England should give me bread.' What did he hope for at that time from an alliance with Marjory? That it might anchor him to the country where alone he could do profit to God's congregation? That it might leave him no choice but to offer an unflinching front to that unthankfulness which already, perhaps, in spite of his protests, he felt would prove too strong for him? We do not know.

For a time, however, he still lived on in London. His salary from the Government being stopped, he was now probably living on the hospitality of his friends, and he had perhaps little liberty of chosing his residence. In December, however, he managed to reach Newcastle and wrote Mrs. Bowes from there 'with troubled heart and weak body.' He hoped to be with her in Berwick in twelve days, though when he thought how her relatives would receive him he was almost inclined to stay away. He wrote her again, but his servant was intercepted on the road and the letters were seized. They only contained religious advice such as he had sent a score of times before, but the lady was alarmed, and Knox set out for Berwick to reassure her. The roads by this time were being watched and he had to be conveyed in secret from one place to another. During all these days his friends were urgently persuading him to leave the country, and he was in great anguish and uncertainty. The fight with Popery was only beginning. His flight from the centre of conflict in London already filled him with remorse.

'The falling back,' he wrote Mrs. Bowes on the 6th

of January, in great haste and troubled heart, – 'the falling back of such men as I hear daily do turn back to the idol again, is to me more dolorous than, I trust, the corporal death shall be, whenever it shall come at God's appointment. Some will ask then,' he added, 'why did I flee? Assuredly I cannot tell; but of one thing I am sure, the fear of death was not the chief cause of my fleeing. I trust the one cause hath been to let me see with my corporal eyes that all had not a true heart to Christ Jesus that in the day of rest and peace bare a fair face. But my flying is no matter; by God's grace I may come to battle before that all the conflict be ended.'

'I cannot express,' he wrote in the same letter, 'the pain which I think I might suffer to have the presence of you, and of others that be like troubled, but a few days. But God shall gather us at His good pleasure; if not in this wretched and miserable life, yet in that estate where death may not dissever us.'

Along with this letter he sent the first half of an Exposition of the 6th Psalm of David, intended for her particular case, on which he had been working for some time. He did not succeed in reaching Mrs. Bowes; meanwhile he composed the second half of the Exposition. The first had been a straightforward piece of Protestant exegesis; into the second he poured all his hesitations, his struggles with himself, and his remorse for the step which he was about to take. He sent it to Mrs. Bowes on the 28th of February on the eve of his flight to France.

Once more, and almost for the last time, his nature softened and became human under a deep affliction. Since his arrival in England, about five years before, success and recognition had been making him more and more overbearing. The Church of England had given him freedom within ample limits to preach the Gospel; he had become an enemy to her while in her service. Cranmer had armed him with power; he had compelled Cranmer on ignominious terms to alter his own Prayer Book. Northumberland had stood by him when he was accused of treason; he had abused Northumberland to his face and before the King. Protected by the laws of England and paid by her Government, he had boasted openly that he did not owe her obedience. But now the state of things in which he could beat Cranmer at his own council table and insult Northumberland to his face was so completely reversed that it might never have been. There was no use in reiterating now that he would 'give place to neither man nor angel'; he had to give place to Mary Tudor. Rage and perplexity alternated in his mind when he thought of his flight; but even now his conviction that he could not be wrong still stubbornly remained. 'Why did I flee?' he asked. He could not tell, but of one thing he was certain: that it was for a different reason from that which causes flight. And now that he had, as he said, proved 'the faint-hearted soldier,' that he had run from the enemy, that he had deserted God and felt deserted by Him, it was not really Knox who had done these things and was suffering remorse and shame for them; strangely enough it was King David and Mrs. Bowes. *They* felt that God 'was altogether departed from them'; *they* cried, 'God is angry, and therefore is there neither help nor remedy to be hoped for at His hands.' Why he had fled he did not know, but he knew that they had been weak. What must have been their feelings!

The passage which he had chosen from David as particularly applicable to Mrs. Bowes' case now stirred him with unexpected power. 'O Lord,' David had cried, 'rebuke me not in Thine anger, nor chasten me in Thy hot displeasure. Have mercy upon me, O Lord, for I am weak: O Lord, heal me, for all my bones are vexed.'

'David felt the wrath of God,' Knox wrote now, 'and therefore desired the same to be removed. He had offended, and therefore desired mercy. He was fallen in most dangerous sickness, and therefore he cried for corporal health. God appeared to be departed from him, and therefore he desired that the comfort of the Holy Ghost should return unto him. And thus was David not as commonly are the most part of men in their prayers, who, of a consuetude and custom, oftentimes do ask with their mouths such things as the heart does not greatly desire to obtain.'

But, he reflected, if David's sufferings were great what must be those of Mrs. Bowes, who was, if anything, a still weaker vessel? 'I confess, indeed,' he wrote, with a profundity of truth which he never attained again, 'that if our troubles come by man's tyranny, then the most sure and most easy way is to run to

God for defence and aid. But let God appear to be our enemy, to be angry with us, and to have left us, how hard and difficult it is then to call for His grace and for His assistance none knoweth, except such as have learned it by experience: neither yet can any man do so, except the elect children of God. For so strong are the enemies that with great violence invade the troubled conscience in that troublesome battle, that unless the hidden seed of God should make them hope against hope, they could never look for any deliverance or comfort. In time of trouble the flesh doth reason, "O wretched man, perceiveth thou not that God is angry with thee? He plagueth thee in His hot displeasure, therefore it is in vain for thee to call upon Him." The devil chimes in, "God plagueth thee for thy iniquity; thou hast offended His holy law; therefore it is labour lost to cry for mercy or relief; for His justice must needs take vengeance upon all inobedient sinners." '

'These things,' he continued, recollecting himself, 'put I you in view of, beloved mother, that albeit your pains sometimes be so horrible that no relief nor comfort ye find, neither in spirit nor body, yet if the heart can only sob unto God, despair not, you shall obtain your heart's desire; and destitute ye are not of faith. For at such time as the flesh, natural reason, the law of God, the present torment, and the devil, at once doth cry, God is angry, and therefore is there neither help nor remedy to be hoped for at His hands: At such time, I say, to sob unto God is the demonstration of the secret seed of God, which is had in God's elect children; and that only sob is unto God a more acceptable sacrifice than, without this cross, to give our bodies to be burnt, even for the truth's sake.'

Having reminded Mrs. Bowes that to sob to God was more acceptable than to be burned, a contingency which he momentarily forgot that she was in no need of fearing, he went on: 'David moreover prayeth, "Turn again, O Lord." It appeareth unto David, being in the extremity of his pain, that God was altogether departed from him; for so always judgeth this flesh (yea, the whole man) when trouble worketh by any continuance of time. David had sustained trouble many days; he had prayed, and yet was not delivered. And therefore judgeth he that God, being offended for his sins, had left him. Whereof it is plain, that the very elect sometimes are without all feeling of con-solation; and that they think themselves altogether destitute, as may be seen in David.'

'The very elect sometimes are without all feeling of consolation, as may be seen in David.' It was only too true, and Knox felt that Mrs. Bowes must feel it. But deprived of solace, the elect evolves a more consoling idea of God. For the time, strangely enough, the image of a 'faint-hearted soldier' did not evoke in Knox's mind the corresponding image of a prophet calling down the wrath of God on faint-hearted soldiers. Saul's disobedience and Jeremiah's curses did not come thronging into his mind; he turned rather to David, for now he was not preaching God, he was seeking Him, and it appeared in vain. When God had been behind him, supporting and guiding, God had been implacable, terrible; but now that, through a mythology composed of King David and Mrs. Bowes, he was seeking God and interceding for His grace, insensibly the divine lineaments began to soften. Suddenly, in a revelation, Knox saw that to God one sob from the heart was more acceptable than the offering of one's body to the fire; it was the truth he had been seeking. At a breath all the plague-foretelling prophets, all the fearful examples of God's vengeance: Jeremiah, Ezekiel, Achitophel, Ahab, Jezebel, Athaliah, melted away; and on the distant horizon, somewhat encumbered by mists, God with an almost paternal expression appeared. Knox, the symbolical sufferer with David and Mrs. Bowes, expiating an offence which had happened for some mysterious reason, 'assuredly he could not tell why,' had descended to earth and to the common state of humanity. He suffered; but his utterance acquired a depth which it was never to recover again.

Before he left England, his prayers, it was evident, had been answered. 'And in conclusion, I would not bow my knee before that most abominable idol for all the torments that earthly tyrants can devise, God so assisting me, as His Holy Spirit moveth me at present to write unfeignedly. And albeit that I have in the beginning of this battle appeared to play the faint-hearted and feeble soldier (the cause I remit to God), yet my prayer is that I may be restored to the battle again. And blessed be God the Father of our Lord Jesus Christ, I am not left without comfort, but my hope is to obtain such mercy, that if a short end be not made of all my miseries by final death (which to me were no small advantage), that yet I shall be encouraged to fight, that England and Scotland shall both know that I am ready to suffer more than either poverty or exile, for the profession of that heavenly religion, whereof it has pleased His merciful providence to make me, among others, a simple soldier and witness-bearer among men.'

Soon after writing those words Knox was on board the boat; he was on the sea; he was in France. His struggles of conscience and his fear of persecution seemed to lie alike behind him. God's face changed again, and the troop of Hebrew prophets, kings, murderers and harlots streamed back, more dreadful than ever. He discharged them, in a concentrated broadside, against the land that had driven him out.

CHAPTER IV

THE PROPHET

EVER since he had met Wishart nine years before Knox had been in the habit of prophesying. He prophesied on grave and on trifling occasions; he prophesied reasonably and unreasonably; he prophesied above all wherever he could not get his own way. He had prophesied against the Castilians in St. Andrews because they were the weaker side; he had prophesied against Northumberland because Edward VI was dying; he had prophesied against Sir Robert Bowes because Sir Robert would not accept him as a suitor for Marjory's hand: there was a variety of reasons now why he should prophesy against England. He prophesied, however, with greater fury than before, because he felt quite alone. The instrument was as eager as ever to be used, but there was nobody to use it. The Scottish Protestants had used it in St. Andrews Castle; the English Protestants had used it in Berwick and Newcastle. Now there was no one to use it save God. God accordingly took on more terrifying powers than ever. The prophecies arose to wild heights of fantasy. It was only natural. English Protestantism, if strong, had been limited in its powers; Knox's last remaining Employer was omnipotent. So

while to the Castilians in St. Andrews he had foretold defeat, to Northumberland his fall, both normal
and predictable fates; alone in Dieppe with God he
prophesied for England plague, fire, slaughter and
desolation. With the guiding control removed the
instrument struck wildly around it, and did not know
what to do with itself.

The man, too, was in an exacerbated temper. He
had left London almost penniless; he had managed to
get enough, it is true, to take him out of the country;
but now he was in a foreign land with no prospect for
the future. His comfortable state salary was gone; the
power that had accompanied it was gone; and Sir
Robert Bowes' refusal still rankled in his mind. His
old neighbour and enemy, the Bishop of Durham, was
flourishing; his friends were bowing their knees to the
idol. He had been chased out of England by a woman,
and he had fled while others more faithful had remained
behind.

All those feelings, public and private, religious and
profane, poured themselves into an extraordinary
epistle, 'A Godly Letter of Warning and Admonition
to the Faithful in London, Newcastle and Berwick,'
which he wrote while he waited at Dieppe. It is one of
the strangest Christian documents ever conceived. It
was written ostensibly by the instrument, but the
spirit that breathed in it was that of a man almost out
of his mind with rage. In that fury of anger, pure and
spontaneous, the powerlessness of the man and the
fanaticism of the prophet were mingled in one devouring torrent.

The two elements had been fused, forming a new person, in his weeks of self-questioning before he left England; now they were fused again, but by a more terrible chemistry. Then the prophet had become the man; now all the passions, all the envies, the hatreds, the cruelties of the man were triumphantly subsumed in the prophet. These passions, envies, hatreds, cruelties, by the same transmutation became the passions, envies, hatreds, cruelties of God. The letter is a sustained pæan of fury.

'Albeit,' he burst out, 'that abominable idolaters triumph for the moment, yet approaches the hour when God's vengeance shall strike not only their souls, but even their vile carcases shall be plagued, as before He has threatened. Their cities shall be burnt, their land shall be laid waste, their enemies shall dwell in their strongholds, their wives and their daughters shall be defiled, their children shall fall on the edge of the sword; mercy shall they find none, because they have refused the God of all mercy, when lovingly and long He called upon them. Ye would know the time, and what certainty I have thereof. To God will I appoint no time, but that these and more plagues shall fall upon the realm of England (and that or it be long, except repentance prevent), I am so sure as that I am that my God liveth.'

He went on passionately to remind them of what he had said in Berwick and Newcastle before the outbreak of sweating sickness. He gave as his authority for prophesying the plain Word of God, and the ordinary routine of God's plagues and punishments from the beginning. He ranged the Old Testament for plagues and threats of plagues. He reminded them that Grindal had prophesied the King's death; that Lever had prophesied desolation and pestilence; that Bradford had foretold God's wrath upon the rulers of England; that Haddon had explained the causes of their former pestilences and had affirmed that worse would come. But had the nobles listened? No, they had called the preachers indifferent fellows, yes, some had actually called them prating knaves.

His rage died down for a little, and he proceeded to an almost reasoned exhortation against meddling with idolatry. If they bowed to the idol, God's vengeance might strike them among the idolaters and they might not escape. Had not the whole tribe of Benjamin perished with the adulterers? Yet they had not all committed adultery. Moreover, 'idolatry so angers God that His wrath is never quenched till the offenders and all they possess are destroyed from the earth; for He commands them to be stoned to death, their substance burned, and even if a city offend, that it should be destroyed utterly without mercy.' But some would naturally demand, 'Shall we go and slay all idolaters?' 'That were the office, dear brethren,' he replied, 'of every civil magistrate within his realm.' In ideal conditions he contemplated an orderly and exhaustive slaughter of the Catholics; but 'the slaying of idolaters,' he had to admit at present, 'appertains not to every particular man,' and 'of you is required only to avoid participation and company of their abominations, as well in body as in soul.'

61

That being so, however, he looked round him for reasons why they should avoid idolatry. They should avoid it if not for their own salvation's sake, then for that of their neighbour, whom they kept voluntarily in ignorance; they should avoid it, above all, for the sake of their posterity. 'I speak to you, O natural fathers,' he wrote, rising suddenly to a strain of noble eloquence. 'Behold your children with the eyes of mercy, and consider the end of their creation. Cruelty it were to save yourselves and damn them. But O, more than cruelty and madness that cannot be expressed, if, for the pleasure of a moment, ye deprive yourselves and your posterity of that eternal joy that is ordained for them that continue in confession of Christ's name to the end, which assuredly ye do, if without resistance altogether, ye return to idolatry again. If natural love, fatherly affection, reverence of God, fear of torment, or yet hope of life, move you, then will ye gainstand that abominable idol; which if ye do not, then, alas! the sun is gone down, and the light is quite lost; the trumpet is ceased, and idolatry is placed in quietness and rest.'

'But yet grudgeth the flesh (say you), for fear of pain and torment.' But yet grudgeth the flesh (he might have reflected) when it has a sudden 'foresight of troubles to come.' That, however, was past now, and 'why,' he asked himself in Dieppe – 'why ought the way of life be so fearful by reason of any pain, considering that a great number of our brethren has passed before us by like dangers as we fear? For some were racked, some hewn asunder, some slain with swords, some

walked up and down in sheep-skins; in need, in tribulation, and vexation; in mountains, dens, and in caves of
the earth! Did God comfort them, and shall His
Majesty despise us if in fighting against iniquity we
shall follow their footsteps?' He wrote, he told them,
from 'a sore troubled heart, upon my departure from
Dieppe, whither God knoweth'; whither Knox also
knew, however, for he was on the point of setting out
for Geneva. 'I fear not the tyranny of man,' he said
in valediction, 'neither yet what the devil can invent
against me.'

But the flight from England had not only changed
God's face, and made Him ask from His elect for something a little more substantial than 'one only sob from
the heart.' It had suddenly clarified Knox's political
opinions. In the galleys, paraphrasing Balnaves on
Justification, a work which 'in itself,' he had said, was
'godly and perfect,' he had written: 'No bishop,' by
which he meant preacher or minister, 'should mix himself with temporal or secular business, for that is contrary to his business. . . . The affair of the subject is,
to obey his prince and rulers placed over him; giving
unto them honour, custom and tribute, not requiring
the cause why they receive the same; for that pertaineth
not to the vocation of a subject.'

And later in England, in the reign of Edward,
he had reminded his Berwick congregation that due
obedience must be given 'to magistrates, rulers and
princes, without tumult, grudge or sedition.' He
warned them that they were not 'to pretend to defend
God's truth or religion, ye being subjects, by violence

or sword, but patiently suffering what God shall please be laid upon you for constant confession of your faith and belief.' Of such things as these he was so sure at the time that he would give way in them neither to men nor angels.

But now, turning over the pages of his favourite prophet Jeremiah again, he had been illuminated by a new truth. When Nebuchadnezzar was threatening Jerusalem Jeremiah had foretold to the king that unless the people went over to the enemy and sought their favour, the town would not escape God's wrath. Those who stood by it, he had said, would die by the sword and by pestilence; but those who deserted to the enemy would be saved. Knox had merely affirmed in his letter that if Jezebel were maintained in authority London would be made a desert, and England given into the hands of strange nations. Was his treason, then, he asked, any greater than Jeremiah's? The conclusion was irresistible. 'Let a thing be here noted,' he said, 'that the prophet of God sometimes may teach treason against kings, and yet neither he, nor such as obeys the word spoken in the Lord's name by him, offends God.'

With this final defiance Knox set out for Switzerland. When he arrived at the city of God it was still giving Calvin some trouble. It was true, he had burned his enemy Servetus the year before, but in spite of that the Church of God was 'tossed about,' as he wrote to a friend, 'like the ark of Noah in the waters of the deluge.' At present he had his hands full with the recalcitrants, but he received Knox cordially and listened to the

MARY QUEEN OF ENGLAND

Mary Tudor, from a painting in the possession of the
Society of Antiquaries.

Facing p. 65.

doubts which the example of Jeremiah had raised. Knox wanted to know whether obedience was due to idolaters, when they were kings, whether the faithful, assuming they had power, might lawfully draw the sword, and whether a woman could rule by divine right, and could transfer her powers to her husband. The questions were general; but Mary was Queen of England, and Philip of Spain was about to marry her. Calvin remained prudently non-committal.

Knox went next to Zurich to see Bullinger. Bullinger was equally unpromising. The Helvetian cities did not yet feel quite securely in possession of power; it was a hazardous business, he reflected, even for the faithful to resist authority. In the case of impious queens, there was the consolation of the example of Athaliah. It was, however, 'very difficult to pronounce upon any particular case.' But the more Calvin and Bullinger hedged, the more enamoured Knox became of Jeremiah. He went to see Calvin again, but Calvin had not changed his views, Calvin agreed with Bullinger. Knox returned to Dieppe in May, more sure than ever that he and Jeremiah were right.

But the spectacle of a Protestant country in power had inspired him. Two months before he had written to his old congregations in rage and despair; now he expressed a chastened hope. His hope was, he said, 'that one day or other Christ Jesus, that now in England is crucified, shall rise again in despite of His enemies.'

He had seen all the congregations of Switzerland, he went on, and reasoned with the pastors and the learned

upon matters which he could not then commit to
writing. 'If I thought,' he said mysteriously, 'I
might have your presence, and the presence of some
other assured men, I would jeopard my own life to let
men see what may be done with a safe conscience in
these dolorous and dangerous days; but seeing that it
cannot be done instantly without danger to others than
to me, I will abide the time that God will appoint.
But hereof be assured,' he proceeded, the impregna-
bility of his arguments with Calvin and Bullinger
appearing more and more manifest in retrospect – 'hereof be assured, that all is not lawful nor just that is
statute by civil laws, neither is everything sin before
God which ungodly persons allege to be treason; but
this I postpone to more opportunity, if by any means I
may, I intend to speak with you or it be long.'

He sent this letter to the Afflicted in England on
the 10th of May. On the 31st he sent an amplified
version; but by this time he had repented somewhat of
his hints on treason; perhaps Calvin and Bullinger had
not been so impressed by his arguments after all;
he left out the hints. The letter, too, which he had
written just after his first flight had perhaps been a
little too pungent, and might give an uninstructed mind
the impression that he was actuated by carnal hatred.
These misconceptions had to be cleared away. 'In the
mean season, beloved brethren,' he wrote, 'two things
ye must avoid. The former, that ye presume not to be
revengers of your own cause, but that ye resign over
vengeance unto Him who only is able to requite them,
according to their malicious minds. Secondly, that ye

hate not with any carnal hatred, these blind, cruel and malicious tyrants; but that ye learn of Christ to pray for your persecutors, lamenting and bewailing that the devil should so prevail against them, that headlong they should run body and soul to perpetual perdition.' Yet, remembering his outburst three months before, he did not want now to be entrapped into a counsel of mere lenity. Carnal hatred was a deadly sin, 'but,' he went on triumphantly, 'there is a spiritual hatred, which David calleth a perfect hatred, which the Holy Ghost engendreth in the heads of God's elect, against the unholy contemners of His holy statutes. And it is, when we more lament that God's glory is suppressed, and that Christ's flock is defrauded of their wholesome food, than that our bodies are persecuted.'

This hatred, as it proved, was ample enough to satisfy any Christian. 'With this hatred may we hate tyrants, and earnestly may we pray for their destruction, be they kings or queens, princes or prelates.' And these prayers, moreover, 'made in the fervency of hatred,' were not to be despised, for often they were literally fulfilled. David, Jeremiah and others had seen with their own eyes the hot vengeance of God poured forth on the cruel tyrants of their time. One never knew; he tried to be as sanguine as possible; he saw no reason why if David and Jeremiah had done it, the faithful in England might not do it too by the power of perfect hatred and judiciously directed prayer. He prophesied that some of his readers would see judgment executed shortly on the pestilent Papists.

The letter concluded with an example of spiritual

hatred. 'Let Winchester, and his cruel consort, devise and study till his wits fail, how the kingdom of his father, the Antichrist of Rome, may prosper; and let him and them drink the blood of God's saints till they be drunk, and their bellies burst, yet shall they never prevail long in their attempts.'

Knox stayed on in Dieppe. He was not alone now; other English refugees had flocked there since his first arrival. They watched England from across the Channel, and waited for an opportunity to overthrow the Government. 'If I thought I might have the presence of some assured men,' Knox had written, 'I would jeopard my own life to let men see what may be done with a safe conscience in these dolorous and dangerous days.' No doubt he knew from his fellow-refugees what that was; no doubt, too, it compelled him to think that everything which ungodly persons alleged to be treason was not sin against God. He had bombarded England with exhortations and menaces; now he too watched it from across the Channel to note the effect. There seemed to be none. The faithful were sliding quietly back into idolatry, the Catholics were preparing briskly for a thorough-going campaign of persecution. In spite of the judiciously directed prayers and the perfect hatred of the elect, London could not yet be called a waste, the wives and daughters of the Catholics remained unviolated, and their children were running about as before. The programme had miscarried. Knox knew himself that he was in the right, but as a lover of power he could not bear patiently to remain on a losing side. Yet England, becoming Catholic quietly but systematically before his eyes, behaved as if he were not there. It was intolerable. He gathered himself up for a supreme effort, and launched 'A Faithful Admonition to the Professors of God's Truth in England.'

His first letter to the professors had been a cry of spontaneous rage and despair; the Faithful Admonition was a desperate last bid to make some impression, to evoke some response, no matter what it might be. The letter was finished on the 20th of July and ran through two editions. At last a stir of some kind was clearly perceptible across the Channel. He had hit the mark this time, certainly, or had he overshot it?

His admonition began, reasonably enough, with an inquiry why God had withdrawn His favour from the elect in England. It was because they had been luke-warm, regarding carnal things more than spiritual. He reproached himself bitterly for his own lukewarmness. Perhaps some people had been displeased by his rude plainness, he said, but that day his conscience accused him of not having spoken plainly enough. He should, he knew now, have singled out the impious man by name, and warned him, 'Thou shalt die the death.' But his love for his wicked carcase had held him back, for he did not want to provoke everybody to hate him. 'I dare not say that I was the greatest flatterer,' he added, perhaps remembering poor Northumberland, yet for his mildness he had now unfeignedly to ask God's mercy.

Nor, when he considered, had he been quite impartial. It was true, he had not sought worldly promotion, but carnal affection for certain men had made him stay longer in some places than in others where there were hungry souls to be fed. Besides, he had not been diligent enough even among his friends, for at their advice he had spared himself, had even allowed himself the luxury of exercising his body. For all this, he confessed now, he deserved damnation, if it were not for the power of Christ's blood.

But still his desire for self-accusation was not satisfied. He had desired, he said, the praise of men, he had courted their favour, he had been puffed up, sometimes, so that vainglory almost got the better of him. But the tale, he felt, was not yet quite made up; and conscious of something missing, feeling that the case against himself was not quite black enough, he begged his readers not to think that he accused himself without cause, or out of self-righteousness, or with the intention of reflecting on them. 'O Lord!' he broke out at last, turning abruptly to One who knew why he had fled from England, 'be merciful to my great offence, and deal not with me according to my iniquity, but according to the multitude of Thy mercies; remove from me the burthen of my sin; for of purpose and mind, to have avoided the vain displeasure of man, I spared little to offend Thy godly majesty.'

But if Satan had got the upper hand with him, he was not surprised that Satan was triumphing in England. 'Wonder not, I say, that now the devil rageth in his obedient servants, wily Winchester, dreaming Durham, and bloody Bonner, with the rest of their bloody, butcherly brood: for this is their hour and power granted to them; they cannot cease nor assuage their furious fumes, for the devil, their sire, stirreth, moveth, and carrieth them, even at his will.

'If Stephen Gardiner, Cuthbert Tunstall, and butcherly Bonner, false Bishops of Winchester, Durham, and of London,' he continued, 'had for their false doctrine and traitorous acts suffered death, when they justly deserved the same, then would arrant Papists have alleged (as I and others have heard them do) that they were men reformable, that they were meet instruments for a commonwealth; that they were not so obstinate and malicious as they were judged; neither that they thirsted for the blood of any man. And of Lady Mary, who hath not heard that she was sober, merciful, and one that loved the commonwealth of England? Had she, I say, and such as now be of her pestilent counsel, been sent to hell before these days, then should not their iniquity and cruelty so manifestly have appeared to the world.'

As he thought of Mary, safely lifted above the reach of his menaces, his fury mounted. Athaliah had murdered the seed of Judah's kings; Herodias' daughter had procured John the Baptist's head; Jezebel, the accursed idolatress, had shed the blood of God's prophets; but what was their iniquity to Mary's? Not even Jezebel had ever 'erected half so many scaffolds in all Israel as mischievous Mary hath done within London alone.' But her projected marriage with the Spanish idolater Philip was the final straw. In the Bible there was no lack of regicides. 'God for

His great mercy's sake,' he burst out at last – 'God for His great mercy's sake stir up some Phineas, Elijah, or Jehu, that the blood of abominable idolaters may pacify God's wrath, that it consume not the whole multitude, Amen.' It was a general invitation to the English to assassinate their Queen.

Now that he had hit the mark he remained there fixed in the sustained consummation of his fury. 'Delay not thy vengeance, O Lord,' he implored, 'but let death devour them in haste; let the earth swallow them up; and let them go down quick to hell. For there is no hope of their amendment, the fear and reverence of Thy holy name is quite banished from their hearts; and therefore yet again, O Lord! consume them, consume them in Thine anger, and let them never bring their wicked counsels to effect; but, according to Thy godly powers, let them be taken in the snare which they have prepared for Thine elect.'

He still believed in the power of prayer and spiritual hatred; he ended his letter by a reaffirmation of them. Let his brethren but continue in prayer, God would rise to their defence and confound the counsels of their enemies. 'He shall send Jehu,' he concluded in a comforting tone, 'to execute His just judgments against idolaters, and against such as obstinately defendeth them. Jezebel herself shall not escape the vengeance and plagues that are prepared for her portion.'

To this extraordinary voice England listened at last, but the effect was not what Knox had calculated. A Jehu did not arise. The Protestants, on the contrary, were dismayed, the Catholics in alarm increased the severity of their persecution. Cranmer, Ridley and Latimer were lying in prison, but no one yet had had to die for his faith. By the beginning of next year the fires of Smithfield were burning and the Protestants threw the blame on Knox. Their anger and disgust were natural enough. They were not fanatics, they detested Knox's opinions and his violence in expressing them; yet now, it seemed, they were to suffer for those very opinions which they hated, while he, in Dieppe, raged on in safety. They were, many of them, moderate Anglicans; they had no great wish to be burned slowly to death; and the more intelligent of them showed an understandable enough disposition to recant. Knox was both a foreigner and a man who had refused to conform to the faith for which they were suffering. They did not forget his officious intrusion.

But by this time Knox had perhaps exhausted his fury. He could hardly hope to surpass the Faithful Admonition. Like everybody else, moreover, he saw by now that the Catholic rule was firmly established, and that he could not hope for the present to be on the winning side. At the end of July or the beginning of August he set out for Geneva.

CHAPTER V

THE FRANKFORT INTERLUDE

DURING those months between his landing in Dieppe
in the beginning of March and his second departure
for Geneva in the end of July, Knox, as we have seen,
had been in a state of fury. He had seen England, on
the fair road to becoming a Protestant land, turn back
again to Catholicism, and he had felt himself powerless
to stem the reaction. Yet his fury was excessive even
in a fighter on a defeated side; something more was
needed to explain its violence; and the explanation may
have been, as I have suggested, that still, in spite of
the comfort of seeing other refugees around him, he
was troubled by the scruples which had escaped him
in his incoherent exhortations to Mrs. Bowes before
he left. Scruples are often unreasonable; in flying from
England when he did Knox behaved like many other
men. He may perhaps have felt a natural compunction
at leaving his congregation behind, destitute of their
wholesome food, yet his flight was not inglorious.
His standard biographer, the Reverend Dr. M'Crie,
asserts with his accustomed unction that 'Providence,
having more important services in reserve for him,
made use of the urgent importunities of his friends to
hurry him away from those dangers' and persuade him

to 'retire,' as the doctor so well puts it, to France. To agree with that now would be over-complaisance. But it is true that the instinct which dictated the flight was an essential quality of Knox the man of action, and one which without denying his nature he could not have resisted. For the real desire of the man of action is not so much that things should be done, as that he himself should do them, and this being so, the most important consideration in the world is that he should continue to exist. The man of action does take risks, but they are reasonable risks, embraced for the future enhancement of his power. He sees, with a sureness beyond that of ordinary men, where his chance lies; the instinct of self-preservation in him has the clarity of genius. Accordingly, in spite of his sentimental outpourings to Mrs. Bowes, Knox thought as little of the attractions of martyrdom as Alexander, Cæsar, Napoleon or Lenin would have done. His actions proved it. The consideration which made him pause, as he did more than once in his life, before he threw himself into a Protestant rebellion, was, Could it be carried through successfully? He had been forced against his judgment to become an ordained preacher in the Castle of St. Andrews; he amply revenged himself on his importunate allies later by prophesying defeat to them when every encouragement was needed. In a few years from now he was to hesitate again, before he threw himself into the most signally successful campaign of his life. He was a man of action, then, but unlike most men of action he imagined he owed an allegiance to a power higher than himself. When the Catholics began to assert their supremacy in England, it was that allegiance which sprang into his mind with overwhelming emphasis. The man of action saw the most profitable chance, the only course; the servant of God was filled with dismay at his own defection. For a time the whole man was torn with uncertainty; but one thing was certain now; the man of action had won. The instrument perhaps had played false with his conscience, but the man had remained true to himself. In a real sense, therefore, the man was blameless, yet the flight was not an action upon which he could look back with pride. Somebody had offended God grievously when such a thing could happen; among God's mysterious arrangements there had to be some explanation. By the time he landed in France Knox had found it. The Protestants had been too lukewarm and they were at present too compliant, but the real fountain-head of all the faithful's offences, it was clear, was the Catholics. Accordingly he vented on the Catholics all the rage he felt at having passed through such an ignominious time. His search for God and for comfort, his perplexity over why he had fled, were human and excusable; his rage of resentment tipped him sheer into abysses of self-deception touched with Sadism which no other reformer had plumbed. At their most grandiose his prophecies about the future of England were almost like the ravings of a madman.

Yet they were not the ravings of a madman, for even when they were wildest the man of action, looking around him for favourable chances, was unconsciously directing them. Instructed by God, the instrument had cursed Mary Tudor and had publicly advised her assassination. It was clear then that the politician's former theories, less immediately inspired, must have contained some fallacy; besides, there was little present prospect for the reformed cause if they had not. The Protestants would either have to give up the fight or move with the times. So between the prophet's first unpremeditated outburst and his second, the man of action was adroitly trying to get out of Calvin and Bullinger an admission that obedience was not due to queens, that the faithful might resist if they had the power, and that a queen did not rule by divine right. If he could establish that, Protestantism might still have a chance in the fight in England. Calvin and Bullinger, however, had refused to back him. He returned to Dieppe; he scanned the position in England; he made one last desperate attempt; then he recognized that there was nothing for the moment to be done. The instrument and the man, the prophet and the politician, had used all their weapons and had failed. But it was the politician who had the last word, and took Knox back to Geneva.

Again Calvin received him hospitably, but again his stay was not to be long. At the end of September a letter reached him from Frankfort. It was signed by twenty-one of the English refugees there, and urgently prayed him to come and be their preacher. He hesitated once more.

The religious situation in Frankfort was, in fact, chaotic. The Lutherans and Calvinists had been squabbling for a long time, but early in the year the confusion had been doubled by the arrival of a congregation of Walloons who during Edward's reign had found a refuge in Glastonbury Abbey. They were Calvinists, and their advances had been indignantly repulsed in succession by the Lutheran brethren in Hamburg, Rostock, Wismar and Lübeck. To insist too emphatically on their religious complexion was clearly a mistake; they decided to keep it discreetly in the background. The new plan was brilliantly successful. Not only did the Frankfort magistrates grant them admission to the town; a church was put at their disposal. When the Walloons were comfortably settled, the horrified Lutherans discovered that they had a nest of Calvinists in their midst. But von Glauburg, one of the most influential magistrates in the town, was in favour of the Genevan doctrines, and he backed his fellow-believers. The Calvinists had obtained the church, and now they stuck to it.

The pastor of the Walloon Church, remembering his hospitable reception in England, thought it only a natural return, when presently four companies of English exiles arrived, to pay them a visit of welcome. He called on the very night of their arrival. He told them how cordially the councillors had received him and his flock, and, drawing on his own experience, told them to apply for permission to stay. The permission was granted, but the English had still no place where they could worship. The indispensable von Glauburg came to their help. On alternate days and on Sundays they could have the use of the Walloon Church; there was only one trifling condition: they would be asked to subscribe to the Walloon Confession of Faith and observe its ceremonies. They accepted the conditions, and the disgusted Lutherans found a second colony of Calvinists in existence. But having accepted, the English found now that they would have to let the Prayer Book go altogether. Though hard pressed, some of them hesitated before such a terrible alternative; and, rather than lose them, the Walloons compromised. The responses, the litany and the surplice were scrapped, and a new confession was substituted for the old, but what remained of the Prayer Book the English could have if they wished. The more old-fashioned members mournfully put up with this maimed service; the more radical were highly pleased with the change, and hoped for one still more fundamental.

The English in Frankfort had now a church, a blessing denied to their fellow-countrymen in other German cities. Frankfort, it was clear to them, was the ideal centre for English *émigré* life, and for the English religion. They wrote, therefore, to their countrymen in Zurich, Strassburg, Emden, and other places, asking them to come to Frankfort and share the blessing, but they did not state that their church was not the Church of England. Something in their letter aroused the suspicions of Zurich. Zurich wanted to know whether if they came they would be permitted the free use of the English service. Frankfort replied that it was the duty of the English abroad to provide an example of Christian unity. Zurich remained courteous, but they could no longer conceal their suspicions, and they sent

Chambers, one of their number, to Frankfort to discover the real state of things, and there was no alternative now but the truth. Chambers returned to Zurich with a letter from the Frankfort congregation. They confessed that there were things in the English service which they could not in conscience approve. Zurich did not reply.

Soon after this Knox was ordained in Frankfort. He had hesitated. He knew the state of affairs; in Frankfort there was little scope for his powers; and altogether the enterprise, launched amid such a tangle of pious misrepresentations, and on such a petty scale, did not attract him. Calvin, however, thought he should go, and Calvin was both his host and the supreme power in Geneva. Soon after his coming two members of the Strassburg group arrived. They were willing to waive such ceremonies as the town would not tolerate; all they asked for was the substance of the Prayer Book. Knox and Whittinghame, one of the congregation, asked, 'What did they mean by the substance of the Prayer Book'? It was a difficult question; they replied that they had no commission to debate it; they merely wanted information on three points: What heads of the Prayer Book would the Frankfort congregation accept? Would the English be granted a separate church? And would they be allowed to remain peacefully in the town? Frankfort replied that the parts of the Prayer Book which they could prove were in accordance with God's Word they could have – if the town sanctioned it. As for a separate church, they would have to wait until the Diet broke up at

Augsburg. They could be pretty sure, however, of being allowed to stay in the town. Strassburg decided to follow the example of Zurich.

With Strassburg and Zurich eliminated, the problem of the Frankfort congregation seemed now a comparatively simple one. They sat down to elaborate a church order of their own; this did not require much consideration; it was clear to the majority that the Genevan order was the 'most godly and farthest off from superstition.' Here quite unexpectedly Knox stepped in as a moderating influence. He had arrived during a late stage in the dispute, he was less deeply implicated than the rest, and he saw that if Frankfort took its own way all hope of bringing in the other English exiles would be gone. He had come unwillingly; he was not now inclined to compromise himself by taking the lead in a petty squabble. He insisted therefore that the new order should not be put in operation until the English in Strassburg, Zurich and the other cities were consulted. He refused to employ the new order; he refused equally to employ the English order. He offered to preach as before; if they would be content with that he would remain; if they would not, he begged them to accept his resignation. They would not think of accepting his resignation. There seemed no way out.

At this moment, Lever, Knox's old colleague in England, arrived from Zurich. He proposed a more temperate order, drawn up without reference to the book of Geneva, but the majority would not listen. At last, in desperation, it was resolved that a summary of the English Prayer Book should be sent to Calvin himself, and that he should give his judgment.

The summary was drawn up by Knox and Whittinghame, they made the best of their opportunity, and Calvin's decision was an easy matter. To make doubly sure, however, Knox wrote a letter to Calvin's colleagues in Geneva. He asked them to weigh carefully the letter already sent by Whittinghame, and to do what they could. He hinted that there were several people who wanted to force the English book on the Frankfort congregation, but he would never be pastor of a church in which such a makeshift of religion was accepted. Would not they ask Calvin, he suggested finally – all his first distaste for Frankfort coming out – would they not ask Calvin if he might not leave Frankfort now with a good conscience? His presence, he felt sure, was a cause of disunion rather than strength.

Calvin gave no reply to Knox's petition, but his decision on the Prayer Book was what the majority had hoped. He reproved the exiles for not living in Christian unity. After studying the summary, he went on, he had seen that the English liturgy contained many foolish things that might perhaps be tolerated, but it was ridiculous to insist on them in the exiles' present condition. The supporters of the Prayer Book liked those things merely because they were accustomed to them. They should be reasonable and yield.

But they did not yield. Backed by Calvin's letter Knox and four of his faction drew up an ultra Genevan service; the minority of the congregation rejected it with horror.

Knox stepped in as mediator again. A committee, drawn from both parties in the congregation, met to decide upon a service which would please everybody, and at last the old English service emerged, much battered and torn. But though everybody had to be content, nobody was pleased. The compromise was agreed to on the 6th of February; it was to hold only till the end of April; and if any disagreement arose before then it was to be submitted to five umpires, among whom were Calvin and Bullinger.

Not even this poor confession, however, was to last. Well acquainted as it was with the wisdom of the serpent, the congregation was soon to encounter a surprising example of it. On the 13th of March another band of English exiles arrived in Frankfort, led by Dr. Richard Cox, an Anglican who knew his mind. The minority, still hoping for an undiluted Prayer Book, were much cheered; the Puritan majority were filled with dismay. Cox and his friends soon made their intentions clear. On their first visit to church they uttered the responses with emphasis, nor did they show any repentance; they meant to worship as they had done in England, they said. Next Sunday they managed to get possession of the pulpit, had the litany read, to the horror of the original congregation, and went inexorably through the responses from beginning to end. This was on the Sunday morning; Knox was to preach in the afternoon.

But once again he behaved with admirable, with surprising moderation. Once, he said, he too had had a good opinion of the Prayer Book, but even at that time he had not thought it should be observed on all points. Later, shocked by the obstinacy of those who would hold to it absolutely, but more particularly reflecting that nothing was sure that had not the warrant of God's Word, he had been driven from his first opinion. Now he discovered in the English Book things superstitious, unclean and imperfect. It was clear to him, besides, that among the sins which had moved God to punish England, one was slackness in the necessary reform of religion; for example, in England the minister had no power to discipline his congregation, while some men were allowed to hold five benefices, to the scandal of the flock.

The last was a good hit, for there were pluralists among Cox's party. They attacked Knox as soon as he was out of the pulpit, and that night denounced him before the congregation at such length that there was no time left for him to reply. On Tuesday, after Knox's sermon, the old congregation met to decide whether the Cox faction should be admitted. The majority wanted to settle the affairs of the church first, when the new-comers might come in if they liked. Once more Knox behaved with the most perverse magnanimity. He asked the Cox party to be admitted, he was so secure of the justice of his position, he said, that he did not fear them. Cox and his company came in, the Prayer Book party were now in a majority, and Knox was dismissed from his post and told to take no further part in the affairs of the church. He had twice shown his distaste for his position in Frankfort, and he had asked somewhat plaintively a few weeks before whether he could not leave it with a good conscience. He certainly could now.

The Cox faction had shown their hostility to any politic lopping of the Prayer Book; their fiercest hostility, it was now to appear, was to Knox himself. They had only recently left England, they had felt the greater severities which had followed the publication of 'The Faithful Admonition to Professors,' and they drew the consequences. Meantime Whittinghame ran to the indefatigable Glauburg; Glauburg decreed that the church should be closed next day, and ordered Whittinghame and Knox, for the one side, and Cox and Lever, for the other, to meet and find a basis of agreement. The negotiations broke off on the third day over the matins. The spokesmen of the old congregation asserted that certain phrases in the liturgy were borrowed from the Papists. There was nothing more to be said.

During the conference Knox had received a curious visit from a Mr. Isaack of Kent. He advised Knox to relax his opposition to the Prayer Book, it would be to his advantage; if he did not he had better look out. Knox paid no attention to the threat, and meantime it took shape. Whittinghame was sent for by the Town Council and asked what kind of man Knox was. A learned, wise, grave and godly man, Whittinghame dutifully replied. Was he aware, a magistrate asked him, that certain of the English had accused this godly man of treason against the Emperor, his son, and the Queen of England? And he showed the astonished Whittinghame certain marked passages of the Admonition, and asked him to bring a translation of them at one o'clock. Though inefficiently chosen, these passages were found to be damaging enough, and Knox was commanded to cease preaching. He appeared next day in the church as a listener, however, and the hostility of Cox and his party blazed up for a last time. They left the church in a body; they would not stay in the same place as Knox. In the meantime the Puritan congregation had been trying to get round the Town Council of Frankfort. The controversy had now acquired an almost cosmic importance in their eyes; they pleaded not merely for themselves, but for their whole posterity, for the whole English nation, which would be damned if this matter were not settled in accordance with scriptural truth. The methods of the Cox faction were quieter and more effective. They too went to the Council. If the Council would not proceed against Knox, Augsburg was near, they would lay their information before the Emperor. The Council had no ambition to be charged with the harbouring of traitors, and Knox was quietly advised to leave the city. On the night before he left fifty of his friends met in his lodgings for a last 'most comfortable sermon.' Next day they saw him safely outside the city, and with many tears said good-bye. It was on the 26th of March 1555. Knox made once more for Geneva.

Thus was decided, in circumstances which were not wholly unsymbolical, the first passage of arms between the great Puritan and Church parties of England. Knox was quite unaware of the importance of the occasion.

THE FRANKFORT INTERLUDE

He had gone to Frankfort against his will; he had tried to be relieved of his post; he finally succeeded by a most providential stroke of Quixotism. He had intended from the first to have his way; he had got it at last.

CHAPTER VI

THE SCOTTISH VISIT

K<small>NOX</small> arrived in Geneva in April. His stay this time was to be a little longer. Calvin received him cordially, for his colleague, he considered, had been badly treated. Knox spent much of his time in study. He was not yet so sure of his Greek and Hebrew as he was of certain propositions which had been enunciated in them. He now applied himself to the languages in which God had originally spoken; but hardly had he begun when he was interrupted by urgent calls from Scotland and Mrs. Bowes. He hesitated again, but Mrs. Bowes, at any rate, would not be denied. At the end of August accordingly, he tore himself away from his studies and set out for Berwick. He wrote to Mrs. Bowes that she alone had sent him out on a journey so contrary to his judgment. He was making this journey for two purposes: to be married to his betrothed, Marjory Bowes, and to see what chances there were of a successful reformation in Scotland.

On the first of these objects particularly Mrs. Bowes had set her mind. The religious pressure of her family was becoming insupportable, and she had now resolved to leave her husband and come to Geneva, where she could worship in peace and near her spiritual adviser.

As a wife fleeing from her husband she could scarcely
do so without scandal; as Knox's mother-in-law she
could do so with comparative propriety.

Knox went straight to Berwick and was married.
That done he set out for Scotland, arriving at the end
of the harvest. It was eight years since he had left
Scotland a prisoner; since then he had known that
Protestantism was growing rapidly; but his reception
exceeded all his expectations. 'This day,' he wrote
Mrs. Bowes jubilantly, 'I praise God for them who was
the cause external of my resort to these quarters; that
is, I praise God in you, and for you, whom He made
the instrument to draw me from the den of my own
ease to contemplate and behold the thirst of our
brethren, night and day sobbing and groaning for the
bread of life. If I had not seen it with my own eyes in
my own country, I could not have believed it. The
fervency here doth far exceed all others that I have
seen; and therefore ye shall patiently bear, although I
spend here yet some days; for depart I cannot, until
such time as God quench their thirst a little. Yea,
mother, their fervency doth so ravish me that I cannot
but accuse and condemn my slothful coldness.'

He ran little risk, indeed, in coming to Scotland
when he did. Mary of Guise was Regent. A Catholic,
but a princess of extreme moderation, she needed the
support of the powerful Protestant Lords for her policy
of making Scotland subservient to France. Archbishop
Hamilton, the head of the Church in Scotland, was for
different reasons as anxious to do nothing to offend the
Protestants. The period of toleration had seen a rapid

growth in the power of the new religion, and the persecution in England had helped greatly to hasten it. The dread of persecution had driven a number of English reformers over the border; they went preaching about the country, and one of them, Harlaw, a tailor, had distinguished himself by converting great numbers in Edinburgh itself. A little after Knox's arrival Mary's toleration restored Henry Balnaves and the lairds of Grange, Ormiston and Brunstone to their estates. Knox, it is true, had made himself notorious by his Faithful Admonition, but all these men had been concerned in one way or another in the murder of Cardinal Beaton, and Brunstone himself was an almost professional traitor.

Knox preached, therefore, to his heart's content in Sime's house in Edinburgh, almost within shouting distance of Holyrood. His audiences were people of importance. 'The trumpet blew the auld sound three days together,' he wrote Mrs. Bowes, 'till private houses of indifferent largeness could not contain the sound of it. O sweet were the death that should follow such forty days in Edinburgh, as here I have had three!' He found himself surrounded again by an adoring circle of women – women of a certain social standing. A Dean of Guild's wife was one of his most faithful adorers, but he was soon to meet people of even greater consequence; for presently to one of his meetings came Maitland of Lethington, the brilliant, restless young adviser of Mary herself, not yet thirty, but already in a position of influence.

At this meeting the question whether a true believer

might outwardly take part in the celebration of the Mass was brought up and settled. Knox began the discussion by affirming absolutely that in no circumstances was it lawful for a Christian to present himself to that idol. Some of those present, probably reflecting that, unlike him, they would have to stay in Scotland for a long time, tried to find some loophole of escape from this uncomfortable doctrine which would so irrevocably commit them. In their need they turned to the Bible; they were repaid. Paul, with the concurrence of other brethren, had once, it seemed, been so tender to the superstitions of the Jews as to make an offering along with some of his followers in the Temple. But Knox saw the danger and forestalled it with two replies. Firstly, he said, paying a vow was one thing, assisting at the Mass was another: the one was idolatry, the other had been sometimes commanded by God. Secondly, even though it had been commanded by God, he was not convinced that Paul's participation in the Temple offering had pleased the Holy Ghost. Why did he think so? Because soon afterwards a mob had put Paul in fear of his life. Lethington was flabbergasted by this logic and could do nothing but say: 'I see perfectly that our shifts will serve nothing before God, seeing that they stand us in so small stead before man.' The brethren left, stunned into assent by Knox's arguments, and Lethington returned a trifle thoughtfully to continue his good work for Mary of Guise.

After this successful meeting Knox went on. He was for some time at Erskine of Dun's house near

Montrose, where the most influential men in the county came to hear him; he was with Sir James Sandilands of Calder where he had talks with Lord Erskine, later to be Earl of Mar, Lord Lorn, the future Earl of Argyll, and young Lord James Stuart, the illegitimate son of the late King. He was in Ayrshire, for a long time now a stronghold of the Protestant faith, encouraging the lairds, and at Finlayson, where the Earl of Glencairn showed him great favour. At most of those places he administered the Lord's Supper. The Catholics at last began to be alarmed.

Knox returned to Edinburgh and went on to Dun for a second visit. While there he received a summons to present himself in the Blackfriars' Church in Edinburgh to answer accusations of heresy. The Protestants were now in a strong position; he resolved therefore, to appear, but in the company of Erskine of Dun and a band of other gentlemen. The Catholics were not prepared to meet such a large party, and the summons was withdrawn. It was a score for the Protestants.

Things were going so well now indeed that the Lords began to have hopes of the Regent herself; her toleration recently had been extraordinary. They commissioned Knox, therefore, to write her a letter, 'something that might move her to hear the Word of God.' Resolutely banishing from his mind those images of Jezebel and Athaliah which the proximity of queens was so apt to evoke, Knox sat down doggedly resolved to be mild. For the first paragraph, it was true, he could not get into the proper flow. He wished Mary to show loving-kindness to the elect, but he doubted very much that she would; and the most plausible examples he could offer her for imitation were the Egyptian midwives who preserved the men-children of the Israelites, Pharaoh's daughter who saved the infant Moses, Nebuchadnezzar who granted his captives their lives, and, somewhat desperately, Rahab, the prostitute, who had been so surprisingly 'loving, faithful, and gentle.' But after that things went better for a while. He could not wonder enough, he said, at this great opportunity offered to him, 'a worm most wretched.' 'I doubt not but the rumours which came to your Grace's ears of me have been such, that if all reports were true, I were unworthy to live on this earth. I am traduced as a heretic, accused as a false teacher and seducer of the people, besides other approbies, which, affirmed by men of worldly honour and estimation, may easily kindle the wrath of magistrates when innocency is not known. But blessed be God, the Father of our Lord Jesus Christ, who, by the dews of His heavenly grace, hath so quenched the fire of displeasure in your Grace's heart that Satan is frustrate of his enterprise and purpose.' 'Superfluous and foolish,' he insisted again, 'it shall appear to many that I, a man of base estate and condition, dare enterprise to admonish a princess so honourable, endowed with wisdom and graces singularly.' Yet that is what he must do, he went on, his mildness suddenly ceasing and the prophet breaking out into his accustomed amplitude of speech, and he had to inform her that unless in her government she were found different from the common ruck of princes her power would land her in torment and pain everlasting. This proposition was hard, he admitted, curbing the prophet again, but if he were to conceal it from her he would be committing treason no less grievous than if he were to abstain from warning her when he saw her prepare to drink a poisoned cup.

So the letter went on in a laborious see-saw between the courtier and the prophet. Her religion, he told her, was poison, and whoever drank it drank damnation and death. But he warned her of this out of love. A messenger of God, he went on, might justly expect from her a motherly care for her subjects, inflexible justice, a heart void of avarice and partiality, with the rest of those virtues which even Pagan writers required of good rulers. But it was vain, he reflected immediately, to expect reformation in manners where the religion was corrupt. He wrote to her in hope, but he could not help showing that he considered her hopeless. He exhorted her to reform religion and to give greater freedom to the Protestants, and he adduced persuasive reasons for his advice; but he could not refrain from adding that if she did not take it, then she and her posterity should suddenly feel the heavy hand of God. The courtier did his best, but the prophet would not be kept under.

The letter was presented to the Regent by Glencairn. She handed it to the Archbishop of Glasgow a few days later with the words: 'Please you, my lord, to read a pasquill.' All Knox's pains had evidently been wasted.

While things were shaping so splendidly, letters

came from Geneva commanding him in God's name to return; and God's voice could not be resisted. Knox saw that though Scotland was ripening for a decisive change, it was not yet quite ripe; he had also, perhaps, some 'foresight of evils to come.' This time at any rate he did not hesitate. He left in July 1556, and he had scarcely reached Geneva when he was summoned a second time to answer at Edinburgh to the former charge. As he could not appear the Catholics contented themselves with burning his effigy at the public cross. This insult outraged him, and he was to nurse it in silence for two years.

He arrived in Geneva with Mrs. Knox, Mrs. Bowes, a servant, and a pupil called Patrick. He was now married to Marjory, and accordingly we hear nothing more of her, except that she bore him two children, and that she died. The same silence henceforth covers the irrepressible Mrs. Bowes. It was not in her nature to be uncommunicative, yet no sound from her escapes the extraordinary blankness which surrounds Knox's domestic life. There is only an occasional complaint from himself to Mrs. Locke, from now on the most maternal of all his women friends. Daily, he told her, he had domestic troubles, to which he had not till then been accustomed, troubles, too, with his poor flock. He earnestly yearned for the comfort of her presence.

Mementoes of his successful ministrations in Scotland continued to pursue him. The sisters in Edinburgh plied him with questions of conscience and dress. 'In all matters concerning your conscience,' he

wrote to Janet Adamson, the daughter of the Dean of
Guild, 'I must refer you to my former letters, which
I trust be common betwixt you and the rest of our
sisters, for to me ye are all equal in Christ.' Janet
had been complaining about her husband. 'Your
husband,' Knox replied with tact, 'is dear unto me, for
that he is a man endowed with some good gifts, but
more dear, for that he is your husband. Charity moveth
me to thirst his illumination, both for his comfort and
for the trouble which ye sustain by his coldness, which
justly may be called infidelity. But, dear sister,' he
went on in a tone of firm discouragement, 'the prophets
of God are oft impeded to pray for such as they
love unfeignedly. This I write, not that any such
thing I find as yet within myself, but that I would
advertise you that I dare promise nothing whereof the
promise is not within my power.' In short she was to
stick to her husband. 'If God will have you exercised
under that kind of cross, which is most bitter, to wit,
to have your head appointed to you by God for your
comfort, to be your enemy, with patience ye must
abide His merciful deliverance, determining with
yourself never to obey manifest iniquity for the
pleasure of any mortal man; which if ye do, your tears
shall be turned into joy, and the bitterness of your
dolour in sweet comfort, which now cannot be felt.'
In the same letter he acknowledged a welcome
contribution.

On the question of dress his advice was more ample,
but less emphatic. What apparel should be used 'of
such as profess godliness,' he confessed, 'is very

difficult and dangerous to appoint with any certainty, lest in so doing we restrain Christian liberty, or else loose the bridle too far to the foolish fantasy of facile flesh. If we shall say that to the clean all is clean, and that the external apparel doth not defile the inward conscience, then I fear that we shall be patrons to such as by their vanity doth witness and declare that they little understand what is Christian purity, which does not only study to keep the self clean in God's presence, but is also most careful to give good example to others, and to avoid all occasion of offence and slander. There be some who will not be seen altogether ignorant of God's Word, and yet, nevertheless, armed as it were with the example of the multitude in apparel, are more like to courtesans than to grave matrons.' Descending to particulars, he went on: 'In cloth, silks, velvet, gold, and other such, there is no uncleanness, but because that unclean persons do abuse the same to ostentation; some to allure the eyes of men, some for pride, and some because they will not be unlike their fellows. I cannot praise the common superfluity which now is used among women in their apparel. For where the Apostle forbiddeth the embroidering and wresting of the hair, the attiring with gold and other such, he condemneth all affectation and appetite, of trimness, fairness, beauty, and decking, other than nature hath given and simple honesty doth require; and therefore such as either labour and study continually to correct natural beauty, or yet that be led away with every new guise of garment, do greatly offend against the precept of the Apostle in my judgment. If the broidering of the hair be evil, as it is pronounced to be, assuredly the anointing and colouring of it cannot be good.' But he did not feel his accustomed assurance in dealing with such a difficult subject, and he enclosed a sermon of 'the man of God,' John Calvin, which he had translated expressly for the edification of the sisters. The sumptuary laws of Geneva were extremely rigorous; Knox was writing to rich burgesses' wives who could afford to dress well; he probably reflected that severer counsels might come with better grace from someone other than himself. The letter is one of his most tactful effusions. Calvin's sermon has unfortunately been lost.

CHAPTER VII

GENEVA

K NOX was settled in Geneva now with a household, and he was to remain there, except for one long absence, for over two years. When he arrived he found that an English Church had sprung up, and that he was one of its pastors. He was now, therefore, a public representative of the Calvinist faith and an active member of the Calvinist community. The time has come to give some account of the extraordinary doctrines which he held from now on, and the strange society within which for these years he moved.

When he had emerged from his apprenticeship to Wishart, Knox was still more inclined to Luther than to Calvin. At the time when Archbishop Hamilton was searching for him in Midlothian, it was Germany that he had thought of as the true place of refuge and centre of light. Even while he lay in the galleys he still had ideas so distasteful to Calvinists as that man in his fallen state retained 'a little of that knowledge and power with the which he was endowed by God,' and that God loved men because they were His own handiwork. During his prosperous years in England, as we have seen, his certainty of his election hardened and with that his whole mind and character; and when he had to fly from Mary it was not to Wittenberg or Frankfort, it was to Geneva that he inevitably directed his way. Lutheranism had wakened him to the truth; Calvinism formed his mind and character. From his discipline in Geneva he emerged with his original obstinacy of nature, his certainty of his own righteousness, and his intolerance fortified by an objective and triumphant sanction. He emerged from it too with a resolve to turn the world into a greater Geneva.

The religious system of Calvin is one of the most extraordinary achievements of modern theology. It is in essence the work of one mind; it is the work, moreover, of a mind which was never shaken from its first formulated position. It is contained complete in *The Institutes of the Christian Religion*, finished when Calvin was twenty-six. Amplified by the same hand several times afterwards, it was never essentially altered. It remained for almost three hundred years a complete and impregnable system, and to the present day the edifice has never fallen: it has only been deserted, all but a forlorn handful of worshippers have vanished. During its age of power it formed the characters of great men, and changed the destinies of peoples. It was the discipline which moulded William the Silent, Coligny, Cromwell, and Knox himself; which saved the Dutch Republic, raised England to be the greatest power in Europe, founded the commonwealth of America, and in a few years turned Scotland into a Puritan country, to remain so until this day. It inspired revolutions and imposed tyrannies; it brought with it prosperity and repression; it assisted at the birth of

Capitalism, and was present at that of Democracy; it gave peace to the Netherlands, and to Scotland a hundred and twenty years of civil turmoil and persecution. It affected the lives of every class of people, from the humblest to the most exalted. As a system it has almost passed away; as an influence it still remains in various parts of the world.

The ideas which made up Calvin's system were not originally his own. Luther had already proclaimed the doctrines of justification by faith and of predestination. But Luther could never resist the temptation of contradicting himself; he saw intuitively, and he had a horror of confining his intuitions within a logical framework. Justification by faith to him was merely the recognition that submission of the heart to God, participation in the Godhead through Christ, was the beginning of all goodness. The Roman Catholic priesthood and ritual stood between him and that immediate and necessary communion. Instead of inward repentance, a movement of the heart, the Church imposed a mere form of penitence, which consisted in the performance of prescribed works and set prayers. To Luther the virtues it enjoined seemed official and dead. The act of faith, justifying the sinner, was everything; but, his experience told him, it was not within the scope of the will; it came unasked, yet with overwhelming certainty, as if straight from the heart of God. But as no one could stretch out his own hand and grasp it, justification could only be the sign of God's free election of the sinner. And yet not all were chosen; to a great number God's hand was never stretched out, and these died in their darkness and went to hell; this was the incomprehensible mystery of divine justice, and for Luther there was no solution of it. 'It is impossible,' he wrote, 'that any but God should be free; His prescience and His divine Providence determine that all things should happen in accordance with His immutable, eternal and inevitable will, which smashes to pieces the free will of man.' Consequently, 'God created the evil in us as well as the good; and the supreme perfection of faith is to believe that God is just, even when He necessarily sentences us to damnation by His free will, and seems to be pleased by our torments.' The supreme perfection of faith for Luther, thus, was to believe the unbelievable. In this form the Protestant doctrine was a possible one only for men as heroic or as illogical as Luther himself. It was the work of Calvin to accept the impossible and build upon it a remarkably persuasive structure of reason.

Justification by faith, election and damnation were to Luther, then, mysteries which he could face only by a faith stronger than his reason. But to Calvin they were self-evident facts. He built his system on two realities: the Bible and human nature. Looking at the world as it was he could not but see that some men were well wrought and others warped; that some went the way of life and others the way of destruction; that some turned their faces towards God and others lived in blind indifference to Him. But if God had once revealed Himself to these, if they had seen His glory and been assured of the eternal happiness which they were to share with Him, was it conceivable that they should have remained indifferent? If it were a matter to be decided by man's will merely, would any one consent to be damned? It was inconceivable; and therefore the irresistible conclusion followed that God only chose whom He willed, and voluntarily left the rest to darkness in this world and torment in the next. This was Calvin's reading of human destiny, but the Bible supported it, and the Bible was his infallible guide. There he found that in the beginning God had chosen one people alone out of many to be His elect to everlasting; there he found, too, as Luther had done, that God was omnipotent, omniscient and just. Being omnipotent, however, God had fashioned the world to His complete desire; being omniscient, His fore-knowledge of all things was in perfect agreement with His fore-ordination of them; and being just, His election of certain souls and His damnation of others was necessarily in accordance with an equity which it was blasphemy to question. But God was eternal as well, and therefore He had already ordained Adam's fall before He created him; He had ordained, in addition, all the consequences which ensued; His will had damned all the multitudes of the lost and chosen every member of the elect before the foundations of the world were laid.

Luther had asked for one certitude only: that the sinner stands justified before God when his heart is filled with faith. Calvin claimed a certainty of more awful scope: that the soul, once elected, is God's for ever, in this world and in eternity. While he insisted, therefore, that his reading of human destiny bore out

God's Word, the supreme rock of his certitude was God Himself. No pledge less great than this could give the elect the everlasting assurance which they desired. The truth which Luther sought was a subjective one, the awareness within his own heart of reconciliation with God; the truth which Calvin demanded was objective, the certainty of his everlasting salvation. Luther tried to justify a mystical feeling; Calvin strove to verify a fact.

It was a fact, however, which from the elect's point of view it was extremely important to verify. God's Word was immutable, but men's hearts were infirm; and after their definitive acceptance by God the weaker vessels were still apt to be tormented by doubts and other sins. Accordingly Calvin maintained that, once elected, the sinner never lost the faith which saved him; no, not even if he lost his fear of God. Calvin went further; faith in the elect was sometimes buried; they lost all consciousness of it, they no longer even possessed it; yet in spite of that faith was not extinct in them, it was still effectual to salvation. He went further still; he held that the children of the faithful were born in grace, and that salvation passed on like an acquired characteristic from father to child, the elect automatically producing the elect, as Jews produce Jews, or Germans Germans. Children born in this dispensation were accordingly generated and regenerated by the same extraordinary act. Calvin's source for this somewhat extreme dogma was the promise to Abraham: 'I shall be thy God and the God of thy children.' It was an extraordinarily comforting theory, for, as Bossuet pointed out a century later, if salvation is transmissible from father to son, then it may pass on, widening, to infinite generations. But Calvin had here to contradict himself for once, and somewhat to modify his doctrine. It was true that baptism was the right of all children born in the faith, but baptism was not always effectual, for two reasons: first, because it did not have its effect on everyone, but only on those who were predestined; and secondly, because some who were baptized in their infancy were not regenerated until their manhood. The contradiction was palpable; but whenever they could, here in veiled, there in more explicit terms, the Calvinists stuck to this first and more comforting theory of infant baptism.

Their reason for doing so was clear enough. Calvinism has been condemned as a gloomy religion, and its view of the world as one of almost unrelieved horror; but to do so is to overlook the fact that the one gleam of hope in that world was confiscated by the Calvinists as their own. To a soul convinced that he was ordained to burn in everlasting fire such a view would indeed be terrible, and if the Calvinists had believed in their own damnation, all the opprobrium which their enemies have cast upon them would be merited. But the Genevan religion was founded by a man who considered himself certain of his election, and the supporters it drew to itself had of necessity the same cheerful assurance. No healthy-minded Calvinist could think for long that he was a vessel of wrath; no one at all could be adopted by the Genevan communion who was fixedly of that opinion. Yet, as doubts were bound to arise, some step had to be taken; and it was to neutralize these that Calvin built up his impregnable line of defences around the certainty of election. The great aim of Calvin's theology was, in short, to instil certitude, confidence and strength into its adherents.

As a system of belief, then, Calvinism was so far from being severe that it might almost be termed complaisant. With his usual insight, indeed, Calvin saw the dangers of complaisance. The elect had been blessed with the special favour of God; their task on earth, however, was to prove that God had chosen them. The harshness of the discipline imposed by the Genevan Church was accordingly as extreme as the indulgence of its creed. Calvin was pitiless to his enemies; he was almost wantonly severe on his followers. During his rule in Geneva the mildest offences were dignified into crimes. To sing was a crime, to wear clothes of a certain cut was a crime, to serve up too many dishes at a dinner was a crime, to dance at weddings was a crime. Offences such as these were punished by mere fines and imprisonment, but incontinence put the offender in danger of banishment or even of drowning, and the penalty for adultery was death. Justice sometimes took even more peculiarly Calvinistic forms. On one day thirty-one people were burned for the crime of spreading the plague, and once a child was beheaded for striking its parents.

In a class by themselves stood crimes against Calvin. It was a crime to laugh at Calvin's sermons; it was a crime to argue with Calvin in the street. But to enter into theological controversy with Calvin might turn out to be a very grave crime. Gruet, one of his opponents, was tortured for three years and finally executed, for having affixed a scurrilous placard to Calvin's pulpit. The terrible fate of Servetus is better known. Servetus had once met Calvin in Paris, when they were both young men, and had maintained his position against him. This unexampled insolence rankled in Calvin's mind, and years after, when he was settled in Geneva, he wrote to a friend saying that if ever Servetus came to that town he would see that he did not leave it alive. Seven years after this letter Servetus stopped at Geneva on his way to Italy. He was seized, tried for heresy by judges who had no legal jurisdiction over him, and condemned to the flames.

But if the penalties in Geneva were severe, the regulations were almost incapable of being kept. Everybody was compelled to attend church; everybody was forced to partake of the Lord's Supper; if a sick man did not send for the minister before the fourth day of his illness he found himself in the terrible hands of the law. No one could leave the town without giving reasons acceptable to the Council. Bands of the faithful had power to enter the houses, put servants through their catechisms, order parents to send their children to school, and forbid nurses to sleep in the same bed as the children they were feeding at the breast. But, in spite of such privileges as these, the Councillors themselves were not let off easily. On certain days they were compelled to attend an

Extraordinary Council, where, 'in good order, all enmity and rancour laid aside,' they had to point out each other's faults and vices, 'proceeding from the first to the last.'

While it was the duty of the magistrates to rebuke one another, the humbler office of the ordinary citizen was to inform. Geneva was a town of about sixteen thousand inhabitants, and the great majority of these consisted of the elect. Yet, between the years 1542 and 1546, fifty-eight people were executed in it and seventy-six banished; while in Knox's last year there and the one following there were four hundred and fourteen prosecutions for such crimes as singing and wearing clothes not cut in the right fashion. Torture added a customary terror to the criminal trials, and the smallest deviation from orthodoxy was dealt with at once. In sixty years one hundred and fifty heretics were burnt in Geneva.

The severity of this rule, which made Geneva the admiration of the faithful and earned for it the name of 'The City of God,' had the disadvantage of making new crimes spring up wherever an old one was eradicated. Vice concealed itself and throve underground; in spite of the magistrates' watchfulness there was an inexplicably large number of illegitimate children whom their horrified mothers were forced by terror to expose in the streets; while through fear or sycophancy many people added to the general tyranny: fathers and mothers accused their children not of minor offences merely, but of crimes, and informers were everywhere.

Calvin's theory of ethics, which dictated the form which his government took in Geneva, was as remarkable as his system of theology. The ways of God had been a mystery to Luther; to Calvin they were perfectly clear, but they were at the same time perfectly arbitrary. 'God not only foresaw,' he laid down, 'the fall of the first man, but also arranged all by the determination of His own will.' That is to say, His action was quite simple, but quite arbitrary. In the same way God chose His elect by 'His gratuitous mercy, totally irrespective of human merit,' and damned the rest to everlasting fire 'by a just and irreprehensible, but incomprehensible, judgment.' Once more everything was clear, but quite arbitrary. But if the judgments of God were 'just and irreprehensible, but incomprehensible,' then the moral judgments of His elect would tend to acquire the same qualities. The school of Calvinist virtue was the Bible, and Calvin accepted the Bible more unconditionally than any of his predecessors had done. But the greater part of the Bible, and by far the richer in examples for imitation, was the Old Testament. In a gallery of the chosen of God which comprised Abraham, Jacob, Noah, Moses, Joshua, Samson, Elijah, David, and Solomon, the elect were given a wide choice for imitation. Certain among them, indeed, preferred minor figures as most possible of emulation. Knox, as we have seen, took Jehu as his guide when he wanted to have Mary of England put away, and Jeremiah when he wished to prove that treason was acceptable to God. For the Protestant, but for the Calvinist in particular, these kings and

warriors of a bloodthirsty Jewish tribe were literal
types of the elect, and men after God's heart. Even to
Luther, the sanest of the reformers, Abraham and
Moses were 'two good Christians,' while Jacob 'lived
in faith in Christ' and was consequently pleasing to
God in all his works, including his theft of Esau's
birthright. But the difficulty as well as the advantage
of such a text-book of morality as the Old Testament
was that it offered such a variety of examples that it
was hard for the faithful to choose. The inevitable
consequence was that they often chose the example
which was most convenient. Reading Calvin one has
a feeling that morality is a mystery as arbitrary as God
Himself. Charity can by a sudden turn become an
offence and hatred a duty. A lady who wrote him was
bold enough to maintain that David's hatred of his
enemies was not a sentiment to be imitated by those
who had had the advantage of reading the New
Testament. 'Such a gloss,' Calvin replied indignantly,
'would upset all Scripture.' David, he went on, had
been set before us as a pattern. 'And, in fact, it is
declared to us that in this ardour he is the type of our
Lord Jesus Christ. Now, if we assume to surpass in
sweetness and humanity Him who is the fountain of
piety and compassion, woe be unto us!'

The Calvinists guarded themselves effectually
against that danger. For no matter how opportunist
their morality might be in particular instances, the
Bible showed them one uniform rule of conduct in the
consistent severity of its punishments. Jacob might
steal his brother's birthright, Noah might act in a

manner unseemly in a patriarch, Samson might forni-
cate at large among the heathen, David might behave
very like one of the more decadent popes; but one
thing remained clear in the Bible, that every offence
against God was to be punished with the most extreme
rigour. In punishing, therefore, the Calvinist could
always feel that he was right, and even when he erred
in imitating one of the more questionable heroes of the
Old Testament, he generally erred on the godly side.

Along with this extremely practical theory of ethics
there existed, it is true, a more academic one drawn up
by Calvin himself. There it was laid down that every
member of the community was to understand the
duties of his position, but in practice this really meant
that he was to be subject to interference by everybody.
Calvin, indeed, made that perfectly clear. 'No member
of Christ,' he said, 'holds his gifts to himself, or for his
private use, but shares them among his fellow-members;
nor does he derive benefit save from those things
which proceed from the common profit of the body
as a whole. Thus the pious man owes to his brethren
all that it is in his power to give.' It was an excuse for
tyranny on the most comprehensive and the most
minute scale.

There was obviously a contradiction at the very
heart of the Calvinist system, and Calvin saw it, and
did his best to reconcile it. On the one hand there was
a God who freely ordained that certain souls should be
saved and others damned, without respect to their
merits or their desires; on the other, there was the fact
that the damned were responsible and were punished.

Nor was there any doubt in the mind of a Calvinist of
the reality of the punishment; these unfortunate people
were 'damned to unquenchable fire.' Calvin reconciled
the contradiction to his own satisfaction, if not to
that of his opponents. He was resolved to make the
strength of his religion overwhelming by incorporating
in it two mutually destructive beliefs: the belief in the
irresistible omnipotence of God working through His
instruments, and the belief in the power and responsibility of the individual. In clinging to this contradiction Calvin showed his profound knowledge of
human passion and vanity; for it was the contradiction in their faith that most of all nerved the Calvinists to their extraordinary successes. Though reason
denied the possibility they did feel within themselves
the irresistible power of God using them as instruments, and at the same time the responsibility and
initiative of free human beings. They fought with all
the greater ardour because it was predestined that they
should win. Victory stood almost in front of them,
and they were impatient until they reached it. The
ardour of God drove them on; the wrath of God confounded their enemies.

As for the reprobate, it was necessary, for a different
reason, that responsibility should be assigned to them.
To fight against people who were merely unfortunate
would have been inhuman even by Calvinistic standards;
to fight against the stubbornly obdurate, on the other
hand, was a task which might be embraced with zeal.
What the nature of the idolater's responsibility was,
however, remained vague even in the lucid pages of

Calvin. Perhaps the best image of it is given in the figures of the poor wretches who were burned for spreading the plague. In a sense, no doubt, it was not their fault that they spread the plague, yet the responsibility for it was mysteriously yet indelibly attached to them. The Calvinistic religion, as we have seen, was essentially a more objective one than the Lutheran. The very existence of the reprobate, in the eyes of a Calvinist, increased evil in the world, and to that extent the reprobate were responsible for it. Finally, the Calvinists had in themselves an objective criterion of what was good and evil. The elect were the visible army of God; the unfaithful were the manifest horde of darkness. The army of God were, moreover, His instruments; they fulfilled His objective judgments; they did not merely win victories, they carried out sentences. To oppose them was blasphemy; to inflict a military reverse on them was rebellion against God. Such effects as these were produced by the auto-suggestion of the Calvinist creed.

To what class of people did this extraordinary religion appeal, and what was its operation on them? It appealed most effectually to the class who were already beginning to realize that the future of power in society lay with them; it appealed to the merchant and banking classes, the progenitors of modern Capitalism. These had not yet gained the coveted perquisites of power in this world, honour and glory, yet they were conscious that power was theirs; somewhere, then, that power must surely be recognized and esteemed; it was esteemed, they discovered, in heaven.

The vocation of the trader was still, in fact, regarded with moral distaste by the Roman Catholic Church, and Luther had been equally contemptuous of it. A stigma, then, rested on the class to whom Calvin chiefly appealed; a mysterious and peculiar hope, therefore, superior to that accorded to any other class, was needed to blot it out. In the eyes of the world the children of God were under a cloud, as the Israelites had been in Egypt and Babylon, as the early Christians had been in Rome; but they felt the growing certainty of a sure deliverance.

Moreover, the virtues which Calvinism inculcated appealed with peculiar force to them. These were the virtues of thrift, frugality, perseverance, work – virtues which were to remain till within living memory the distinguishing virtues of the commercial classes. On these the capitalist system arose; it has now to a large extent dispensed with them, but it still accords them a retrospective veneration. Calvinism took root most profitably in places like Amsterdam, Antwerp and London. In England it led to that rapid growth of the commercial classes which was first crowned for a while by the triumph and dictatorship of Cromwell. In the Netherlands it inspired the successful resistance to the aristocratic power of Spain. In Scotland it appealed to a different class, but one which, too, felt potentialities sprouting, and appreciated to the full the Genevan virtues of thrift and frugality. It appealed to the lairds of Ayrshire and the Mearns and the rising burgesses of Edinburgh, and these remained the chief stay of the new faith when the nobles proved lukewarm or inconstant. But later still Calvinism was to extend its appeal to lower classes and finally to the lowest of all: to the resentful, the desperate, and the insane. In the rabble of criminals and zealots which composed a part of Cromwell's army it showed a portent to the world, while in Scotland during the same century it assumed some of its most richly comic as well as heroic forms; provided many examples of immovable fortitude, several of bloodthirsty crime, and the spectacle of Donald Cargill, the 'prophet,' excommunicating Charles II in a field before a handful of rustics. In the end the unconditional affirmation of the will of God found expression in the most wildly fantastic affirmations of the will of the individual. It was inevitable. Calvin had stuck to the omnipotence of God and to the responsibility of man, and how was a prophet so queer as Donald Cargill to distinguish between God's voice in him and his own? The more dull-witted of the brethren, it was certain, could scarcely keep a firm hold on that subtle compromise by which Calvin secured for himself the practical advantages of two antithetic beliefs; they were sure only of one thing, that God would exalt them and destroy their enemies. It was, indeed, the gist of their faith, and such men had no need of the nicer subtleties of Calvin's theology. Yet they loved the theological terms which they misapplied. Casuistry became popular. A woman abused Calvin in the street for making God the author of evil. She discovered afterwards that to corner a prophet of God might be a crime.

Like every other religion, in short, Calvinism appealed not only to its specific audience, but to some instinct of good or of evil in everybody. Its appeal, like that of every other religion, was twofold: it attracted or it repelled. It attracted a narrower circle than the Roman Catholic Church, but into that circle, as into the Catholic circle, were drawn, for every variety of reason, men of almost every degree of virtue and of vice. Calvinism appealed to the strong who felt assurance, and to the feeble who needed it; it ratified pride and fed vanity; it was an indulgent religion for the unscrupulous, and the strictest of all schools for the righteous; it encouraged interference and stiffened independence. But though it had a place for the strong and the weak, the learned and the simple, the humble and the arrogant, the ascetic and the sensual, it had no place at all for the merciful or the generous. It could no more have produced a figure like Saint Francis than it could have produced one like Socrates. Judged by the best in humanity, its figures seem narrow, sick, and almost pathological. Judged by the best examples of Protestantism even, they make up at best a peculiar people. To turn from Calvin or Knox to Socrates is to turn from obsession to sanity. To turn from them to Luther himself is to pass from the spectacle of an incurable spiritual malady to that of a spiritual struggle, painful perhaps, but human and brave. Calvinism inspired great changes, but it remained the religion of a sect.

To Knox, for many reasons, the appeal of Calvinism was bound to be irresistible; he, if anybody, was

obviously predestined to be a Calvinist. From his first
adherence to Protestantism he had found it hard to
conceive that he could be in the wrong: Calvinism
assured him that none but Calvinists were in the right,
and that God had so ordained it. He was naturally
of an obstinate temper: Calvinism encouraged obstinacy. He had an inconquerable desire to impose his
will on others: Calvinism told him that it was his duty
to do so. He hated the necessity of acknowledging
any earthly authority higher than his own: Calvinism
proclaimed that God's will was supreme, and that it
was his office to enforce it. He had, in spite of all this,
a native timidity and caution whose effects had often
perplexed him; he could only feel invincible when he
recognized himself as the instrument of a mightier
power: Calvinism left him in no doubt that he was the
instrument of God. He was finally a choleric and
violent man: Calvinism flung open for him the portals
of the Old Testament, which had so expediently been
ignored both by Catholics and Lutherans, and revealed the full scale of God's judgments: dotards,
women, children and cattle put to the edge of the
sword, infants' brains dashed out against the stones,
cities levelled to the ground, races exterminated to the
last man, plagues of boils and running sores, plagues
of locusts, lice, serpents and cockatrices, floods,
tempests and earthquakes, rains of fire and lakes of
blood, and the still more terrible, because unnameable,
abomination of desolation. To a man who had been a
priest; to one who had lived in St. Andrews Castle,
the galleys, and Berwick, and had known in these

places the worst off-scourings of Protestantism and of
the professional criminal classes, the Old Testament
presented as well, however, a picture of life which must
have struck him by its truth. Fornication, abomination, adultery, idolatry: these were to remain till the
end of his life Knox's favourite terms.

For these general reasons, then, the appeal of
Calvinism to Knox must have been decisive. There
were more particular causes, however, which rein-
forced it. Till the hour when he left the Roman
Catholic Church Knox's position in it had been obscure.
After that, when he cast in his lot with the Protestants,
he rose quickly to pre-eminence; but at once his
success was snatched from him and he was compelled
to lie inactive for nineteen months in a French galley.
He had risen again in Edward's brief Protestant reign,
but again he had been forced to give up all the power
he had won. He had next been sent to Frankfort, to a
petty community which gave no scope for his powers;
he had tried to evade the new task, and at last, deliberately or accidentally, had succeeded in doing so;
yet his manner of leaving the town had had some
touch of ignominy. He had last of all scored an immense success in Scotland, but at the final moment
prudence or necessity had compelled him to draw back
once more. Both in England and in Frankfort his
thwarted desire for power had been refused the opportunity it urgently demanded. He had complained in
both places that the preacher was not allowed to impose discipline on his flock. He was now fifty; nothing
he had taken part in had succeeded; not once yet had he

attained a position in which his word had to be feared,
and his will obeyed. In Geneva he succeeded at last;
he was a minister of a Calvinist church, and the
Calvinist discipline was extremely rigorous. A man
who feels within him the necessity to rule will exercise
it by managing a few obscure rustics in a small
village rather than not exercise it at all. Knox had
begun his reforming career as a dominie; now, after
waiting for ten years, he was at last permitted to direct
and punish adult human beings. If he showed a disinclination to leave Geneva when greater opportunities
beckoned, it was natural enough. He was prone to
sudden attacks of timidity, and in Geneva, on however
small a scale, he was fulfilling his nature.

His time there was busily occupied. He had to
preach three sermons a week, each of which, as the
usage of the time prescribed, would last from two to
three hours. He admonished and chastised his
congregation. He studied Greek and Hebrew. He
wrote, and ruled his household. He had never been so
happy in his life. Geneva, he said to Mrs. Locke, was
'the most perfect school of Christ that ever was on the
earth since the days of the Apostles.'

Yet, in spite of all this, in spite of his power in the
congregation and the solace of Mrs. Bowes' and Mrs.
Knox's company, he still longed for the comfort which
only other men's wives, it seemed, could give him in
full measure. 'Ye wrote that your desire is earnest to
see me,' he said in a letter to Mrs. Locke in London,
a few months after he had settled in Geneva with his
family. 'Dear sister, if I could express the thirst and

languor which I have for your presence, I shall appear to pass measure. Yea, I weep and rejoice in remembrance of you; but that would evanish by the comfort of your presence, which I assure you is so dear to me that if the charge of this little flock here, gathered in Christ's name, did not impede me, my presence should anticipate my letter.' What was the comfort which he longed for so earnestly? It was the same which he had found once in Mrs. Bowes' friendship, a friendship which, it was clear, however, no longer quite satisfied his needs. Writing to Mrs. Locke and her friend, Mrs. Hickman, jointly, he revealed what it was: 'God, I doubt not, brought us on such familiar acquaintance,' he said, 'that your hearts were incensed and kindled with a special care over me, as the mother useth to be over her natural child.' His urgent necessity during these years, in fact, seems to have been to surround himself with mothers. He had secured Mrs. Bowes already; to secure another a trifling relaxation of principle would surely be justifiable. On the 9th of December accordingly he suddenly broke out in the middle of a letter to Mrs. Locke: 'Were it not that partly ye are impeded by your head, and partly by so good occasion as God hath now offered you to remain where ye are, in my heart I would have wished, yea and cannot cease to wish, that it would please God to guide you to this place.' He enclosed, he said, a tract on the first temptation of Christ, written in Edinburgh, by means of which some had been, so they said, 'brought from the bottom of hell.' It pleased God to bring Mrs. Locke to Geneva in the following May, in spite of the opposition of her 'head,' who was left behind in London. She appeared with her son Harry, her daughter Anne, and a maid called Katherine. The adventure began disastrously. Anne died a few days after arriving, and her death filled the poor mother with remorse.

It was, it may be remembered, in the year that Mrs. Locke came out to Geneva that Janet Adamson had written from Edinburgh complaining also about her 'head.' But Janet was the Dean of Guild's daughter; she must have been quite young. Knox was certain, he told her, that 'with patience ye must abide His merciful deliverance, determining with yourself never to obey manifest iniquity for the pleasure of any mortal man.' The cases were obviously different.

CHAPTER VIII

HESITATION AT DIEPPE

S INCE his arrival in Geneva in September 1556, Knox had been hearing fairly regularly from Scotland. In May 1557 he received a message which once more threw him into a prolonged fit of hesitation. It was from Glencairn, Argyll, Erskine and Lord James Stuart, the greatest nobles on the reformed side. It urgently requested him in the Lord's name to return to his native land, where he would find everyone as zealous as he had left them. Persecution had not increased; on the contrary, the priests were daily in less estimation with the Queen as with the nobility; there was every prospect that God would augment His flock. The signatories added that they were ready to hazard their lives and their goods in the forward setting of the glory of God; the substance of what they proposed Knox would learn from the faithful bearers of the letter.

The opportunity had come, and Knox was free to accept or reject it – he did neither. He consulted with Calvin and the other ministers in Geneva. No help there; he could not refuse the call, they said, 'unless he would declare himself rebellious unto his God, and unmerciful to his country.' It was obvious that he could not show himself rebellious to God, but a little deliberation would be permissible surely before one threw oneself into such a great task. Knox deliberated at length. He received the urgent summons in May; he hurried from Geneva, amid the sobs of his apprehensive congregation, at the end of September. Dieppe was the first halting stage in his long journey. He set out with the inflexible determination of reaching it, and successfully accomplished the journey in four weeks. Further deliberation, however, was now demanded. He was assisted in it by two letters, one to himself, one which a friend of his had received. The first informed him that the matter proposed in Scotland was now finally to be decided upon, and advised him to stay where he was until the decision was reached. The second contained a warning that the supporters of the adventure had not the boldness and constancy required; that some were sorry it had ever been proposed, some were ashamed of it, and others were prepared to deny that they had any connexion with it at all. Knox had given the matter several months' thought, and he had actually reached Dieppe. The news, he now wrote to the Scottish nobles, confounded him and pierced him with anguish and sorrow. He had come to Dieppe of full mind to sail for Scotland with the first ship; now he was compelled to put it off. He reminded them of the length of time he had spent in consulting with the godly and learned, that he might have their judgments for the assurance of his own conscience and those of his correspondents. 'And then, that nothing should succeed such long consultation,' he went on, 'cannot but redound either to your shame or mine; for either it shall appear that I was marvellous vain, being so solicitous where no necessity required, or else that such as were my movers thereto lacked the ripeness of judgment in their first vocation.' But it was plain to him where the fault lay, and plain too that, after all his care, he would have to bear the brunt of it. 'To some it may appear a small and light matter,' he told these men who were only prepared to hazard their lives, 'that I have cast off, and as it were abandoned, both my particular care and my public office and charge, leaving my house and poor family destitute of all head, save God only, and committing that small (but in Christ dearly beloved) flock, over which I was appointed one of the ministers, to the charge of another.' Yet to him, he said, 'more worldly substance than I will express could not have caused me willingly to behold the eyes of so many grave men weep at once for my cause, as that I did in taking my last good night from them.' The brethren in Geneva, it appeared, had been led to expect that he was going to the glorious dangers of a possible martyrdom in Scotland, and after all he had only gone to Dieppe! If he should return to them now, he asked, and they were to inquire why he had not reached Scotland, what was he to answer?

But this was a minor grievance. The real cause 'of my dolour and sorrow (God is witness),' he assured the nobles, 'is for nothing pertaining either to my corporal contentment or worldly displeasure; but it is for the grievous plagues and punishments of God, which

assuredly shall apprehend not only you, but every
inhabitant of that miserable realm and isle, except that
the power of God, by the liberty of His Evangel,
deliver you from bondage. I mean not only that
perpetual fire and torment, prepared for the devil,
and for such as denying Christ Jesus, and His known
verity, do follow the sons of perdition; but also that
thraldom and misery shall apprehend your own bodies,
your children, subjects, and posterity whom ye have
betrayed (in conscience I can except none that bear the
name of nobility), and presently do fight to betray
them and your realm to the slavery of strangers.'
By strangers he meant the French, to whom the
nobility were as inveterately opposed as he was
himself.

The air was cleared, however, the nobility were
rebuked, the prophet was triumphantly rehabilitated,
and Knox had leisure to break into one of those
passages of exalted eloquence which he could command
so easily. 'I am not ignorant,' he said, 'that fearful
troubles shall ensue your enterprise; but O joyful and
comfortable are those troubles and adversities which
man sustaineth for the accomplishment of God's will,
revealed by His Word. Your subjects, yea, your
brethren are oppressed, their bodies and souls holden in
bondage; and God speaketh to your consciences (unless
ye be dead with the blind world), that you ought to
hazard your own lives (be it against kings and emperors)
for their deliverance; for only for that cause are ye called
princes of the people, and ye receive of your brethren
honour, tribute, and homage at God's commandment;

not by reason of your birth and progeny (as the most part of men falsely do suppose), but by reason of your office and duty, which is to vindicate and deliver your subjects and brethren from all violence and oppression, to the uttermost of your power.'

The appeal to hazard life and goods was couched in the noblest strain, but the Scottish nobles may have reflected that Knox stood somewhat apart from the danger, and that to inspire heroism in Scotland and England while he stayed in Dieppe had become something of a habit with him. At any rate they did not send any immediate reply.

On the 1st of December, Knox, still sitting stubbornly in Dieppe, sent out a further epistle, this time to the brethren generally. He had received no reply, he began, to various letters which he had written since May, but he attributed this to the uncertainty of the times rather than to their negligence. He warned them against a danger which was having two grave consequences. Their loose living gave a handle to the Papists, and was causing some of the nicer brethren to secede and separate into pernicious and damnable sects. Although neither the Catholics nor the over-nice should escape sharp punishment, yet he exhorted his brethren to avoid offence.

The defections, however, were quite unjustifiable, he went on. They sprang from two errors: first, those sectaries judged a religion by the lives of its professors; secondly, they required an impossible justice and purity of conduct. From these misconceptions followed the most horrible absurdities. For if goodness of life were made the criterion of true religion, it followed that the idolatry of heathens and Mahometans must be approved, and, by the same standard, that the holy law of God must be rejected as false and vain. Among the Pagans there had been men of singular external virtue, and the Turks lived a stricter life even than God's Word required. But on the other hand, what period could be found in Biblical history in which iniquity was not plentiful? Abraham himself, the father of the faithful, had denied his wife; the Israelites, after they received the law, had committed horrible fornication; David had been guilty of adultery and murder; God's people, in short, had been liberally inoculated with every possible vice. But did this prove that their religion was false? 'Far be such cogitations,' he declared, 'from the hearts of Christians.'

Yet after the coming of Christ the Church might be expected to show greater purity, it would be argued. This, too, was an error. Paul, or rather the Holy Ghost speaking through him, had saluted the congregations of Corinth, Galatia and Thessalonica as members of the true Church of Christ. How had those congregations spent their time? In 'fornication, adultery, incest, strife, debate, contention, and envy.' Paul, it is true, had denounced those vices, yet none the less he had reverenced the churches themselves as truly Christian. 'And therefore,' Knox went on triumphantly, 'I say that the life and conversation of man is no assured note, sign, or token of Christ's visible Kirk.' The real mark of that Kirk was 'the substance of that doctrine and religion, which is publicly preached and universally received in any congregation.' Knox had learned his Genevan lesson thoroughly.

Nevertheless he told the brethren a second time that they must behave themselves and then went on to the more congenial task of refuting the seceders. Their heresies were incredible. By their godly and pure lives they denied the power of justification, which came by faith alone. Some denied that Christ was the Son of God. Others held that it was possible to fulfil the law of God in this life. Others again thought that Christ's justice was of no avail unless the believer lived justly himself. But the supreme error common to them all was that God had given everyone a free choice to work out his salvation. The moral to be drawn was obvious. 'Suffer no man,' Knox said in conclusion, 'without trial and examination to take upon himself the office of a preacher.'

On the 17th of December he wrote in a somewhat different strain to the nobles. This time he was addressing a more intelligent and less impressionable audience, and he drew exhaustively on the support of Holy Scripture. His object was to point out the benefits which accrued to princes who took messengers of God under their wing. Pharaoh's kindness to Joseph had been amply returned, he pointed out, during the lean years in Egypt. Nebuchadnezzar's promotion of Daniel had been repaid, for after a long punishment the king was not only restored to his own shape, but to his former dignity. The conclusion Knox left the nobles to draw for themselves. He hoped they were still resolved to hazard all in the cause of Christ. He counselled them meanwhile to moderation. He had heard that there had been rebellion against the established authority in the realm. He commanded them not to disobey the authority in anything lawful; they should rather seek its favours, while openly confessing their faith. If their requests were refused, then, while giving the Queen obedience in every other respect, they should strive to establish the true Church whether she consented or not. Above all, he warned them against the Duke of Châtelherault, and the Hamiltons generally. The letter was a judicious mixture of prophecy and practical advice. Knox had now no intention of going to Scotland, and he could take a reasonable view of the situation.

He stayed on in Dieppe till March. There was a large Calvinist congregation in the town, and he probably preached on occasion. But he had a great deal of time on his hands, and he determined to employ it in exposing what, his experience told him with more and more urgency, was a crucial evil. Mary Tudor, a Papist, ruled in England; Mary of Lorraine, another Papist, reigned in his own land. The first had made him fly the country, the other, he must have learned by now, had called his letter a pasquil. Women were thus the sole cause why Protestantism was being persecuted in two countries, and why he was stranded in Dieppe. There may have been other reasons which spurred him to his protest. He had a sincere appreciation of the qualities of motherly women; he had left two of them behind in Geneva. But the maternal instinct is possessive, and a proprietrial air, charming in a correspondent, may become annoying in a member of one's household. Mrs. Bowes in England had sometimes blamed him for not writing oftener to her; in Geneva her importunate demands and her spiritual trials alike may already have begun to pall. He had had domestic troubles daily. On every count the case against women was decisive. He sat down and wrote *The First Blast of the Trumpet against the Monstrous Regiment of Women.*

He began magnificently: 'Wonder it is that amongst so many pregnant wits as the Isle of Great Britain hath produced, so many godly and zealous preachers as England did sometime nourish, and amongst so many learned, and men of grave judgment, as this day by Jezebel are exiled, none is found so stout of courage, so faithful to God, nor loving to their native country, that they dare admonish the inhabitants of that isle, how abominable before God is the empire and rule of a wicked woman, yea, of a traitress and bastard; and what may a people or nation left destitute of a lawful head do by the authority of God's Word in electing and appointing common rulers and magistrates.' 'I am assured,' he went on, 'that God hath revealed to some in this our age, that it is more than a monster in nature that a woman shall reign and have empire above man.' Enemies of God, it was true, would find reasons enough why such doctrines should not be published, but if it were wisdom to conceal the truth the ancient prophets of God had been fools. His readers feared persecution, but had any of the prophets and apostles drawn back for fear of persecution? 'If any think that the empire of women is not of such importance,' he continued, 'that for the suppressing of the same any man is bound to hazard his life; I answer, that to suppress it is in the hand of God alone. But to utter the impiety and abomination of the same, I say, it is the duty of every true messenger of God to whom the truth is revealed on that behalf. I shall be called foolish, curious, despiteful, and a sower of sedition; and one day perchance I may be attainted of treason. But seeing that impossible it is, but that either I shall offend God or else that I shall displease the world, I have determined to obey God, notwithstanding that the world shall rage thereat.'

With this splendid flourish the book began, but the sound of the first blast quickly died away, and Knox began to look about him anxiously for all those proofs of woman's infamy which the exordium promised. These turned out to be disappointing. Man, he found, drawing on his knowledge, was strong and discreet. Woman, on the other hand, was mad and phrenetic. Was it reasonable that the passionate should rule the calm and the strong? Women, moreover, had been known to die of sudden joy, to commit suicide, to betray their country to strangers, and to be so avid of dominion that they murdered their husbands and children. Besides, Aristotle had pronounced against woman; Tertullian had called her 'the portal and gate of the devil'; Augustine and

Ambrose had pointed out that through her sin came
into the world; and the natural world gave further
examples: did the lion, for example, 'stoop before the
lioness?' Paul, moreover, had called man woman's
head. But 'who would not judge that body to be a
monster,' Knox reasoned, 'where there was no head
eminent above the rest, but that the eyes were in the
hands, the tongue and mouth beneath in the belly, and
the ears in the feet.' It was all wrong, but his fund of
arguments unexpectedly ran dry. He could only
reiterate variously that the domination of woman was
'a monster,' that it was 'monstrous,' and that it was
indeed 'monstriferous.' It was with relief that he came
to his peroration, and after so much reasoning could
prophesy again. 'Cursed Jezebel of England,' he
wrote, 'with the pestilent and detestable generation of
Papists, make no little brag and boast, that they have
triumphed not only against Wyatt, but also against all
such as have enterprised anything against them or their
proceedings. I fear not to say that the day of vengeance, which shall apprehend that horrible monster
Jezebel of England, is already appointed in the
counsel of the Eternal', and so on, in his familiar vein.
'And therefore let all men be advertised,' he concluded,
'for *The First Trumpet hath once blown*.'

Knox's attitude to woman, it will be seen, sometimes changed with extraordinary rapidity. On Mary
Tudor's accession to the throne he had begged God to
illuminate her heart with pregnant gifts of the Holy
Ghost and to repress the pride of those who would
rebel; after his flight his prayer was to send a Jehu to

cut off her days. When Mary of Guise was behaving with great toleration to the Protestants in Scotland she had been 'a princess honourable, endowed with wisdom and graces singularly,' but now that he had heard about the pasquil she, like all other queens, was a monster. The one class of women who still had his modified approval was mothers, but he made it clear in *The Blast* that they should have no power over their sons. His mother had perhaps died when he was young; he had known his stepmother, however, and, the Papists declared indeed, in a sense which would at once suggest itself to a theological mind. Two mothers were at present waiting for him in Geneva, but their authority, like that of his stepmother, must have appeared in his eyes a usurped one. His first taste of feminine discipline had reached him from an illegitimate source; he now felt that all feminine rule was illegitimate. Though they were as solicitous for him 'as the mother useth to be over her natural child,' Mrs. Bowes and Mrs. Locke were obviously not real mothers. Mary of England and Mary of Guise, he was equally convinced, could not be real queens.

He had been in Dieppe for five months; he might as well return to Geneva again, where, in his absence, he had once more been elected minister. He took *The First Blast* with him. What Calvin's opinion of it would be he was not at all sure, but the book was too good to be lost. Accordingly he had it printed secretly, with no indication of the author's name or of the publisher's. Copies were sent to England. Calais had just been lost; the country seemed ripe for seditious propaganda. The book was accordingly condemned by royal proclamation, and possession of it was made punishable by death. Calvin in Geneva sat on, serenely unaware that such a notorious work had been printed in the city of God.

CHAPTER IX

DOUBTS, THREATS,
AND PREDESTINATION

Now that he had returned to Geneva, Knox was
assailed with doubts. While he had been in Dieppe he
had been at least technically on the road to Scotland;
but now he had definitely turned his back on it. Had
he been wrong? Had too much deliberation made him
lose an opportunity which might not return again?
Why, really, had he hesitated? Once more he did not
know.

In his first letter to the Lords from Dieppe he had
cast the blame on them, and had declared that they
would be punished. But afterwards he had exhorted
them to continue in the course which they had chosen,
and he could not but see that there was some show of
illogicality here. Besides, people might imagine that
he had drawn back because he was timid, or even that
he was more intrepid in counsel than in action. Doubts
had already begun to trouble him before he left
Dieppe. 'If any object,' he wrote to Mrs. Guthrie, an
Edinburgh sister, on the 16th of March – 'if any
object, I follow not the counsel I give to others, for my
fleeing the country declareth my fear; I answer, I bind
no man to my example. Yet I trust to God that I do not

expressedly against the Word, which God uttereth to me. If the love of this life, or the fear of corporal death, caused me to deny the known verity, or to do anything in the eyes of men which might seem for fear to favour idolatry, then woe unto me forever, for I were nothing but a traitor to Christ and His religion.' But had he ever denied the known verity in Dieppe and Geneva? Had he done anything there to favour idolatry? Never. 'But if my fear,' he continued, 'be so measured that it compels me not to commit open iniquity, then do I nothing against my counsel, which is not mine but the express commandment of Christ Jesus, commanding us to forsake ourselves and to follow Him. Yet assure yourself of that,' he concluded, 'that whenever a greater number of you shall call upon me than now hath bound me to serve them, that by His grace it shall not be the fear of corporal punishment, neither yet of the fear temporal, that shall impede my coming to you.' 'Whenever a greater number of you shall call upon me than now': it had been the weakness of the Protestant forces, then, that had made him draw back! But this explanation did not satisfy him for long, nor was he altogether pleased with the theory of measured fear. He would have to search the Scriptures for guidance.

'The chosen vessel of Christ Jesus, St. Paul,' he began a letter to the sisters in Edinburgh a month later, 'the chosen vessel of Christ Jesus, St. Paul, appointed to his ministry and preaching, not by man, but by the imperial voice of the Son of God speaking unto him from heaven, ashamed not to confess (dearly beloved), that albeit he had an earnest zeal and desire to have

visited the congregation of Thessalonica in their
greatest necessity, that yet he was impeded by Satan
of his journey and purpose.

'It may appear marvellous at the first sight that
Satan should have such power to impede such a good
and godly work which the people desired so earnestly.
But if we shall mark and consider, dear sisters, that
God sometimes does humble His most faithful servants,
disappointing them of their own enterp. ses, which
they not the less have purposed for promoting His
glory, we shall cease to wonder, and begin to magnify
the providence of our mighty God, Who only disposeth
the times, and alone knoweth the causes why He not
in all things satisfies the desires in this mortal life of
His dearest children.'

Having adroitly transferred the responsibility from
the devil to God Himself, Knox went on: 'Foolishness,
presumption, and arrogance it were in me to compare
myself with that most excellent instrument of the Lord
Jesus, in zeal towards the promoting of Christ's glory,
or yet love towards the salvation and comfort of my
brethren. No, alas! as my heart is corrupt, and the
hypocrisy thereof, in many thousand cases, hid from
myself, so is my zeal cold and my love nothing, if it
shall be tried by the right touch-stone. Only this dare
I say, that sometimes (seldom, alas!) I feel a sob and
groan, willing that Christ Jesus might openly be
preached in my native country, with a certain desire
that my ears might hear it, although it should be with
the loss of this wretched life. And of very purpose to
have visited you,' he continued, coming to the point,

'did I leave this congregation here, and also the family committed to my particular charge; but the cause of my stop do I not to this day clearly understand. I most suspect my own wickedness,' he admitted. He was not worthy, it seemed, 'of so great a joy and comfort as to hear Christ Jesus truly preached,' where his heart most desired it. But why was he not worthy? Because of former ingratitude and disobedience to God. This was clearly the reason why God had made him deliberate so long in Geneva and remain so long in Dieppe. 'And so,' he continued, 'to punish my former unthankfulness, it may be that my God most justly hath permitted Satan to put in my mind such cogitations, as did impede my journey towards you at this present; and they were these: I heard such troubles as appeared in that realm, I began to dispute with myself as follows: Shall Christ, the Author of peace, concord and quietness, be preached where war is proclaimed, sedition engendered and tumults appear to rise? Shall not His Evangel be accused, as the cause of all calamity which is like to follow? What comfort canst thou have to see the one half of the people rise up against the other: yea, to jeopard the one, to murder and destroy the other, but above all, what joy shall it be to thy heart to behold with thy eyes thy native country betrayed into the hands of strangers, which to no man's judgment can be avoided, because that they who ought to defend it, and the liberty thereof, are so blind, dull and obstinate that they will not see their own destruction?' Satan had spoken with great eloquence at the time, it was clear, yet Knox knew now that his arguments had been fallacious. 'My conscience beareth record,' he went on, 'that the salvation of my brethren ought to be so dear unto me that it ought to be sought with the hazard of all that is on earth.' He repeated again that he accused nobody so much as himself and the former ingratitude which had brought on this sanctioned assault of Satan, and he begged the sisters to pray that he might give no scandal to the religion he professed. The two letters, he added, which he had received at Dieppe may have had something to do with his disinclination to go to Scotland.

It was one of the advantages of the Calvinist creed that it could explain the sins of its adherents, and by that explanation put them in a somewhat more favourable light. To the nobles Knox had denied that he had offended at all; to Mrs. Guthrie he had justified his inaction as the result of fearing in measure; to the sisters he confessed his sin, but explained it as a just punishment which, at the most embarrassing moment, God had inflicted upon him. This punishment was certainly his reward for sins, unspecified, of which he had been guilty in the past; but in itself it was less a sin than a misfortune, and so sin was mysteriously pushed farther into the background. Thus his theory that God had prevented him from going to Scotland was a justification of the immediate offence, even if it was an indirect confession of a former weakness; and the weakness it acknowledged, moreover, was that general species of weakness to which all human beings are subject. From specific blame, therefore, he stood exonerated. He could not have been wrong, his confused apology insisted, even while he was accusing himself. Yet his explanation did not quite satisfy him. 'The cause of my step do I not to this day understand,' he said. He had said something very like it to Mrs. Bowes when he fled from London.

That he should acknowledge Satan's arguments, so overwhelming at the time, to be erroneous at present, was inevitable, however. Satan had asked him if Christ could be preached where sedition was engendered, and inquired what comfort he could have in seeing one half of a people rising against the other. Knox was presently to have the comfort of commanding one half of the people not merely to rise against, but to exterminate the other, and of preaching sedition and Christ in one breath. His letter to the sisters was written in April; his Appellation to the Nobility and Estates of Scotland was finished in the first half of July.

His appeal was against the insult he had received two years before, when his effigy had been burned at the market cross in Edinburgh. Could Satan, to enforce his arguments, otherwise so humane, have held up before Knox during those long deliberations in the safety of Geneva that affrighting symbolical ceremony, and have whispered that the same fate might overtake the living prophet? It may have been so; Knox did not mention it; but the incident had rankled in his memory for two years, and he now denounced the cruelty of the Catholics in burning an effigy. 'From all judgment of that wicked generation,' he announced, 'I make it known to your honours, that I appeal to a lawful and general council,' in other words, to the Lords themselves.

His Appellation had two objects: to convince the nobles of their legitimate powers, especially in protecting messengers of God, and to instruct them how those powers should be used. The first was easy; to the second he bent all his powers of persuasion. The duties of the nobles, he discovered, were three: first, to punish malefactors and protect the innocent; secondly, to instruct the people in the true religion and root out abuses; and thirdly, to punish with death any who taught false doctrine. If any one should object that the true church should reform itself, they were expressly to know that this was heresy. The reformation of religion, he said, 'doth especially appertain to the civil magistrate.'

While he had been in Scotland in 1555 he had sprung on the astonished Scottish Protestants his favourite theory that Catholics were idolaters. He found this theory particularly useful now. From the Old Testament it was easy to prove that idolatry should be punished by death, but in Deuteronomy he came across a passage of really ample ferocity for all purposes. 'If,' the Holy Scriptures declared – 'if thy brother, son, daughter, wife, or neighbour, whom thou lovest as thine own life, solicit thee secretly, saying, Let us go serve other gods, whom neither thou, nor thy fathers, have known, consent not to him, hear him not; let not thine eye spare him, show him no indulgence or favour, hide him not, but utterly kill him: let thy hand be the first upon him, that he may be slain, and after that the hand of the whole people.' From this passage Knox drew three logical conclusions, 'appertaining,' as he truly said, 'to our purpose.' First, that even those who solicit to idolatry must be put to death; secondly, that idolaters must suffer no matter what their rank may be; and thirdly, that their punishment appertains not to 'kings and chief rulers only, but also to the whole body of that people, and to every member of the same, according to that possibility and occasion which God doth minister to revenge the injury done against His glory.' Any Protestant had obviously, therefore, the right to kill any Catholic; it was the collective duty of the Protestants, however, to exterminate the Catholics *en masse*. He supported this theory with the most indefatigably persuasive and the most portentously prolix arguments, and by a miracle of ingenuity succeeded in being at once monstrous and boring. He drew his most convincing reasons from the Old Testament. God had commanded all the inhabitants of idolatrous nations to be destroyed. He had, moreover, strictly enjoined any city which was even declining into idolatry to be put to the edge of the sword. For a moment Knox himself was awed by the horrors he had called up. 'To the carnal man,' he said in parenthesis, 'this may appear a rigorous and severe judgment, yea, it may rather seem to be pronounced in rage than in wisdom. For what city was ever yet, in which, to man's judgment, were not to be found many innocent persons, as infants, children, and some simple and ignorant souls who neither did nor could consent to such impiety? And yet we find no exception, but all are appointed to the cruel death. But in such cases wills God that all creatures stoop, cover their faces, and desist from reasoning when commandment is given to execute His judgments.' He considered this mystery for a little, but the attractions of his original theme drew him back again. Whenever God put the sword into the hands of His elect, they were bound to remove enormities. 'In such places, I say, it is not only lawful to punish to the death such as labour to subvert the true religion, but the magistrates and people are bound so to do, unless they will provoke the wrath of God against themselves. And therefore I fear not to affirm that it had been the duty of the nobility, judges, rulers, and people of England, not only to have resisted and gainsaid Mary, that Jezebel, whom they call the Queen, but also to have punished her to the death, together with all such as should have assisted her, what time that she and they openly began to suppress Christ's Evangel.' He became more loathsomely reasonable as he went on. He addressed himself, he said, to 'the sober and godly reader.' If the Scottish nobles accepted his 'reasonable and just advice,' the world would see that the very angels of the Eternal would fight on their side. If they refused it, however, the Almighty in His turn would refuse them. His words were not his own, he declared, but those of God, Who would perform the promises of His prophet. 'I have offered unto you,' he said, to sum the matter up, 'the verity of Christ Jesus.' He prayed that the Holy Ghost might rule their hearts, and the spirit of Jesus Christ guide them to the end.

The tone of this extraordinary letter is very different from that of the frenzied denunciations which four years earlier Knox had sent out from Dieppe. Deprived of his former position, alone in a foreign town, help-lessly witnessing the destruction of a religion which he thought the only true one, he had written in impotent rage, and prophesied terrors which he rather hoped for than believed in. But now he wrote from the security of the greatest stronghold of the elect, and he wrote to a party who were not visibly oppressed, but were, on the contrary, confidently enhancing their power. He wrote to them in a strain, not of wild prophecy, but of sober advice. He wrote, moreover, to men far younger and less experienced than himself. The policy he out-lined for them was one which could only have been carried out by fiends, yet his reasonable and persuasive style showed that he had no consciousness that this was so. He was appealing, finally, against one of the minor effects of a policy whose cruelty, in comparison with what he counselled, was almost humane.

His letters from Dieppe showed an ungovernable temper and an imagination delighting in cruelty. His Ap-pellation from Geneva could only be the work of a mind corrupted by a monstrous doctrine. Any generous and humane qualities which Knox had ever possessed had withered during two years spent in the close and demor-alising atmosphere of Geneva, and four years of passion-ate brooding over the obscene violences of a tribal god and a bloodthirsty people. His letter showed not merely an extreme insensibility to human sufferings; it lingered sickeningly in a delighted contemplation of them.

At the same time that he was drawing up the Appellation, he was preparing for perusal a new edition, with notes, of his letter to Mary of Guise. In its new dress it could no longer be mistaken for the work of 'a worm most wretched.' 'It shall not excuse you to say or think,' he told the Regent, 'that ye doubt whether I be sent of God or no.' To deny his requests was to rebel against God. Her religion, he continued, was as odious to the Almighty as the acts of murderers and harlots. Her authority was borrowed. God, moreover, had already visited His judgments on her, for it was not by chance that she had lost her two sons within six hours of their birth, and that her husband had died ignominiously. 'God move your heart to understand my petition,' he said in valediction.

The letter which he presently despatched to the commons of Scotland was comparatively mild. They, as well as the nobles, it seemed, were responsible for the reformation of religion, but their power was less, and accordingly their tasks were more modest. They had the right, however, to choose preachers for themselves and to maintain them against persecution, and they might justly refuse the tithes demanded by the false church, for poor as they were, Christ had died for them. Knox's distribution of advice to Scotland was by his standards judicious. To the powerful he counselled violence and cruelty, to the subordinate a moderate dose of independence.

While he was admonishing Scotland and caring for his flock, however, he was already seeking other triumphs. The Anabaptists were becoming troublesome; they were a menace to true religion in Scotland, as he had already warned his colleagues; they were also publishing books, and it was imperative that these should be confuted. One book in particular, called *Careless by Necessity*, had been singled out by the English brethren, and a request sent by them to Geneva that it might be answered. Knox took on the task, a little, it seems, to Calvin's discomfort. Calvin refused to have Geneva mentioned on the title-page, and ordered two members of the English congregation to vouch that the reply should contain nothing contrary to the orthodox doctrine.

The beliefs of the Anabaptists have perhaps been most judiciously characterized by Knox's standard biographer, the Reverend Dr. M'Crie. 'The radical error of this sect,' he says, 'was a fond conceit of a certain ideal spirituality and perfection by which they considered the Christian Church to be essentially distinguished from the Jewish, which was, in their opinion, a mere carnal, secular society. Entertaining this notion, they were naturally led to abridge the rule of faith and manners by confining themselves almost entirely to the New Testament, and to adopt their other opinions concerning the unlawfulness of infant baptism, of civil magistracy, national churches, oaths and defensive war. But besides these tenets, the Anabaptists were, at this period, generally infected with the Pelagian heresy, and united with the Papists in loading the doctrines which the reformers held respecting predestination and grace with the most odious charges.' The Anabaptists believed, in other words, that Christianity had its origin in Christ, that God loved rather than hated His creatures, that salvation was free to whoever believed in and imitated Jesus, and that it was the Christian's duty to love his fellow-creatures. They held besides that war was odious, that the legal system had not descended from God, and that no man should be persecuted, far less burned, for obeying his conscience. It was these errors that Knox set himself now to refute.

Careless by Necessity was the work of a naïve, mobile, disinterested and witty mind, but of a mind untrained in theological speculation. Knox's mind was neither disinterested nor mobile, but he had behind him the greatest theological genius of the age, Calvin. The Anabaptist who wrote *Careless by Necessity* sought to understand God by the light of reason and nature; Knox held inflexibly to the God of revelation as interpreted by Calvin. There were other differences between the disputants which made the controversy even more profitless than it might otherwise have been. The Anabaptist looked for the attributes of God in his own spiritual aspirations and in his conscience; Knox found them in God's objective judgments, derived chiefly from Old Testament history. In everything he wrote the Anabaptist implied the existence of free-will; in all his replies Knox assumed the truth of predestination. The Anabaptist could not have understood Knox, and it was clear that Knox did not understand the Anabaptist.

Yet the Anabaptist gave Knox a great deal of trouble. He asserted, for instance, that according to the Calvinists God created the greater part of mankind that He might damn them. Knox was indignant at this iniquitous misrepresentation; God damned the reprobate, he replied, not for the mere sake of damning them, but for His own glory. God, the Anabaptist began again, had given all creatures a natural inclination to love their offspring; man was the child of God, formed in His image; therefore it was inconceivable that God had damned man before his creation. Knox replied that, as the Book of Job witnessed, the ostrich left its eggs unprotected in the sand, which was no great sign of its love for its offspring, and that, moreover, the similitude was blasphemous, because it implied that God had the same affections as brute beasts. The Anabaptist asserted that Calvinists did more harm than atheists; for 'they are less injurious to God which believe that He is not, than they which say He is unmerciful, cruel, and an oppressor.' Knox retorted that the lie was so outrageous that he would not deign to reply. The Anabaptist next pointed out that if God with His revealed will, as the Calvinists held, willed that Adam should not fall, and with His secret will willed that Adam should fall, then God had willed two contraries, and, moreover, had spoken one thing and meant another. 'For answer,' Knox replied, 'I ask of you, if ye will bind God to that law which He hath imposed to His creatures.' God, in fact, was perfectly at liberty to practise deception if He liked, and His ingenious behaviour, it presently turned out, was only another of His means for enhancing His glory. Whenever the Anabaptist gave him a particularly violent anomaly to explain, Knox's reply was that it was one of God's ways of enhancing His glory. The damnation of sinners enhanced His glory; the contradictoriness of His statements enhanced His glory; but His supreme means for the enhancement of His glory was His incomprehensibility. When Knox was too hard pressed, therefore, this incomprehensibility could always meet every particular argument. 'The pride of those,' he said, 'shall be punished, who, not content with the will of God revealed, delight to mount and fly above the skies, there to seek the secret will of God.' 'Nature and reason,' he said later, 'do lead men from the true God. For what impudence is it to prefer corrupt nature and blind reason to God's Scriptures!' With all the privileges of comprehensibility and incomprehensibility in his reach, with Calvin at his elbow and the Old Testament open before him, Knox, indeed, could do nothing but win. Yet the Anabaptist had the last word. 'And as for you, Careless Men,' he ended his book, 'you ought to take it in good part whatever I have said. First, because it is truth; secondly, because ye hold that all things be done of mere necessity; then have I written this of necessity.' Knox could not think of a relevant retort.

Once, however, the controversy became serious. During the course of his treatise Knox had conscientiously called his adversary a liar, a blasphemer, a dog, and even a devil incarnate, as he was bound to do; but at one point he became angry. It was when the Calvinists were accused of preferring the elect to be wealthy if possible, and 'for a perpetual memorial of

their cruelty' of publishing books, 'affirming it to be
lawful to persecute and put to death such as dissent
from them in controversies of religion ' – 'Be these, I
pray you,' the Anabaptist burst out, 'Be these the
sheep whom Christ sent forth in the midst of wolves?
Can the sheep persecute the wolf? Doth Abel kill
Cain? When ye walk even after the lusts of your
hearts, thirsting after blood and persecuting poor men
for their conscience' sake, ye be blinded, and see not
yourselves, but say, Tush, we be predestinate.' Knox
cited the executions, burnings, tortures and imprison-
ments of Geneva as an ample proof of the Calvinists'
zeal for virtue, and stated that those who disagreed
with Calvin did not follow their consciences, as his
opponent believed, but were blasphemers and therefore worthy of death. Near the end of the book,
the accusation still rankling in his mind, he returned
to it. He instanced the fact, which happened to be
true, that certain of the Anabaptists had, half a century
before, themselves been guilty of violences. He
described these at length, and then, showing for the
first time his genuine debating skill, turned aside and
addressed himself directly to princes and governments.
'As ye have rebelled and dishonoured God,' he said,
'so will He pour forth contempt upon you, in the
which ye shall perish both temporally and forever.
And by whom doth it appear that temporally ye shall
be punished? Of us, whom ye banish, whom ye spoil
and rob, whom cruelly ye persecute, and whose blood
ye daily shed? There is no doubt, but as the victory
which overcometh the world is our faith, so it behoveth

us to possess our souls in our patience. We neither
privily nor openly deny the power of the civil magistrate. Only we desire the people and the rulers to be
subject unto God, and unto His holy will plainly
revealed in His most sacred Word. And therefore of
us, I say, ye are and may be without all fear.' 'And
what instruments can God find in this life more apt to
punish you,' he continued, 'than those that hate and
detest all lawful powers?' Than the Anabaptists, in
other words. 'God will not use His saints and chosen
children to punish you,' he concluded. 'For with them
is always mercy, yea, even although God have pronounced a curse and malediction, as in the history of
Joshua is plain.'

With the elect there was always mercy, Knox said,
yet to the Scottish nobility he had calmly advised a
policy of general slaughter. From the elect rulers had
nothing to fear, yet he had denied the authority of the
rulers of England and Scotland, and had prayed for the
assassination of Mary Tudor. His predictions were
no better founded. It was not the Anabaptists who
were presently to drive Mary of Guise out of her
capital, and a little later to hound Mary Stuart from
her country into the hands of her greatest enemy. It
was not the Anabaptists who, later still, were to involve
Scotland in a century of civil war and persecution, cast
down the throne of England, and execute a king.
Knox knew the intentions of the Scottish nobles;
he was encouraging them already to greater excesses
than they themselves contemplated. In diverting
the attention of men in authority to the Anabaptists,

therefore, he was deliberately encouraging the persecution of a sect, at the time harmless, while throwing his mantle over men prepared to go to any lengths of violence. To stand by his own party was justifiable enough; to intensify the persecution of a sect already persecuted on every side by Roman Catholics, Lutherans and Calvinists alike, was inhuman; but to intensify it by a dishonest charge was almost reprehensible by Genevan standards. A very important change, however, not yet noted, had taken place when Knox did this.

CHAPTER X

EXASPERATION AT DIEPPE

On the 17th of December 1558 Mary Tudor died, and presently Elizabeth ascended the throne. England was Protestant again, and the English exiles in Geneva began to make preparations to return. By the end of January 1559 all but one or two had left the city. Knox left with the others. His family, increased by the birth of two sons, remained in Geneva. He made, as usual, for Dieppe. As he was not heading directly for Scotland this time, his journey probably took him about eleven days. From Dieppe he wrote Cecil asking permission to reside for some time in England, and especially to see his flocks in Berwick and Newcastle, before he went on to his native country. Cecil laid the matter before the Queen: the petition was ignored.

In the circumstances the tacit refusal was exasperating. Knox had learned from a friend in Scotland that Protestants were quite safe there now and that the Regent actually thought of reforming religion publicly on an appointed day. England, moreover, was a Protestant country, and where, if not in a Protestant country, was he entitled to every licence? But Elizabeth had read *The First Blast* and had somewhat perversely applied its consequences. Missing its object the book, indeed, had just come in time to be a letter of introduction of the most doubtful value to Elizabeth. During his enforced delay in Dieppe Knox consoled himself by writing those pages of his treatise on Predestination in which the Anabaptists were distinguished as the real enemies to be feared, and the elect were shown in such a roseate light.

Meanwhile he wrote again to Cecil. 'I purpose to discharge, in few words,' he said, 'my conscience towards you.' Cecil, it appeared, had not applied his powers to the glory of God; he had, by his silence, consented to the setting up of idolatry and the persecution of God's saints; he was accordingly worthy of hell, even though God had promoted him to honour: would he not give Knox permission to come to England? The book against the government of women, Cecil had objected, was treasonable; Knox thought it would be extremely hard to prove it. Besides he wanted to communicate certain things which he did not wish to commit to writing. But even this temptation did not fetch Cecil.

The First Blast was causing some inconvenience to Calvin, it appeared, as well. In the beginning of the previous year he had sent a copy of his *Commentaries on Isaiah* to Elizabeth with a dedication. The gift was not accepted with effusion; on the contrary he received a letter from Cecil pointing out that *The First Blast* had been printed in Geneva. Calvin replied that he had had no inkling of the book and for a year had been ignorant of its publication. When it was brought to his notice he had amply expressed his displeasure at such paradoxes, but then it was too late, and he would only have made matters worse by doing anything. He referred bitterly to 'the thoughtless arrogance of one individual,' and admitted that there might have been a danger that through this man's action 'the wretched crowd of exiles would have been driven away not only from this city, but even from almost the whole world.' He was very annoyed with Knox.

Yet between the death of Mary and his departure from Geneva, Knox had taken the opportunity of decreasing still further his chances of being accepted with open arms by Elizabeth. In the first enthusiasm of seeing England once more a Protestant country he had sent out 'A Brief Exhortation for the speedy Embracing of Christ's Gospel.' He began, as usual, with menaces; he wrapped everybody in England, he said, in idolatry, murder and every iniquity – everybody, that was to say, except those who had suffered death for the truth, those who had abstained from idolatry, and those who had run away; the rest had deserved all they had suffered. Having dilated on this idea, he went on to point out the only way of salvation. They must expel all dregs of Papistry and idolatry, remove all glistering and vain ceremonies (in other words, the ritual and ceremony of their church), divide every large bishopric into ten small ones, and impose universally the Genevan discipline. If they did not do this, God's hot displeasure would burn and destroy the head and the tail, the Prince and the false prophet, root and branch.

But in spite of this and his reminders to Cecil that he merited hell-fire, the permission did not come. Meanwhile he preached to the Dieppe congregation with such ardour that they summoned courage to worship during the day-time. His correspondence with Cecil had convinced him by now that all he had said in *The First Blast* was true. Accordingly he taught his congregation that women were incapable of reigning, and the chief pastor of the Genevan congregation in Paris became alarmed. The Protestants in France were living in the constant shadow of persecution; any unconsidered act might bring it down. Accordingly the chief pastor wrote to Calvin: 'Knox was for some time in Dieppe, waiting on a wind for Scotland. He dared publicly to profess the worst and most infamous of doctrines: "Women are unworthy to reign; Christians may protect themselves by arms against tyrants." I fear that Knox may fill Scotland with his madness. He is said to have a boon companion at Geneva, whom we hear that the people of Dieppe have called to be their minister. If he be infected with such opinions, for Christ's sake pray that he be not sent; or if he has already departed, warn the Dieppe people to beware of him.' A week later the persecution broke out, but Knox was already in Scotland.

He had remained in Dieppe for three months, demolishing the Anabaptist, proving that the elect were obedient to princes, denouncing queens, and waiting in ever greater exasperation for a sign of grace from the Queen of England. He became surly even to Mrs. Locke, who was still in Geneva, and complained of his silence. 'Oft to write where few messengers are found,' he rejoined, 'is but foolishness. My remembrance of you is not yet so dead, but I trust it shall be fresh enough, albeit it be renewed by no outward token for one year. In answering to your question,' he went on, perhaps remembering that he had once foolishly encouraged the lady to leave her husband and come to Geneva, 'I know I shall be judged extreme and rigorous.' But now he had to advise her not on a point of conduct merely, but of doctrine. In spite of his companionship, in spite of her knowledge of his views, she was actually asking him whether she could justifiably partake of the Anglican communion! 'Sister,' he replied, 'now is no time to flatter, nor to dissemble. Our Master calleth upon His own, and that with vehemency, that they depart from Babylon; yea, severally He threateneth death and damnation to such as, either in forehead or in hand, bear the mark of the Beast. And a portion of his mark are all these dregs of Papistry which were left in your great Book of England, any jot whereof will I never counsel any man to use. One jot, I say, of these diabolical inventions, viz.: crossing in baptism; kneeling at the Lord's Table; mumbling, or singing of the litany,' and so on. But he tried to soften somewhat the severity of the reproof. 'Of nature I am churlish,' he said, 'and in condition different from many: yet one thing I ashame not to affirm, that familiarity once thoroughly contracted was never yet broken on my default. The cause may be that I have rather need of all than that any hath need of me.' Yet as he wrote most of those whom he needed so much were apparently leaving him in hosts, for in the same letter he complained that his *First Blast* had blown away all his friends in England. 'The Second Blast, I fear,' he continued, 'shall sound somewhat more sharp, except men be more moderate than I hear they are. England hath refused me; but because, before, it did refuse Christ Jesus, the less do I regard the loss of that familiarity. God grant that their ingratitude be not punished with severity, and that ere they be aware.'

England was plainly obdurate, persecution was threatened in France, his protracted wait in Dieppe was becoming unendurable. On the 23rd of April he sailed at last and arrived in Edinburgh on the 2nd of May. Scotland was in a greater turmoil than it had known for several years.

CHAPTER XI

MARY OF GUISE

The scene upon which Knox now entered was very different from any he had known during the last nine years. In England he had occupied an honourable Government post; he had seen himself a prominent agent in a great national change; he had known the highest dignitaries of the State and Church, and had preached at Court. In Geneva he had lived in a society almost as cosmopolitan as that of Rome, and more intellectually alive. He had had exasperating intervals in Dieppe and Frankfort, it was true, but Geneva had been always in the background, his real home and his permanent centre of reference. Now he found himself in a small, poor, tumultuous and semi-dependent country in the far north, and among people who in point of civilization were as far behind the English as they were behind the Genevans in intellect. Large parts of that country were inaccessible. A line of mountains which ran slanting from the west near Glasgow up to Aberdeenshire cut off more than half of the area of Scotland. Along the southern borders there was the Debatable Land, given over to robbers and outlaws. All that was left were the counties in the centre and east; the Mearns, Angus and Fife, the strip stretching from Glasgow to Edinburgh, the Lothians, and Kyle and Ayrshire in the south-west. In this circumscribed area the important points were all in the east, and all within a small radius. Stirling, Perth, Dundee, St. Andrews, Leith, were towns of trifling size. Edinburgh was the centre, and most of it lay round the steep main street which led from Holyrood at the foot of the hill to the Castle at the top.

To maintain itself Scotland had had for more than a decade to draw alternately on the assistance of England and France, assistance which always put it in a half-dependent situation. While the Castilians were being besieged at St. Andrews, they were intriguing, as we have seen, with England, but France managed to arrive first. England did appear later, however, during the Protectorate of Somerset, to overrun the south and burn and slay at their leisure. No sooner had they done so than Scottish feeling veered round to France again. Mary of Guise freed the country from the English, but now the French, having done their work, were indisputably present, and they in turn became the enemies of Scottish freedom. The Scottish Lords accordingly looked hopefully towards England again. This was the state of things when Knox arrived.

The men with whom he had to work were, first, the Scottish nobility and lairds, and secondly, the preachers. Among the former were two men of great talent, Lord James Stuart and Maitland of Lethington, and one man of undoubted integrity, Erskine of Dun. An illegitimate son of the late king, the Lord James was at once in a difficult and a privileged position.

Had he been born on the right side of the blanket, his talents might have made him one of the most remarkable of the gifted Stuart line; but he was to have greater ambition than opportunity. In his early youth he had shown bravery and military skill. By nature cold, he had a more genuine enthusiasm for the new doctrines than any of the other nobles, and was more truly solicitous for the good of his country; yet his secretiveness made him distrusted by all except the preachers and the people, who recognized his desire to be just. He sacrificed some of his wealth to advance the Reformation and he was involved in most of the deeds of violence which marked it; yet his caution was such that, while precipitating events, he succeeded in appearing to ignore them. Once he took a resolution he was cold-bloodedly insensible in carrying it out, but his participation in violence and crime had always an appearance of reason rather than of passion. His aims were public-spirited; his ambitions were so secret that people did not know whether he even acknowledged them to himself. He attained finally to the supreme control of the country through the ruin of his half-sister, Mary Stuart, who had from the first loaded him with benefits. He became known by the people as 'The Good Regent'; he was assassinated by one of his enemies for an act barbarous and inhuman even for those days. His ingratitude and treachery towards Mary, his inveterate cruelty to the enemy who shot him have both an appearance of cold-bloodedness, and might both have been the effects of a policy deliberately followed for large public ends. Lord

James remains a mystery; his talents, his secretiveness, his coldness of temper: these alone are certain.

Maitland of Lethington, the second in importance of Knox's colleagues, is a more comprehensible figure. A few years older than the Lord James, he was baffling only in the intricacy of his policy. He appeared to like perfidy for its own sake, and seemed resolved to explore all the possibilities which a complete intellectual and moral licence laid before his delighted eyes. He is one of the earliest native representatives of that Renaissance type in which a complete disbelief in morality is logically accompanied by a complete freedom of action. He was listened to with respect when he argued on theology; he plotted and fought with ardour for the new faith; yet he looked upon his colleagues' aims as childish imaginations. He had the most subtle and mobile brain in Scotland, and he used it in turn to betray Mary of Guise and Mary Stuart after taking everything they could give him. He could be on no side without intriguing against it. To plot, to counterplot; to build up, to undermine what he had built up; to invent ever deeper intricacies of perfidy out of the sheer intellectual pleasure it gave him; this was his nature. His entire freedom from moral inhibitions made no step, however infamous, appear impossible to him. Yet on any general issue his arguments were all for mildness and humanity. A piece of infamy which justified itself by principle rather than immediate utility seemed to him stupid, and even aroused his indignation. When Knox wished to punish and execute, Lethington repeatedly took up the cause of mercy. He had no objection to assassination; he was indirectly involved in the murders both of Rizzio and Darnley; but to murder judicially, for reasons taken from the Old Testament, was objectionable to his feelings and his intellect.

Of far less influence, Erskine of Dun was perhaps the most single-hearted figure on the reformed side. His religion was free from rancour, his conduct was disinterested, and his sweetness of temper endeared him even to his opponents. He was a man of culture, and he was one of the first men of rank to turn Protestant in Scotland. Apart from some of the preachers he was probably the only Protestant of consequence in Scotland who could be trusted.

Of the other leaders, Glencairn and Kirkcaldy of Grange were perhaps the most respectable, though Kirkcaldy consistently betrayed the Regent while he was in her pay. The young Earl of Argyll remained faithful, but his life was a scandal to the brethren. Morton was violent, greedy and treacherous. Arran was almost a half-wit, and in a few years went insane. His father, the Duke of Châtelherault, the chief of the Hamiltons, was so notorious for his instability of character that the Protestants could neither be happy with him nor without him. But Ruthven, it is generally agreed, was the worst as well as the most abnormal of the Lords of the Congregation. He was later to be one of the chief murderers of Rizzio, and he rose from his sick-bed in order to share in that gruesome deed. He twice betrayed both parties within a few days, deserting

from the Protestants to the Regent and from the
Regent to the Protestants. He seems to have taken a
gloomy, half-mystical pleasure in bloody acts. He was
accused by some of his colleagues of sorcery, but if he
practised it he also scorned it as a superstition. He
died at last in exile, seeing visions of angels. In an age
which could boast of Morton and Bothwell he was
described by an English observer as the worst in
Scotland.

These were Knox's chief colleagues; his enemy was
one woman, Mary of Guise. No queen could be more
unlike Knox's portrait of woman in *The First Blast*, or
more unlike himself. Seeing the deplorable state of
the country, and feeling within her the capacity to rule
it better, she had in 1554 ousted Arran, now the Duke
of Châtelherault, from the Regency, and taken it over
herself. With French troops she had driven out the
English, and now with French counsel she ruled the
country. Her object was to bind Scotland and France
in close alliance, and finally to make Scotland subject
to France. She worked for this end with immense
patience and skill, with considerable success, and
against the wishes of her subjects. She succeeded so
far as any ruler could have done in the circumstances.
But her policy, however unpopular, was in a certain
measure forced upon her. The Hamiltons, the most
powerful family in Scotland, were hostile because she
had taken the government out of the ineffectual hands
of their head. The Lord James and Morton were
still very young, and the one was a Protestant,
the other not to be trusted. There was left

Maitland of Lethington, but he betrayed her as he was to betray everybody else. She had to rule, therefore, mainly with French advisers, and their advice was inevitably in favour of France. Yet she had a genuine care for her subjects. She sent strong protests to France against the brutal conduct of the French soldiers. She opposed an undisturbed mildness to the perpetual provocations of the Protestants. She had in an extraordinary degree self-control, patience, coolness and magnanimity. Her policy was a disastrous mistake, but she pursued it with high aims and with a skill and perseverance which might have excited the admiration of opponents more generous. If one were to accept the description of the sexes in *The First Blast*, she might stand as the masculine type and Knox himself as the feminine. In the battle between them calmness, self-control, reason, dignity were all on Mary's side, frenzy, vituperation and back-biting all on the side of Knox. She has been accused of excessive duplicity. She certainly lied for her ends, as every ruler did then and will always do, but her lies were more skilful and less gross than those of Knox himself, who, as a man of notorious probity, was set up by his party to tell them.

Since the winter of 1557, when Knox was hesitating in Dieppe, the tension between the Protestant party and the Regent had been steadily increasing. The Regent, however, succeeded in her chief design. On the 24th of April 1558 young Mary Stuart was married to the Dauphin of France at the Church of Notre Dame in Paris. All the ancient liberties and

privileges of the Scottish nobility were protected by
the act of settlement; the marriage, therefore, had the
approval of the Scottish Parliament; and eight Scottish
commissioners attended the marriage ceremony. As
they were leaving Paris, however, it was suggested that
they should send the Scottish crown to France to be
put on the head of the Dauphin. They already knew
that the Regent wished to make Scotland subject
to France; the request aroused their suspicions. They
replied that their instructions did not go to such
lengths, and that the demand might make the
young queen unpopular with her subjects. Four
of the commissioners died before they got out of
France; the rumour went that they had been
poisoned.

The Estates met at the end of November, and the
problem of the Scottish crown was debated at length.
Several of the nobles were in the pay of France, and
the Regent's French soldiery carried a certain weight.
Parliament decided, therefore, to send the crown to
France, and appointed the Earl of Argyll and Lord
James Stuart to convey it. But it was never sent.
Protestant Elizabeth was now on the throne of
England, she, too, had several of the Scottish nobles in
her pay, and many of the others were already beginning to think that a too close alliance with France was
a mistake. The French soldiery employed by the
Regent were unpopular everywhere. The French
influence had to be checked. The nobles began to
throw out feelers to Cecil and Elizabeth.

Meantime, under the protection of the nobility,

Protestantism had been steadily growing. In December 1557 the Lords had bound themselves to give their lives to the advancement of the reformed religion and the support of the preachers. 'We shall maintain them, nurse them, and defend them,' they swore, 'the whole congregation of Christ and every member thereof, at our whole powers and risk of our lives.' Their first demands were moderate. They asked that 'The Book of Common Prayer' should be read on Sundays and Saints' days, and that preaching should be allowed in private houses until public services should be sanctioned by law.

But the preachers systematically exceeded the Lords' demands. Harlaw the tailor preached openly in Edinburgh and Leith; Paul Methuen pulled down images in Dundee and requisitioned a church thus purified; and meetings were held freely in Angus and the Mearns. The sermons of the preachers were frequently followed by image-breaking and riots. At the request of the Catholic Clergy the Regent at last summoned the preachers to appear in Edinburgh on the 19th of July 1558. They appeared with a following large enough to overawe their judges, and were ordered to go away again. On the same day a party of Protestants came in from the west to see that no harm happened to their favourites. They forced themselves into the room where the Regent and the bishops were sitting, and one of them, the laird of Gartgirth, addressed his sovereign with, 'Madam, we know that this is the malice and device of these jailbirds, and of that bastard[1]

[1] The Archbishop of St. Andrews.

that stands by you; we avow to God we shall make a day of it. They oppress us and our tenants for feeding of their idle bellies; they trouble our preachers, and would murder them and us. Shall we suffer this any longer? No, Madam, it shall not be.' The Regent replied disingenuously that she meant no harm to the preachers, and reminded them that they should love their neighbours. The preachers were allowed their freedom.

A month later, as the priests were carrying the image of St. Giles through Edinburgh on his name-day, they were assaulted by the Protestants, the image was seized and broken, and the priests were chased through the streets. This seemed a suitable time for the Protestants to prepare a statement of their grievances. Mary received it courteously, but excused herself from putting it before Parliament; meantime what she could do for them she would. The Lords of the Congregation were not satisfied. They protested again that they were not allowed to worship according to their conscience, and asserted that if any tumult should arise on account of differences of religious opinion, the responsibility should rest on her.

On the 1st of January 1559 an extraordinary placard was found nailed to the door of every ecclesiastical establishment in Scotland. It began: ' The blind, crooked, lame, widows, orphans and all other poor visited by the hand of God or may not work, to the flocks of all friars within this realm, we wish restitution of wrongs past, and reformation in times coming, for salutation.' The widows and orphans painted their wretchedness and the avarice of the priests with considerable literary skill. They warned the clergy that they must vacate their monasteries and priories before Whitsun, so that the poor, the true proprietors, might enter and enjoy their riches, wrongfully withheld from them. 'If ye fail,' the blind and lame concluded, 'we will at the same term, in whole number and with the help of God and assistance of His saints on earth, of whose ready support we doubt not, enter and take possession of our said patrimony, and eject you utterly forth of the same.' The 'saints of earth' whose help the oppressed were so sure of were the Protestants, and the Protestants had some weeks before warned the Regent that if tumults should arise the fault would be hers. The Regent was roused at last. She called the bishops together and commanded them to reform the Church; she made them put off a summons which had been sent out against the preachers; she issued a proclamation enjoining the keeping of Lent and forbidding any one to disturb religious services or bully priests; she ordered that Easter should be observed after the Roman Catholic fashion, and that no unauthorised person should preach. The bishops made a feeble attempt at reform; the preachers paid no attention to her edicts. Whitsun was close at hand; the blind and lame might presently take matters into their own hands; there might be riots, looting and bloodshed. Mary herself now commanded the preachers to appear before her at Stirling on the 10th of May, and this time she would not listen to the arguments of the Congregation. The preachers were summoned not merely for disobeying her proclamation, but for sedition and tumult. She was probably weary of her struggle with the Protestants; she was ill of the malady which was finally to kill her; and her chief wish at the time was to get to France. She never saw it again.

It was eight days before the preachers were due to appear that Knox arrived in Edinburgh. 'I see the battle shall be great,' he wrote Mrs. Locke, 'for Satan rageth even to the uttermost; and I am come (I praise my God) even in the brunt of the battle. Assist me, sister, with your prayers, that now I shrink not when the battle approacheth.' News of his presence was sent to the Regent in Glasgow, she ordered him to be publicly proclaimed a rebel and outlaw. Knox fled to Dundee, which was crammed with excited Protestants who had come in from Angus and the Mearns resolved to protect the preachers. They consulted. The Regent had commanded the preachers to appear before her at Stirling. For the Protestants to march there in a body would have been open rebellion. But Perth was on the road, it was, moreover, the only walled city in Scotland, and it had access to the sea. The Protestants resolved to go there and send Erskine of Dun forward to Stirling to parley with the Regent. Knox went with the Protestants to Perth.

Mary could only depend at the moment on a small French army of 1500 to 2000 men. Accordingly she kept Erskine dangling with promises, and many of the Protestants, thinking their demonstration had been successful, returned to their homes. On the 10th of May, she suddenly outlawed the preachers for not appearing. Erskine returned to Perth with the news; the indignant Protestants were more resolved than ever to stand by the preachers and to resist the Regent. Knox preached a furious sermon against idolatry.

It was this sermon that precipitated the civil war which was to last with intervals for over a year. Before that some composition was still possible between the two parties: afterwards there could be none. In this sermon, the last of a series, Knox 'denounced,' as Professor Hume Brown, the most learned and benevolent of his biographers, has said, 'the idolatries of the Roman Church, and pointed out the duty of Christian men in regard to them.' Most of the Christian men present, however, had left without performing their duty, and the few who remained were suddenly recalled to it by a priest who, 'with a curious fatuity under the circumstances,' to quote the same author, went up to the altar and boldly prepared to celebrate Mass. 'A forward boy commenting on his action,' Professor Hume Brown goes on, 'he struck him a blow on the ear. It would seem that the youth on coming to the church must have had some notion of possible mischief, since he at once retaliated by throwing a stone, which missed the priest and broke an image.' The foresight of the forward boy recalled the congregation at last to their duty. The church was wrecked in a few moments, and a mob composed of the faithful and the hooligans of the town, filled with zeal and desire for loot, looked round for other places where images might be smashed, and gold and silver and jewels and meat and wine stolen or enjoyed. There were two monasteries in the town and an abbey. In two days the silver and gold, the lead from the roofs, meats and wine, sheets, blankets, coverlets, beds, napery – everything had disappeared, and only the walls were left standing. Bonfires were made of the images; the trees were pulled up by the roots; the priests were threatened with death. The destruction began on the 11th of May, four days before the date on which the blind and lame had promised to occupy their property.

Mary could not overlook any longer the actions of the Protestants, but she did not move at once. The Lord James and the Earl of Argyll were on her side, the Hamiltons had come in; she now summoned the levies of Stirlingshire and Clydesdale. With these she began her march on Perth on the 22nd of May.

The Protestants took what measures they could, and employed Knox to write four letters; to Mary herself, to the French soldiery, to the nobility, and to the Catholic Clergy. In the first two the Protestants fiercely protested their loyalty; all they asked was liberty to worship as they liked. If the Regent refused them this right, she did so, they suggested, against the wishes of those faithful Protestants, their young sovereigns in France. In the letter to the nobility they threatened those who did not join them with excommunication. 'Doubt ye nothing,' they said, 'but that our Church and the true ministers of the same,' some five or six, 'have the power which our Master, Jesus Christ, granted to His apostles in these words, "Whose sins ye shall forgive, shall be forgiven, and whose sins

ye shall retain shall be retained." ' The letter to the
Catholic Clergy began: 'To the generation of Antichrist, the pestilent prelates and their shavelings within
Scotland, the congregation of Jesus within the same
saith.' The congregation of Jesus complained of the
Papists' cruelty, and warned them that if it continued
they would be arrested as murderers. 'Yea,' the
brethren said, 'we shall begin that same war which
God commanded Israel to execute against the Canaan-
ites, that is, contract of peace shall never be made till
ye desist from your open idolatry and cruel persecution
of God's children.' The Catholics, in other words,
were neither to interfere with the Congregation's
liberty of worship nor to have any of their own.

Meanwhile the Protestants of Dundee and the
lairds of Fife came in to support Perth. Mary marched
from Stirling, but halted at Auchterarder fourteen
miles from her goal, and sent Argyll and Lord James
on to open negotiations. Once more the Protestants
protested their loyalty and said that they only asked for
religious liberty, but Knox gave the Lords an extraordinary personal message for the Regent. They were
to tell her that the brethren whom she persecuted in
such blind rage were God's servants and her obedient
subjects; that her religion was the contrary of Christ's;
that her designs would not succeed; that though she
might humble the servants of God for a little, she was
fighting against the Almighty; and that her end would
be confusion if she did not repent. He required them
to say this in the name of the eternal God, adding that
he was a better friend to her than those who flattered

her corrupt appetites. Argyll and Lord James returned to Auchterarder; they outlined the Protestants' conditions, but did not give Knox's message. Lord Semphill, however, who had accompanied them, repaired the omission and this was reported to Knox. Semphill, he wrote indignantly, was 'a man sold under sin, enemy to God and all godliness.'

The protestations of the brethren did not seem to Mary a sufficient explanation for the looting of monasteries and the desecration of churches, and she sent a herald to Perth ordering everyone to leave under pain of treason. Two or three days later news came to her that Glencairn and Ochiltree had marched up from the west with 2500 Protestants, foot and horse, and were within six miles of the town. Knox's party did not know this; and at about the same time they were sending assurances of their future obedience if the Regent would amnesty the offenders in the riots, give the reformed religion liberty to grow in the town, and leave no French soldiers behind. When Lord James and Argyll reached Perth to conclude this agreement they found Glencairn and Ochiltree there with their men.

The agreement was accepted, and in such congenial company Argyll and Lord James stayed long enough to promise that they would join the brethren if the Regent did not keep her word. Knox foretold with certainty that she would not keep her word, and the two nobles signed with a lighter conscience a new bond pledging themselves along with the others to wreck churches and loot monasteries. They had just concluded a treaty in the name of one whose duty it was to protect churches and monasteries. If, after all, she should keep her word, their action might look premature.

She did not keep her word, they soon discovered. At her entry into Perth her soldiers let off their hackbuts and a shot killed a child standing in a window. This was her first offence. After that she quartered Scottish soldiers in the town; these soldiers had seen French service under Scottish officers; it was clear to the Congregation, therefore, that in spirit if not in appearance they were French soldiers. Besides this she had Mass celebrated in some of the desecrated churches on improvised altars; yet she had promised that the new faith should have leave to grow! Argyll and Lord James abruptly quitted the town. She ordered them to return, but they refused. They could not approve of her present conduct, they said.

A little after this Knox wrote to Mrs. Locke again. He told of the duplicity of the Regent, and said that the brethren had sought the next remedy. 'And first they put their hands to reformation in Saint Johnstone, where the places of idolatry of Grey and Black friars, and of Charterhouse monks, were made equal to the ground; all monuments of idolatry that could be apprehended, consumed with fire; and priests commanded, under pain of death, to desist from their blasphemous mass.' The boy who had been shot at the Regent's entry was now referred to as children. Knox went on to speak of other image-breaking crusades, and exclaimed: 'Thus far hath God advanced the glory of His dear Son amongst us. O that my heart could be thankful for the superexcellent benefit of God!' Christ, he was convinced, would triumph in Scotland.

Lord James and Argyll, joined by a few other Lords, made for St. Andrews and summoned their allies to meet there on the 3rd of June. Knox meantime had been preaching in Anstruther and Crail. Presently he joined his friends at St. Andrews, but when he arrived he was faced by Hamilton the Archbishop, and a hundred spears. Hamilton informed him that if he dared to preach he should be met with 'a dozen culverins, whereof the most part should light upon his nose.' But Knox's story of his prophecy in the galleys had already gone the rounds, and it was intolerable that now, on the very spot, he should be cheated of its fulfilment. Besides, Lord James had a little over a hundred horse at his back, and the Archbishop's challenge had roused the Protestants. With one voice they proclaimed 'that Christ Jesus should be preached in despite of Satan.' The leaders, it was true, were unwilling to bring on a new tumult, for the Regent was only a dozen miles away, at the pretty royal palace of Falkland. But nothing could shake Knox. He desired only the glory of God, and he was resolved to have it. After thirteen years Providence had at last given him his opportunity. 'As for the fear of danger that may come to me,' he said, 'let no man be solicitous, for my life is in the custody of Him whose glory I seek. I desire the hand nor weapon of no man to defend me.'

It was clear, however, that hand and weapon were at his disposal. Hamilton thought better of his threat.

MARIA.LOTHORINGIA.ILLIVS.IN.SECVNDIS.NVP
TIIS.VXOR.ANNO ÆTATIS SVE.Z 4

MARY OF GUISE

Artist unknown.   From a portrait in possession of the
Duke of Devonshire.

Facing p. 177.

Knox preached next day, a Saturday, to an audience which included many of the Catholic clergy. His theme was the driving of the money-changers from the Temple, and he applied the moral so skilfully that the Catholics sat dumb both during his sermon and during the sequel, when their images were burned before their eyes. Knox preached for three days more, and all the other churches were dismantled.

Once more the effects of Knox's presence forced Mary to take action. She marched from Falkland with a small force. But the Lords had gathered from Lothian and Fife an army of over 3000 men. 'Finally,' says Knox, 'God did so multiply our number that it appeared as men rained from the clouds.' The two forces met near Cupar, about six miles out from St. Andrews. The day was misty, and D'Oysel and Châtelherault, who led the Regent's army, could not make out where their opponents lay. As soon as they did so they saw they were hopelessly outnumbered. They had expected an easy victory. 'Who had been at Falkland the night before,' Knox wrote, drawing on his fecund imagination, 'might have seen embracing and kissing betwixt the Queen, the Duke and the Bishop.' Now there was no course left for the Regent but to treat again with her rebellious subjects. She offered a free amnesty to the Protestants if they would promise not to wreck monasteries and abbeys, and would stop preaching in public. The brethren indignantly refused both conditions. At last an eight days' truce was settled, during which neither party should give occasion of offence. The brethren began it by

M   177

wrecking the abbey of Lindores, overthrowing the altars and burning the images, vestments, and vessels in the monks' presence. Meanwhile Mary, who had promised to send envoys to St. Andrews to treat, did not send them. This, Knox wrote, was another proof of her craft and deceit. She had obviously broken her word again.

The uneasy truce expired. Meanwhile the Lords had heard from the brethren in Perth that Christian liberty was once more oppressed. Gathering a numerous force the Protestants marched to Perth, and on the 20th of June entered without resistance. Again the looting began. The ecclesiastical possibilities of Perth were already exhausted, it was true, but a mile away lay the village of Scone with its ancient abbey and palace. The first two days of the new regime were passed in their destruction. The Protestants of Dundee and Perth distinguished themselves particularly this time, but Argyll, Lord James, and Knox himself unsuccessfully intervened to stop the rioting. The burning and looting were by now, in fact, getting the Protestants a bad name. 'The reformation,' Knox wrote to Cecil, 'is somewhat violent, because the adversaries be stubborn; none that professeth Christ Jesus usurpeth anything against the authority; neither yet intendest to usurp, unless strangers be brought in to suborn and bring in bondage the liberties of this poor country. If any such thing be espied, I am uncertain what. shall follow.' He was somewhat reassured, however, by an incident during the sacking. 'A poor aged matron,' he wrote, 'seeing the flame of fire pass up so mightily and perceiving that many were thereat offended, in plain and sober manner of speaking said, "Now I see and understand that God's judgments are just, and that no man is able to save where He will punish. Since my remembrance, this place hath been nothing else but a den of whoremongers. It is incredible to believe how many wives hath been adulterate, and virgins deflowered, by the filthy beasts which hath been fostered in this den; but especially by that wicked man who is called the Bishop. If all men knew as much as I they would praise God; and no man would be offended." ' At these words, Knox added, 'many were pacified, affirming with her that it was God's just judgment.'

Protesting their loyalty, the Lords, as we have seen, had entered Perth and driven out the Regent's men. They now heard that the Regent was at Stirling, preparing with a weak force to bar their progress south. Protesting their loyalty again, they made a rapid night march on Stirling, to find that the Regent had fled before them to Edinburgh. With a last tearful expression of loyalty they went on to Edinburgh, but the Regent had taken refuge in Dunbar, where she could easily get away by sea. The Protestants' pursuit had been marked by destruction. In Stirling the mob, taking their opportunity while it lasted, had wrecked the churches and monasteries before the brethren arrived. In Edinburgh nothing was left, Knox said, 'but bare walls, yea, not so much as door or window; wherethrough we were the less troubled in putting order to such places.'

The destruction of the religious buildings and works
of art in Scotland has been debated by historians,
antiquarians and theologians at length and with
acrimony. Two examples, showing the fluctuations
of opinion among Knox's admirers, may be cited.
Dr. M'Crie's apology is perhaps the most extraordinary. He begins by treating the matter with
elephantine facetiousness. 'Antiquarians,' he said,
'have no reason to complain of the ravages of the
reformers, who have left them such valuable remains,
and placed them in that very state which awakes in
their minds the most lovely sentiments of the sublime
and beautiful by reducing them to – ruins.' But,
becoming serious, he was 'satisfied,' he said, 'that the
charges usually brought against our reformers on this
head are highly exaggerated.' He next argued that
even had the 'irregularities' been greater, he must still
'reprobate the spirit which disposes persons to dwell
with unnecessary lamentation upon losses which, in
the view of an enlightened and liberal mind, will sink
and disappear in the magnitude of the incalculable
good which rose from the wreck of the revolution.' He
concluded by approving flatly Knox's maxim 'that the
best way to keep the rooks from returning was to pull
down their nests.' The enlightened *Edinburgh Review*
of his time, the time of Keats and Shelley, agreed with
him. But, writing eighty years later, Professor Hume
Brown took up a different attitude. 'In these blind
outbursts,' he said, 'there was no expression of real
religious feeling; it was simply the instinct of plunder,
the natural delight in unlicensed action which in

ordinary times is kept in check by the steady pressure
of law.' This was not so, and indeed the same writer
contradicts himself in another passage, for these blind
outbursts had, he admitted, Knox's 'cordial approval.'
They had more; they had the approval of the Protestant Lords. It was for the destruction of churches
and monasteries that more than one 'band' of the nobles
was made; it was in part because they were asked not
to destroy churches and monasteries that they refused
Mary of Guise's terms at Cupar. The liberty which
the Protestants demanded from the Regent, in fact,
was twofold; they asked leave to worship as they
liked, and to pull down monasteries and churches. By
open profession they considered both those claims
equally legitimate.

The destruction, then, was essentially a policy rather
than a blind outburst. It began as early as 1540; it was
continued by Paul Methuen, the first man in Scotland
to set up a purified Church. Nine days after his arrival
in Scotland, Knox set the work going on a large scale.
It went on sporadically for another century, and Andrew
Lang says bitterly: 'The fragments of things beautiful
that the Reformers overlooked were destroyed by the
Covenanters.' The destruction, then, was systematic
and was on a vast scale, but it presented irresistible
temptations to many besides the earnest professors. It
was a policy, but it was one which had all the insensate
attractions of a riot. Thus, while the real objects of
reformed fury were, of course, the images of Christ
and the Virgin, in moments of exaltation it rose to
embrace all statuary. A monument to Robert the

Bruce among other things was destroyed in the religious frenzy.

The whole affair now is so displeasing chiefly because it seems insensate and meaningless. But at the time, and from the Protestants' point of view, there can be no doubt that it was an effective policy. There were thousands of statues of Christ, the Virgin and various patron saints in Scotland; some of them must have been beautiful; all of them must have had the power of evoking reverence in the people. The reformers wished to kill that reverence, and to kill it the most drastic means were also the best. If any man could drag down an image of the Deity and break it to pieces, then clearly no supernatural power inhered in images. The campaign of destruction was symbolical; in seeing abbeys and monasteries pulled down the people were witnessing in effigy the overthrow of the Catholic Church itself. As a doctrine Knox's theory of idolatry seems now ridiculous; as a political weapon we can still acknowledge its skill and effectiveness. It was all the more effective because, as far as can be discovered, nobody in Scotland on either side had any great appreciation of beauty, or felt any reluctance at destroying the monuments of it which existed.

Yet Knox was the only reformer of great reputation who encouraged a general destruction of works of art, and he felt his isolation. Calvin was severe enough in his reprobation of beauty, but robbery and pillage, even of Catholic property, his orderly mind could not abide. A preacher at Nîmes called Tartas had made himself notorious by his zeal, asserting that destruction was a

matter of conscience with him. This was insupportable, Calvin said. '*We*,' he went on, 'know that it is
not the case, for God never commanded anyone to
overthrow idols, except every man in his house, and
those who are armed with His authority in public.
Let the fire-brand tell us what title *he* has to be ruler
of the land where he burns things.' Tartas had none,
it was clear, as little as Knox and the Protestant Lords
had in Scotland. While encouraging destruction at
the time, therefore, Knox was careful – when later he set
out a history of the Reformation for public approval –
to insist that the monasteries were destroyed by the
mob, and that the churches were purified by the lawful
authorities. In his letter to Mrs. Locke he told, as we
have seen, how the brethren had sacked the religious
houses in Perth and threatened the priests with death.
In his *History* the priests were not threatened, and the
looting was the work of the 'rascal multitude,' not of
the brethren. Perhaps – so full of intricacies was his
character – he actually believed by then that the mob
were the real offenders. His side could not be in the
wrong, but if what he had said to Mrs. Locke was true,
then, according to the best opinion of the elect, they
had been in the wrong. His mind refused to rest under
such a monstrous accusation; the whole business in
Perth now seemed more confused than ever, but the
probability steadily grew that the mob had destroyed
the monasteries. When he took up his pen they *had*
destroyed the monasteries.

CHAPTER XII

DEATH OF MARY OF GUISE

The completeness of Knox's first metamorphosis from a Catholic priest into a perfect type of Protestantism has baffled his biographers. The second change his character underwent as soon as he put his hand to the Scottish revolution is, at first sight, almost as difficult to explain. The man who for several years, from Dieppe and Geneva, bombarded England and Scotland with seditious pamphlets, was a man of extreme views and violent passions, but one who, at the threat of danger, was apt to be timid. The man who threw himself into the revolution, while equally violent in his opinions, showed a furious daring which outshone the boldest of his colleagues. Before the prospect of danger full of terrors and excuses, in its actual presence he was cased in unassailable intrepidity. He invited perils; he created them; he rushed upon them, as if something else, which he dreaded more, were pursuing him.

To create this consummated Knox, this intrepid figure, many influences, some heroic and some not, must have combined. The extremes of daring, it has often been shown, are attained oftenest by men conscious of their weakness. They have to prove themselves, and the only proof that will satisfy them is some act which goes beyond the ordinary courage of practised men of action. Knox confessed that he was a timid man; in shaking off his fears now, therefore, he overcame himself and was re-born a second time. Yet the change, while it ennobled his character, did not essentially alter him. It was fear partly that drove out his fear. He found himself pitched headlong into a country on the eve of civil war; he found himself at the same time a proclaimed outlaw. To join the Protestant insurgents was not so much rebellion as prudence; to make the revolution certain was his only hope of safety. Nine days after his arrival the revolution broke out, and his preaching in Perth was the cause. The quarrel was settled for a time. Then he preached at St. Andrews, and it broke out again. He was only secure so long as the country was split into two factions, and he was in the centre of one of them. He split Scotland into two factions. Compared with any common standards his courage remains extraordinary; but it was, at the same time, his only hope of winning safety.

Of winning safety, but not only for himself, for his religion as well, and he was nothing without his religion. It was the seventeenth chapter of the Gospel of St. John which had created him anew, and the figure which emerged was partly personal, John Knox with his passions, his furies, his self-distrust, his hesitations, and partly the impersonal and unassailable instrument of God. In himself he was nothing, as the instrument he was the equal of the greatest. His second nature, consequently, sat more easily on him than his first. As a man, meeting his contemporaries on the ordinary human level, he said and did nothing which showed originality, wisdom or great personal force. He only came to life in the pulpit or the debating-chamber, or when, with a pen in his hand, he reported God's judgments to a general audience. His true utterance was preaching; his natural conversation was argument. As an instrument alone, then, did he manage to establish contact with his fellow-creatures, or to impress them with his powers. The religion which discovered to him that he was an instrument, therefore, created him, and in fighting for it he was fighting for all that made him remarkable. His faith in it had that piercing conviction which could only come from gratitude for something as dear as life.

Yet a man who had a need to clothe himself with the apparel of God before he could face his fellow-men must have had at the bottom of his soul a profound feeling of inferiority. This feeling, which had always to be conquered anew, came out in his timidity, in the violence which was its complement, and in his morbid resentment of all authority higher than God's or his own. It had made him in England, and in Geneva itself, challenge whatever was set over his will. He had disobeyed the mild laws of the Anglican Church; he had disobeyed Calvin, too, whose approval he so much coveted. The same feeling had driven him to denounce the rule of women, and had made his relations to Mrs. Bowes and Mrs. Locke so curiously filial. It now gave him the quality for which for the rest of his life he was best known; his obstinate speaking of his mind in and out of season. He had perpetually to be asserting himself in order to prove that he was there. He had always to be showing that he was the equal of anybody, to demonstrate that he was the equal of somebody. He had continually to be reassuring himself that he was on the side of righteousness, and that his enemies were the servants of the devil. He could never rest so long as his party was not victorious; he was not comfortable in victory if there was the faintest sign of independent spirit on the conquered side. In defeat and in power he was equally unable to endure opposition, then, because opposition hinted at the free existence of wills which threatened his own. The assertion of his will and of God's, with which it was so mysteriously allied, was his perpetual need; for its assertion was its proof, and its proof was the only sure demonstration of his own value. As a man of action his peculiar characteristic is therefore a unique and maddening persistence of will. Other reformers, statesmen, soldiers, are distinguished by an ebb and flow of volition; their will seems to rest and sleep, gathering its energies for a sudden blow, or for a prolonged sequence of aggressive action; in the interval, when it is needed, they put up an impregnable resistance to every stimulus, showing extraordinary patience and self-control. But Knox's will never slept; it was incapable of resisting a stimulus; it drove him on with a frightful automatic compulsion in which there was something meaningless, because pathological. It drove Scotland

on with him. It was a force beyond his control,
and incapable of being controlled by anybody else.
He gave Scotland no choice, because he had none
himself.

Only the fact that his will was the will of God,
however, explains the second capacity which, along
with personal bravery, he found added to him as soon
as he was involved in the revolution, his capacity for dissimulation. It was a capacity which came more easily to
him. As we have seen, he was accustomed to translate
his own disputes into the disputes of God. When he
was angry with England he could only express the fact
by saying that God was angry with England. When
two queens in succession persecuted him and his religion, he could only formulate the truth of the matter
by stating that God disapproved of queens. From the
beginning all his resentments had been falsified by
being transposed into public issues. As soon as the
man suffered the instrument prophesied, but before
the suffering appeared as the prophecy it had suffered
a baffling transmutation. Yet this natural dissimulation
lay so deep in Knox's character that he was as uncon-
scious of it as were all but a few of his contemporaries.
It was a stroke of inspiration now, therefore, for the
Protestant Lords to set him up as the chosen apologist
for their shifty policies. Nobody can tell lies with such
effect as the natural self-deceiver who is convinced that
he is speaking the truth. Nobody could have told the
lies of the Protestant Lords with more conviction than
Knox, or with more certainty that they were true.
He had, indeed, a kind of honesty which stood at the

opposite pole from the common honesty of other politicians of his time. Lethington, Cecil, and Mary of Guise used duplicity deliberately; their honesty consisted in recognizing it as duplicity. Knox used duplicity and persuaded himself that it was the truth, but he was honest enough not to have used it if he had recognized what it was. He did not wilfully deceive others; he did not need to, for he deceived himself.

The Lords made Knox their official prevaricator, first by the simple expedient of making him their secretary, and later by giving him a commission to write a history of the conflict. Already, while he was preaching at St. Andrews or soon afterwards, he had been sending to Cecil in England letters asking aid for the Congregation. About the same time he was assisting in a plot to get back to Scotland Arran, a Protestant and the nearest claimant to the throne after Mary Stuart. By the 14th of June proposals were being made by the Lords for a marriage between Arran and Elizabeth, proposals which would have rendered Mary's succession to the throne superfluous. A plot against the Regent and the young Queen was being prepared therefore, and with Knox's knowledge; yet what he was put up to say was that there was no plot, that the Protestants were perfectly loyal, and that they only desired liberty to worship according to their conscience. 'We mean no tumult,' he wrote to Mrs. Locke, after the Congregation had driven the Regent out of Edinburgh, and were intriguing to get Arran married to Elizabeth – 'we mean no tumult, no alteration of authority, but only the reformation of religion, and suppressing of idolatry.' It was like a sentence which he had learned by rote, for a few days later he wrote to Cecil, who knew perfectly well what the Protestant Lords' intentions were: 'None that professeth Christ Jesus usurpeth anything against the authority.' Yet with another part of his mind he knew that the Lords were trying to usurp the authority.

Through informers in the Protestant party and through her spies in England Mary of Guise knew it as well, however. While the Congregation sat in an Edinburgh purified of idolatry and works of art, while with a last protestation of loyalty they were grabbing the royal Mint, she issued a public accusation of the Protestants. She was prepared to allow freedom of worship, but, she continued, the reformers had seized the royal palace of Holyrood and the Mint, they were daily intriguing with England, and their real intention was to subvert the throne. Knox denied it with the most sincere indignation. He admitted that the Lords had seized the Mint, but that had been to prevent the further issue of the debased money with which Mary paid her French soldiers. There surely has never been a more grotesque quarrel. A queen accuses her subjects of disloyalty; they reply that she is a liar.

As the supporters of the Congregation in Edinburgh deserted in greater and greater numbers to return to their work, the need for intriguing against Mary and proving their loyalty to her became ever more pressing. On the 19th of July Knox wrote to Cecil again protest-

ing his devotion to Elizabeth, who had not yet forgiven
The First Blast. 'The time is near, sir,' he said, 'when
all that either trust Christ Jesus to reign in this isle, the
liberty of the same to be kept to the inhabitants thereof,
and their hearts to be joined together in love unfeigned,
ought rather to study how the same may be brought to
pass than vainly to travail for the maintenance of that,
whereof already we have seen the danger and felt the
smart. If the most part of women be such as willingly
we would not they should reign over us; and if the
most godly, and such as have rare gifts and graces, be
yet mortal, we ought to take heed, lest that we in
establishing one judged godly and profitable to her
country, make entress and title to many, by whom not
only shall the truth be impugned but also shall the
country be brought to bondage and slavery.' The
many mentioned by Knox was Mary Stuart, by whom
the truth was certainly impugned, and for whom at the
time the throne of England as well as of Scotland was
claimed by her supporters. The appeal to Elizabeth
was adroit, therefore, the hint of sedition only a hint.
Meanwhile in the pulpit of the Tolbooth Kirk Knox
was indignantly denouncing as lies the rumours that
the Protestants were guilty of sedition.

The Lords had entered Edinburgh on the 29th of
June with a force of over 6000 men. Now, after three
weeks, their numbers were reduced to about 1500.
The Mint, useful as it had appeared at first, had not
yielded them much. They had no money to pay
their men; they wrote urgently asking for help from
England. On the other hand Huntly, bribed by the

earldom of Moray, had joined Mary; and Châtelherault, though vacillating, remained faithful to her.
Now a rumour was set going that the Lord James, with
the backing of the Protestants, intended to raise himself to the throne; Châtelherault as the nearer claimant
became more faithful than ever. At last, on the 23rd
of July, Mary's forces, under Châtelherault and
D'Oysel, marched from Dunbar. They were twice as
strong as the Congregation, and they knew that Lord
Erskine, who held Edinburgh Castle, was on their
side. They reached Leith early in the morning of the
24th. Leith had promised to support the Protestants;
it fired one shot and surrendered. From their station
on the eastern slope of Calton Hill the army of the
Congregation saw the enemy entering the gates of
Edinburgh.

Mary once more showed moderation. The terms
imposed upon the Congregation were that they should
leave Edinburgh within twenty-four hours, that they
should deliver up the coining-irons and Holyrood,
that they should be loyal subjects in all matters except
religion, and that they should not disturb the Catholic
clergy or wreck churches and monasteries. In return
the Regent promised that Edinburgh should be free to
choose its own form of religion, and that the preachers
should not be molested. This agreement was to last
till the 10th of January 1560, when Parliament would
meet.

The agreement was signed by the leaders of the
Congregation, and the Protestants left the town. But
before they left they made a solemn proclamation of

the terms. In this they omitted all provisions unfavour-
able to themselves, and added two of their own
invention. These declared that idolatry should not be
restored where it had been suppressed, and that the
French should be sent away after a reasonable interval,
not to return except with the assent of the whole
nobility. The Catholics pointed out the brethren's
mistake; the brethren, however, stuck to it. After
the agreement had been signed there had apparently
been a conversation between Huntly and Châtelherault
on the one side, and certain of the Lords of the Congregation on the other. Imitating the precedent of the
Lord James and Argyll, Huntly and Châtelherault
had promised to desert to the other party if Mary
broke her word; Châtelherault had sworn to do it,
moreover, if she did not send away the French army.
Therefore 'we proclaimed nothing,' Knox affirmed
triumphantly, 'which was not finally agreed upon, in
word and promise, betwixt us and those with whom the
appointment was made.' The promise was made by
men who, immediately after treating for Mary, had
betrayed her. She would never have agreed to it, if
she had known. It was not in the treaty to which the
Protestants had just put their hands. Having mis-
represented, therefore, an agreement which they could
not have avoided signing, yet by which they were
secured favours more ample than they could have
expected, the Congregation left Edinburgh certain
now that the Regent must break her word again.

When Mary's forces were setting out for Leith
Knox had been preparing to travel on a diplomatic

mission to England. Several times since his coming
he had written Cecil asking for the necessary permission. From St. Andrews in the beginning of June
he had asked leave to visit the Newcastle district, that
he might communicate to some man of discretion and
solid judgment things which it would be impolitic to
commit to writing. From Perth, after the sack of
Scone Abbey, he renewed his request. From Edinburgh on the 19th of July he renewed it again,
pointing out, among other things, that the longer the
permission was refused the less comfort the faithful in
Berwick and Newcastle would receive. Permission
same at last, but the arrival of Mary's army, the
settlement of the treaty, and the misrepresentation of it
afterwards delayed Knox for a few days. At the end
of July he sailed from Fife to Holy Island, where he
had a secret appointment with Crofts, the Governor of
Berwick and the representative of Cecil. From the
Protestant Lords he carried instructions to treat.
These required that England should send men, gold
and ships in return for a perpetual defensive alliance
between the two countries. In particular the Lords
asked for money to garrison Stirling Castle, which they
would seize, and for ships to capture Broughty Castle,
a fairly easy enterprise. Crofts conveyed Knox to
Berwick and there got somewhat more ample ad-
missions out of him than he had intended making.
Under skilful questioning he confessed that the
Lords would follow Elizabeth's wishes in the
matter of changing the authority in Scotland. He
thought, too, that Arran should be kept in England

until they saw what was in him; his second choice was the Lord James. But now complaints were sent to Cecil that Mr. Knox had arrived with so little secrecy that his coming was known to everybody, including Mary of Guise. Knox suddenly decided that he could not remain any longer away from his flock. He felt, he said, that he was not fit to treat of such great matters, Balnaves might make a better shape. Accordingly on the night of the 3rd of August he left for Scotland along with another messenger from the Congregation called Whitelaw. On the road back Whitelaw fell ill, and Knox went on his way. When Whitelaw resumed his journey he was chased for three miles by Lord Seton, who was keeping watch for the Regent, and a chair was broken over his head: Lord Seton thought he was pursuing Knox, who was safe in Stirling. In his *History*, written later, Knox, however, adduced the incident of the broken chair as a sure proof that the Regent had broken the treaty. He did not say that Seton had mistaken Whitelaw for himself, or that a week after the signing of the treaty he had been arranging with the English for the capture of Stirling and Broughty Castle. Such was the reformer's conception at that time of truth and honesty.

The Congregation, zealously assisted by Knox, were now doing so many things that it is difficult to keep account of them. They were proclaiming their loyalty to the Regent and intriguing with England to depose her. They were falsifying the treaty of the 24th of July, and predicting that she would break it; and they were themselves breaking the treaty thus falsified.

Their general policy, then, was treachery; but many of them embraced the opportunity of private treachery as well. Kirkcaldy of Grange, one of their number, was betraying Mary while he accepted her pay. Lethington, another of them, was writing to England that 'he attended upon the Regent no longer than he might have a good occasion to revolt unto the Protestants.' Lord James and Argyll had already betrayed her after closing an agreement in her name at Perth. Huntly and Châtelherault had followed their example at Edinburgh. Dissimulation had been used abundantly on both sides; but treachery was the unique distinction of the chief figures in the reformed party. It was this sequence of lying and betrayal which Knox was now set up to paint in blameless colours. He did so, not merely with skill, but with conviction. He made out Mary to be a liar, a cruel tyrant, and a woman of light virtue. He portrayed the leaders of the Congregation as men who only desired the purification of religion and the freedom of their country. He wished this to be true, and it became true.

He did not spare himself, however. While he was writing his *History*, he was also preaching up and down the country, and acting as secretary to the Congregation. He wrote to Mrs. Locke from St. Andrews on the 2nd of September. 'Time to me,' he said, 'is so precious that with great difficulty can I steal one hour in eight days either to satisfy myself or to gratify my friends. I have been in continual travail since the day of appointment and notwithstanding that fevers have vexed me the space of a month, yet have I

travelled through the most part of this realm, where
(all praise be to His blessed Majesty) men of all sorts
and conditions embrace the truth. We do nothing,'
he went on, forgetting his secretarial labours for the
Congregation – 'we do nothing but go about Jericho,
blowing with trumpets, as God giveth strength,
hoping victory by His power alone.' He trusted that
his wife would soon arrive. 'Now,' he concluded, 'to
the complaint and prayer of your letter written, say ye,
at midnight. Be of comfort, sister, knowing that ye
fight not the battle alone. Fight, and fruit shall succeed, albeit not such as we would, yet such as shall
witness that we are not void of the spirit of the Lord
Jesus, Who only is our justice, sanctification and
holiness.'

He found leisure about the same time to write
Calvin for advice on two important points. 'Should
the bastard sons of idolaters and excommunicated
persons be admitted to baptism, till either the parents
have by repentance submitted themselves to the
Church, or their offspring are qualified to ask baptism?
Should the yearly revenues of the Church be paid to
Popish monks and priests who neither serve the
Church of God nor from their habits are fit to serve it,
even should they confess their former error?' After
congratulating his brother on the abundant success of
his labours in Scotland, Calvin replied in his mildest
vein. 'As the authority of God,' he said, 'is to be regarded in the right use of baptism, and His appointment should decide what is right, it is here proper to
consider, in the first place, who they are that God by

His Word invites to baptism. But the promise not only comprehends the offspring of each of the faithful in the first degree, but is extended to a thousand generations. Whence also it is the case that the interruption of true religion, which has prevailed under Popery, has not obstructed the virtue and efficacy of baptism. For the origin of baptism is to be considered, and its very reason and nature are to be estimated by the promise. Wherefore we have not the least doubt that the progeny of holy and pious ancestors, although their grandfathers and parents may have been apostates, belong notwithstanding to the body of the Church.' If any relative could be found to act as sponsor, in short, Knox would be well advised to let the bastards in. 'For while the Church,' Calvin argued, 'is being gathered together after a fearful dispersion, since the possession of baptism has through a long series of ages survived even to our times, it ought to be retained, and in process of time the licentiousness which has crept in must be corrected, and parents must be forced to present their own children, and to be their chief sponsors.' Calvin showed his admirable political tact equally in his reply to the second question. 'It is true,' he said, 'that subsistence is not due to monks and priests from a public source, in order that they may live in useless ease. If any, therefore, are fit to edify the Church, let them be called to labour therein. But, seeing they are for the most part unlearned and destitute of all skill, we think they should be humanely dealt with. For, although those who give none of their labour to the Church have no right to claim their maintenance, yet, since they have ensnared themselves through ignorance and error, and have spent part of their life in idleness, it were hard that they should be totally deprived of it.' The questions were those of a callow pupil, the replies those of a master. Knox did not act on them.

Meanwhile Arran had arrived in Scotland. Soon after his arrival his father, the old Duke of Châtelherault, at last came over to the Protestants. Balnaves had been more successful than Knox; he had extorted £3000 out of England and promises of more to come. But in the interval 1000 French troops had arrived at Leith, and while the Protestants were assembled in the west they heard that the Regent was fortifying the town. This was a clear breach of the falsified treaty, and they sent a message to Mary forbidding her to go on with the fortification. In a few days, however, another 800 French troops arrived at Leith. The Protestants summoned their supporters to meet at Stirling on the 15th of October, and Knox wrote urgently to England asking for money.

On the 16th of October the Protestants, 8000 strong, entered Edinburgh. They again ordered Mary to desist from fortifying Leith and to send her French soldiers out of the country. Mary's French soldiers were her only pledge of safety; she replied that the message would have been more appropriate in a prince to his subjects than in subjects to their prince, and that her precautions had been justified, as their presence in Edinburgh showed. On the 21st the Protestant Lords held a meeting in the Tolbooth, to which they invited

Knox and Willock, another preacher. They wanted to know whether they would be justified in deposing Mary of Guise. Willock was enthusiastically affirmative; Knox gave his modified approval. If the Regent should openly repent her conduct and subject herself to the nobility, she must be reinstated; nor must they forget their young sovereigns in France. The Lords did not forget them. On the 24th they deposed the Regent in the name of Francis and Mary, and, clothed thus with royal authority, summoned Leith again, but Leith paid no attention. The Protestants next got a gold-worker to forge the royal seal, and armed with it issued proclamations in which Francis and Mary, with admirable altruism, commanded the more lukewarm nobles to obey their supplanter Arran. These audacious young princes even referred to the Pope as Antichrist. But while the seal was being prepared the Protestant army, raw and untrained, stood powerless before the scientific fortifications of Leith, held by 3000 men. Knox, grown desperate, wrote to Crofts in England again.

'Such is our estate, right worshipful,' he began, 'that unless present support be provided for us, you and we will both lament.' He asked that men and money should be sent with all haste. England, he knew, had four months ago made a treaty of peace with France and could not send help without breaking it. 'If ye fear to offend France,' he argued therefore, 'in secret it is already at defiance with you, and abideth only the opportunity and advantage. If you list to craft with them,' he went on hopefully, 'the sending of a thousand or more men to us can break no league nor point of peace contracted betwixt you and France; for it is free for your subjects to serve in war any prince or nation for their wages. And if ye fear that such excuses shall not prevail, you may declare them rebels to your realm when ye shall be assured that they be in our company. I speak my judgment freely; judge you as God shall move your heart.' 'Our simplicity,' he said later, 'shall appear before God and man.'

Crofts' reply was in a more appropriate vein of hypocrisy. 'I cannot but marvel,' he wrote, elated at any opportunity to get a slap at a prophet, 'that you, being a wise man, should require of us such present aid of men, money and ammunition, as we cannot minister unto you without an open show and manifestation of ourselves to be as open enemies, where, as you know, by league and treaty, we be bound to be friends; praying you to consider how we may, without touch of honour and hurt of our commonwealth, being now in good peace and amity, enter suddenly into open war and hostility, being no cause of breach, no manifest injury offered unto us.' It was not the treachery to France, however, it was the obviousness of it that shocked him. Having reproved Knox for the wickedness of his proposal, he next censured him for its clumsiness. 'To be plain with you,' he said, 'ye are so open in your doings as you make men half afraid to deal with you.' Cecil was told of the rebuke, and remembering Knox's former admonitions to him was greatly delighted. The reformer's 'audacity,' he wrote, 'was well tamed,' and he went on to instruct his

agent to act as Knox had suggested. Knox replied to
Crofts in a chastened mood. 'Your reasonable answer
to my unreasonable request, right worshipful,' he said,
'received I this 28th of October, and have imparted
the contents of the same to such as partly advised me
before to write.' He excused himself by the argument
that it would be more advantageous for England to
break her word than to keep it.

At this time, indeed, he had little time for reflection.
He was trying to get the Congregation out of a critical
position; he was scheming for them and whitewashing
them; he was conducting a large correspondence, and
preaching whenever he could. His wife had returned
at the end of September, but in spite of her assistance
as secretary he was still overburdened with work.
In a letter to Gregory Railton, one of Cecil's agents,
he wrote: 'Make ye advertisement as ye think good,
for I cannot write to any especial for lack of opportunity; for in twenty-four hours I have not four free to
natural rest, and ease of this wicked carcase.' He
added that great watch was laid for his apprehension
and large money offered to anyone who would kill him,
and he begged Railton to ask one of Mrs. Bowes' sons
for a good and assured horse.

Lethington, having at last decided to desert the
Regent, presently took the secretarial work of the
Congregation into his more expert hands. But for a
while everything went wrong; Bothwell intercepted a
thousand pounds of English money intended for the
Protestants; their regular soldiers mutinied; and the
Leith garrison were having all the best of the exchanges.

On the 5th of November the Protestants made an attack and were driven back with great loss. At midnight they hurriedly left the town. 'The despiteful tongues of the wicked railed upon us,' says Knox, 'calling us traitors and heretics; everyone provoked the other to cast stones at us. One cried, "Alas, if I might see"; another, "Fie, give advertisement to the Frenchmen that they may come and we shall help them now to cut the throats of these heretics." And thus, as the sword of dolour passed through our hearts, so were the cogitations and former determinations of many hearts then revealed. For we would never have believed that our natural countrymen and women could have wished our destruction so unmercifully, and have so rejoiced in our adversity: God move their hearts to repentance!' The Congregation did not stop until they were safe in Stirling.

The Congregation had staked everything on their 8000 men; they had lost; and Knox preached next day to the despondent Lords. He took as his text a passage from the 80th Psalm: 'O thou the Eternal, the God of Hosts, how long shalt Thou be angry against the prayer of Thy people? Thou hast fed us with the bread of tears, and hast given us tears to drink in great number. Thou hast made us a strife unto our neighbours, and our enemies laugh us to scorn among themselves.' He began with an exposition of the reasons why God suffered His flock to be exposed to mockery and destruction. These were three: that they might feel the vehemency of His anger; that they might recognize how little strength was in themselves; and that they might leave to later generations a record both of the devil's malice against them and of the marvellous ways which God ordained for their deliverance. Then he turned to one of his favourite ideas, the idea which had comforted him in those weeks before he fled from England. How terrible, he said, was the temptation to think that God turned away His face from their prayers, for that was to conceive God to be armed to their destruction. Then he threw in an adroit piece of flattery. No one could withstand that thought, he informed the hardened Scottish Lords, unless by the power of the mighty Spirit of God itself. The difference between the reprobate and the elect in moments such as this, was that the former, sustained by the secret power of God's Spirit, continued to call on Him even though He appeared to ignore their prayers, and wrestled with Him and in a sense overcame Him, while the reprobate, seeing their requests denied, either ceased to pray or sought the devil's aid.

Having raised the nobles' spirits to this pitch, he burst out: 'Our faces are this day confounded, our enemies triumph, our hearts have quaked for fear, and still they remain oppressed with sorrow and shame. But what shall one think to be the very cause that God hath thus dejected us?' And having made sure of his audience, he began to rebuke them. Returning to the same argument with which he had justified his hesitations at Dieppe he continued: 'If I shall say our sins and former unthankfulness to God, I speak the truth.' It was necessary that he should prove one thing to them, that they had not failed because their present battle was treasonable. 'Seldom is it,' he went on, therefore, 'that man descendeth within himself, accusing and damning in himself that which most displeaseth God. But rather he fancies that to be a curse, which before God is no curse indeed.'

He chose his indispensable Biblical example with extraordinary care. He took the celebrated war of the Israelites against the tribe of Benjamin. Several young Benjamites, it will be remembered, seized the wife of a Levite and raped her; and the wrath of God was kindled so vehemently that He commanded Israel to exterminate the whole tribe. Yet the campaign, curiously enough, was completely unsuccessful for a time. The Israelites, Knox pointed out, were twice discomfited, with the loss of 40,000 men. 'They lamented and bewailed,' he continued, 'both first and last; but we find not that they came to the knowledge of their offence and sin, which was the cause that they fell on the edge of the sword; but rather they fancied that to have been a cause of their misfortune, which God had commanded. For they ask, "Shall we go and fight any more against our brethren, the sons of Benjamin?" By which question it is evident that they supposed that the cause of their overthrow and discomfort was, because they had lifted the sword against their brethren and natural countrymen. And yet the express commandment of God that was given unto them did deliver them from all crime in that case.' The real reason why God had not given them victory at once was that they had declined from Him and suffered idolatry to be maintained. In shedding the blood of their countrymen, Knox continued, 'they offended not; but in this they failed, that they go to execute judgment against the wicked, without any repentance or remorse of conscience of their former offences, and defection from God.' This, then, was one of the causes; but there was another. As their numbers were superior they had vainly trusted in their own strength, instead of invoking the name of God. 'The like,' Knox decided, 'may be among us.'

But the cause of the Congregation's defeat had not yet been fully exposed, and he worked cautiously but steadily towards it. He divided the Congregation into two parts: those who had been faithful from the beginning, and those who had joined recently. 'Let us begin at ourselves,' he said, 'who longest has been continued in this battle. When we were a few in number, in comparison of our enemies, when we had neither earl nor lord (a few excepted) to comfort us, we called upon God; we took Him for our protector, defence and only refuge. But since that our number hath been thus multiplied, and chiefly since my lord duke his grace with his friends have been joined with us, there was nothing heard but "This lord will bring these many hundred spears; this man hath the credit to persuade this country; if this lord be ours, no man in such a bounds will trouble us."' That had been the offence of the faithful; paying too much attention to the needs of the situation, and too little to the ministers. But what was the offence of the Duke? Knox described his own anguish at Perth, Cupar Moor and Edinburgh, when the Congregation had been pursued by those

cruel murderers, the Regent's forces. The Duke, he
said now, had at all these places been a great encouragement to the enemy, and a discouragement to themselves, and he was still uncertain of the Duke's sincere
repentance. But 'I am assured,' he said at last, 'that
neither he, neither yet his friends, did feel before this
time the anguish and grief of heart which we felt,
when in their blind fury they pursued us. And therefore hath God justly permitted both them and us to
fall in this confusion at once; us, for that we put our
trust and confidence in man; and them, because that
they should feel in their hearts how bitter was the cup
which they made others to drink before them.'

The whole address was an extremely skilful performance, and showed Knox at his best. He breathed
spirit into the Lords by persuading them that they
were the elect; he took away any compunction they
may have had at shedding their countrymen's blood
by fixing the offence elsewhere and by antedating it
consolingly; he managed to insinuate two grievances
of his own – his displeasure at the neglect of the
preachers' advice and at the past shufflings of
Châtelherault. He rose confidently to his peroration.
Let them all turn unfeignedly to God and 'I have no
more doubt,' he exclaimed, 'but that this our dolour,
confusion, and fear shall be turned into joy, honour,
and boldness, than that I doubt that God gave victory
to the Israelites over the Benjamites after that twice
with ignominy they were repulsed and driven back.
Yea, whatever shall become of us and our mortal
carcases, I doubt not but that this cause (in despite of

Satan) shall prevail in the realm of Scotland. For, as it is the eternal truth of the eternal God, so shall it once prevail, however for a time it be impugned.'

'The sermon ended,' Knox wrote in his *History of the Reformation*, 'the minds of men began wondrously to be erected.' Nowhere before had Knox shown more clearly the pre-eminence of his spirit and the power of his eloquence. He played with the Lords while infusing life into them. Yet he himself had been driven to despair by the flight from Edinburgh, and he betrayed his real feelings in a letter to Mrs. Locke. 'One day of troubles,' he wrote, 'since my last arrival in Scotland, hath more pierced my heart than all the torments of the galleys did the space of nineteen months; for that torment, for the most part, did touch the body, but this pierces the soul and inward affections.' Yet, in another letter to the same lady the ineradicable ambiguousness of his nature came out again. Repeating his argument to the Lords, which he had convinced himself to be true by now, he wrote: 'We trusted too much, dear sister, in our own strength and specially since the Earl of Arran and his friends were joined to the number. . . . I wrote you before to be suitor to some faithful, that they would move such as have abundance to consider our estate, and to make for us some provision of money, to keep soldiers and our company together; and herein, yet again, I cannot cease to move you.' But the matter did not end there. Mrs. Locke wrote back saying that she had tried to get help, but that the brethren, being of Knox's opinion, had not thought it necessary, seeing

that God would support His people. She implored
Knox to avoid danger and to fight by prayer in some
safe place rather than expose himself. Knox in his
reply noted these points and left them. He complained
bitterly, however, of the illiberality of the faithful, and
said that the Protestants' forces, though relying on
God alone, could not quite dispense with private
support. He feared that if help did not come their
enemies would prevail in the field. 'But God,' he concluded, assuming the prophet again, 'shall support,
even how, when, and by whom it shall please His
blessed Majesty.'

Marvellously as their spirits were erected, however,
and much as they trusted in God, the Lords did not
immediately resume their battle with the tribe of
Benjamin. One man besides Knox was convinced
that all was not lost, Maitland of Lethington. Lethington, Knox wrote to Crofts, introducing his successor,
was now 'delivered from the fearful thraldom of the
Frenchmen'; and Lethington based his hopes for the
Congregation less on the help of God than on that of
England. In his adroit hands the negotiations began
at last to show fruit. While the Congregation separated, while Châtelherault and his following waited
in Glasgow, and the Lord James with the eastern
forces returned to St. Andrews, Lethington threw
aside the pretext of religion and put the revolt on
a basis of patriotism. The Lords were now fighting for the liberty of Scotland against the French.
The new catchword was both more tolerable to
Elizabeth and more popular with the Scottish

people, and it was soon to bring in reinforcements
from both.

Knox had retired to St. Andrews with the Lord
James and his army. For the next few months he had
no guiding influence on the policy of the Congregation,
and that policy, it was clear, displeased him. After
raising the Lords from their dejection at Stirling, he
seems, indeed, to have become somewhat unpopular.
'I am judged amongst ourselves too extreme,' he wrote
to Railton, 'and by reason thereof I have extracted
myself from all public assemblies to my private study.'
But his studies were somewhat disturbed. In the
beginning of the new year D'Oysel began to invade
Fife, and his object was St. Andrews. The Lord James,
Arran and Kirkcaldy of Grange, with a handful of men,
fought heroically. 'For twenty and one days,' Knox
wrote, 'they lay in their clothes; their boots never
came off; they had skirmishing almost every day; yea,
some days, from morn to even.' They did this in the
middle of winter, amid rain and great storms. Yet
Knox was not quite satisfied. He preached at Cupar,
foretelling that deliverance was near; but he criticized
Arran and compared him adversely with that blameless
hero, Jehoshaphat. Jehoshaphat went out and in
among his soldiers, but Arran 'kept himself more close
and solitary than many men would have wished.'
Poor Arran, sleeping in his clothes for three weeks,
had no time for anything so Biblical as going out
and in. He told Knox to mind his own business.

The French troops advanced at last to within six
miles of St. Andrews. 'Where is now John Knox, his

God?' the Regent is reported to have asked her attendants. 'My God is now stronger than his, yea, even in
Fife.' But deliverance unexpectedly arrived; on the
same day that St. Andrews was threatened the English
fleet appeared in the Firth of Forth. 'Those bloody
worms,' the French, now 'retired as much in one day,'
Knox wrote to Railton, 'as they advanced in two.' In
the same letter he expressed once more his great need
for a good horse. Mrs. Bowes had procured one
for him, but she did not know how it could be
sent.

Meantime Lethington's diplomacy was crowned
with success. Nine thousand English troops crossed
the border and joined the Scottish forces at Preston-
pans on the 4th of April. They advanced to Dalkeith
and there sent the Regent a final summons; religion
was not mentioned in it. On the 6th they began the
investment of Leith. Mary had been ill ever since, a
year ago, she had tried to quell the revolt at Perth. She
was now in the first stages of a dropsy which was to
carry her off in a few weeks. She asked leave to be
admitted to Edinburgh Castle, which for the present
maintained its neutrality. She was received there
before the siege began.

While the siege ran its tedious course Knox still
remained in his comparative retirement, preaching
and studying, and writing his apology for the Congregation. He had removed from St. Andrews to
Edinburgh when at last, on the morning of the 11th
of June, the indecisive struggle was ended by the death
of Mary. When all their efforts, when the lying of

their advocates and the assistance of England had
equally failed, this accident was to give the Lords
supreme power in Scotland, and was to establish the
Protestant religion so securely there that it has never
since been shaken.

Knox's detestation of Mary of Guise outlasted her
death. Nobody till now, not even Mary Tudor, had
remained so securely beyond the reach of his admonitions and furies. She had encountered with irony his
claims to prophetship; she had met his fiercest threats
with smiling self-control. Her virtues were so anti-
pathetic to him that he could only see in them a cloak
for deep-seated vices. He hated her self-possession,
her patience, her moderation, for they were virtues
which, as he was quite incapable of them, he neither
understood not trusted. He hated her very physical
appearance; a crown on her head was as seemly, he
said, with his genius for humiliating characterization,
'as a saddle upon the back of an unruly cow.' But
what must have infuriated him most was her calm
refusal to recognize his claims. Against such a woman
he was powerless. There is disappointment, therefore,
as well as spite in his persistent blackening of her
memory. He asserted, against all the facts, that she
only waited the opportunity 'to cut the throats of all
those in whom she suspected the knowledge of God to
be, within the realm of Scotland.' He repeated with
delight a baseless rumour that she had intended to
poison her husband. He insinuated that Cardinal
Beaton had 'got his secret business sped of her either
by day or night.' He insinuated that D'Oysel had

had the same freedom. He threw suspicion on the legitimacy of her daughter, Mary Stuart. He called her the 'wanton widow.' He did this both while she lived and after she was dead.

The passage where his hatred of her comes out most repellently, however, was written several years after her death. He had fled at the time from her incensed daughter to the quietness of Kyle, and he was comforting himself by adding a few touches to his *History*. He came to the siege of Leith; the allies had just been repulsed with loss. 'The French,' he wrote, 'proud of the victory, stripped naked all the slain, and laid their dead carcases before the hot sun along their wall, where they suffered them to lie more days nor one; unto the which, when the Queen Regent looked, for mirth she hopped and said, "Yonder are the fairest tapestry that ever I saw: I would that the whole fields that is betwixt this place and yon were strewed with the same stuff." This fact was seen of all, and her words were heard of some, and misliked of many. Against the which John Knox spoke openly in the pulpit, and boldly affirmed: "That God should revenge that contumely done to His image, not only in the furious and godless soldiers, but even in such as rejoiced thereat." And the very experience declared that he was not deceived; for within few days thereafter (yea, some say that same day) began her belly and loathsome legs to swell and so continued, till that God did execute His judgments upon her.' Knox's hatred and his hope that in the end, if not by direct admonition, then at least by prayer to God, he had got even with Mary, are equally to be traced in that very repellent passage. If he could not claim the credit for having made an impression on her, he was resolved at least to have the responsibility for her dropsy.

CHAPTER XIII

THE BOOK OF DISCIPLINE

Soon after the Regent's death commissioners arrived from France to effect a settlement. They had instructions to treat with England only, for in their eyes the authority of the Scottish nobles was necessarily invalid. The terms, however, were as favourable as the Lords could have gained for themselves. The French troops were to leave the country. During their absence a council was to govern, of which seven members were to be appointed by the Queen in France, and five by the Estates. Religion once more was left unmentioned, but the settlement put the Protestant Lords in full possession of power.

On the 15th of July the French troops left and the English marched back towards the Border, there were public rejoicings and a grand service of thanksgiving in St. Giles. A few days later ministers were assigned to various churches, and Knox was given the charge of Edinburgh. Lethington, who more than anyone had brought about the change, looked on sardonically. They must all deny themselves now, he said, 'and bear the barrow to build the houses of God.' He did not like the prospect.

The fateful Parliament met on the 1st of August; it was the largest that had ever assembled in Edinburgh. The question of religion was given first place. A supplication from certain 'barons, gentlemen, burgesses and others' was presented to the Convention. It begged that the Catholic religion should be abolished by Act of Parliament and that henceforward Catholics should be punished. The members were disposed to grant the request, but before they did so it was necessary to know the doctrines of the new Church in whose name they should persecute. A committee of barons and ministers was accordingly selected to draw up a Confession of Faith; Knox sat on it. The Confession was completed in four days, and it laid down the beliefs which everybody in Scotland must hold thenceforth. It was on the orthodox Genevan model. The nature of God, the mystery of Christ, the destiny of man, were all explained reverently, but with firmness. The Confession described how some were elected to everlasting salvation, and others ordained as vessels of wrath, without reference to their merits or vices; it denied that the individual had any part in his own salvation, or any choice whether he should be saved or damned, and it lauded the incomprehensible mercy of God. Coming to more particular points it admitted only two sacraments as pure – Baptism and the Lord's Supper, and ordained that ministers should be chosen by their congregations, and should have power to chastise them. Princes and authorities, it said, were appointed by God, and to such pertained in chief the reformation of religion.

The Confession was ratified by Parliament in a few days. A new religion was thus set up; the members next turned their attention to the old. In an Act passed on the 24th, shortly after the ratification of the Confession, they meted out appropriate punishments to all who in future should attend the Mass. The penalty for the first offence was confiscation of goods and corporal punishment; for the second, exile; for the third, death. With such energy did the new Church begin its ministrations a week after it had been established. The Confession had been drawn up in four days by a handful of barons and preachers; the punishments were intended to affect thousands of people who had never heard the new faith preached and had not the faintest notion whether they belonged to the elect or the reprobate. Thirty-six years after the passing of this extraordinary Act 'there were above four hundred parishes, not reckoning Argyll and the Isles,' says Dr. Hay Fleming, 'which still hadn't ministers.' But the Act was far too mild for the preachers. From the pulpit, wrote Archbishop Hamilton to a colleague in Paris, they were openly persuading the nobility 'to put violent hands and slay all churchmen that will not concur and adopt their opinion.'

Thanks to the nobles, whose zeal was greater for Church lands than for persecution, the more blood-thirsty provisions in the Act were not put into operation. Knox was meantime given work which would keep him quiet. Before the Parliament dissolved six of the ministers were instructed to draw up a volume

containing the policy and organization of the Kirk, and
Knox was one of the six. Parliament encouraged
him at the same time to continue his *History of the
Reformation.*

He was now fifty-five; the end for which he had
written, preached, lied, and prayed seemed to be
attained at last. It had been attained, moreover, more
quickly and more completely than even he could have
expected. In his sermon at the thanksgiving in St.
Giles he had said, almost in accents of awed surprise,
'Neither in us, nor yet in our confederates was there
any cause why Thou shouldst have given unto us so
joyful and sudden a deliverance, for neither of us both
ceased to do wickedly, even in the midst of our greatest
troubles.' It was but two years before, at Geneva, that
he had written the sisters in Edinburgh: 'Only this
dare I say, that sometimes (seldom, alas!) I feel a sob
and groan, willing that Christ Jesus might openly be
preached in my native country, with a certain desire
that my ears might hear it, although it should be with
the loss of this wretched life.' Now Calvinism was the
official religion of the country, and if anyone felt the
need to sob and groan it was a faithful Catholic here
and there. Yet both as a prophet and a patriot Knox
had many trials to endure in the few months during
which he was assisting in the compilation of the Book
of Discipline. The noblemen to whom the reformation of religion pertained were reforming in a manner
which did not please him. They were not persecuting
the idolaters with any conviction; they were only
annexing here and there tempting portions of the

idolaters' property. Nor were the Protestants' political
plans prospering. The Lords, unwilling to let any
chance slip, had been urging Elizabeth in London to
marry Arran and thus give Scotland a Protestant
king, while at the same time in Paris they were
endeavouring to get Francis and Mary's ratification
for their late Acts of Parliament. Both attempts failed.
The hope of a Protestant king was fading; the refusal
of their sovereigns to ratify the new Acts left religion
insecure. While Knox was being harassed by those
public cares, in December his wife died. Hardly
anything is known of his domestic life; in his few
references to Marjory there breathes approval rising
to a mild affection; he now mourned her loss with
genuine regret. Mrs. Bowes was left in his house to
look after his two young children.

Shortly after his wife's death, however, his spirits
were greatly raised by a piece of good news which
came to him from a friend in France. He describes it
characteristically. 'Lo!' he wrote, 'the potent hand of
God from above sent unto us a wonderful and most
joyful deliverance. For unhappy Francis, husband to
our sovereign, suddenly perisheth of a rotten ear.'
Scotland was freed from the menace of French
influence.

On the afternoon of the day that he received the
news he hurried to the Duke's house near Kirk-o'-
Field. He found the Lord James with the Duke.
While he comforted them with the news, they condoled
with him on his wife's death. They doubted, however,
the truth of what he told them; as they were

talking a confirmatory letter came from Lord Grey at Berwick. Arran's suit with Elizabeth had not prospered; but now there was a young widow in France who, once married to a Protestant prince, would suit the Lords and the preachers as well. Accordingly, less than a month after Francis' death Arran was commending himself to Mary, and the suit had the approval of the Lords and Knox. But Mary followed Elizabeth's example. The Protestants were disappointed again and Arran, twice balked in his determination to marry a queen, went about in great dejection.

Parliament met on the 15th of January 1561. Its main business was the discussion of the Book of Discipline, now completed. The book was debated for several days and with great acrimony, but no decision was reached.

The Book of Discipline is perhaps the most just picture of the aims of Knox and his colleagues. It is a full description of the Church which they thought it possible to set up in 1561; it defined that Church's powers and adumbrated its potentialities. It indicated the boundaries between civil and ecclesiastical jurisdiction. It was a systematic summary of law, not applicable merely to the temporary situation, but designed to last, without alteration, in perpetuity.

The Book was divided into nine sections. The first three were devoted to an exposition of doctrine; that doctrine did not differ in any respect from orthodox Calvinism, of which Knox had become a master in

Geneva, and which has already been treated. The remaining six sections described the means by which that doctrine might create for itself an effective instrument of power. The two corner-stones of that power were to be democracy and authority. The Congregation alone were to have the privilege of choosing their ministers; but the ministers once elected, the Congregation must reverence them 'as the servants and ambassadors of the Lord Jesus, obeying the commands which they speak from God's mouth and Book, even as they would obey God Himself.' The only ceremony required to clothe these men with such power was the public approbation of any congregation, and the sanction of the chief minister.

The preachers were to be paid out of the riches of the Church which they had supplanted. Out of the same source the poor were to be relieved, and a scheme of education was to be set up. This scheme was to comprehend a whole system of elementary schools, secondary schools, and universities. Attendance at the first was to be compulsory for both rich and poor; attendance at the second was to be compulsory for promising students; attendance at the third compulsory again on the best. The course of study in all three was to be rigorous, and pupils, lecturers, and subjects were alike to be under the supervision of the Kirk. By the age of twenty-four every student was to be compelled to leave the university 'and serve the Church or commonwealth.'

The Book considered next the interior discipline of

the Kirk. 'It is this section,' says Professor Hume Brown, 'beyond every other that expresses the essential character and tendency of the Reformed Church of Scotland.' It began by defining the respective spheres of Kirk and State. To the State belonged the punishment of all capital crimes, such as blasphemy, adultery, murder and perjury. But drunkenness, gluttony, the wearing of ostentatious apparel, fornication, oppression of the poor, wanton language and conduct and such like offences, should be punished by the Kirk. The Book next set up a systematic scale of punishments. Personal offences, resting on suspicion, must be checked by a private warning to the offender to abstain from all appearance of evil. If he promised to do so and his conduct showed that he feared God and his brethren, that would suffice. If he disregarded the warning, then the minister must rebuke him; if he still remained recalcitrant the officers of the Kirk must take more drastic steps and proceed by the rule of Christ.

Public and heinous offences, however, such as 'fornication, drunkenness, fighting, common swearing or execration,' must be brought before the minister, elders and deacons in session. There the offender's sin must be pointed out, so that he might be made conscious of it. If he showed signs of unfeigned repentance, then a day should be appointed on which before the whole congregation he should confess, express contrition, and beg the congregation to pray for him and accept him as a member of their communion. If he remained stubborn, he should be dismissed with a warning that he was in a dangerous state, and that other remedies would be employed. If this did not work the congregation should be told that certain crimes were being committed, and asked to pray that the offenders' hearts might be touched. If the man still held out, then next Sunday his name and his crime should be published in church and the congregation asked if such things should go un-punished; at the same time his friends should travail with him and the whole congregation should put up a prayer. The hypothetical offender having now survived to the third Sunday, the minister should inquire if he had shown any signs of repentance. If he had not, then through the mouth of the minister he should be pronounced excommunicate from God and from the society of His Church.

The Book next defined what was connoted by excommunication. After the Kirk's curse nobody, except the offender's wife and family, was to have any communication with him. Everybody would be forbidden to eat or drink with him, to sell him any-thing, or even to speak to him. His children born or conceived after his excommunication should be excluded from the blessing of baptism. His sentence should be published universally so that no one might plead ignorance. By such means, the writers of the book piously hoped, the man, seeing himself abhorred by the faithful, might be driven to repent and so be saved.

The next section related to the reciprocal duties of the minister and the congregation. The congregations were to be corrected by their ministers, their elders and one another. The ministers were to be corrected by their colleagues and their elders. The elders were to be corrected by their ministers, their congregation and their fellow elders.

The provisions of the Book flowed inexhaustibly on. Churches in the chief towns were to hold services every day; those in towns of medium size were to meet twice or thrice a week; those in remote places might meet only on Sundays. During the week-day services all labour, both of minister and servant, was to be intermitted; Sunday should be strictly kept. Every householder should instruct his children and servants in religion. In private houses the common prayers should be used morning and evening. 'Convert us, O Lord,' this section ended, 'and we shall be converted.'

Such, in outline, was this remarkable summary of ecclesiastical polity. In it may be seen most of the virtues and faults of the religion in which Knox believed and which he was instrumental in impressing on Scotland for several centuries. The virtues of that religion were its single-minded enthusiasm, and an intrepid spirit to which no task seemed impossible; its faults were a lack of understanding, an incapacity for human charity, and, above all, a consciously virtuous determination to compel and humiliate people for the greater glory of God. Its most fundamental idea was the corruption of man's nature, and its policy had necessarily, therefore, to be a policy of espionage and repression. Its sole instrument for keeping or reclaiming its members was punishment. The ministers had to correct their congregations; the elders had to correct the ministers; the congregations had to correct the elders. A Church such as this, held together by universal and reciprocal fault-finding, could not but have something ambiguous in its piety, and could not but encourage the self-opinionative and the censorious at the expense of the sensitive and the charitable. It did more, however; it substituted for the particular tyranny of the priest a universal and inescapable public tyranny. It was to show its dual qualities to the full in the next century of Scottish history, with its 'prophets,' its sadistic Kirk Sessions, its instances of intrepid constancy, its intolerance, its murders smiled on, its deeds of moderation execrated, its array of villains and of martyrs, but, above all, its stiff-necked blindness to the more spacious ideas which were moving mankind. It shows these qualities in many of the habits of Scottish life which persist unbroken to the present day. The 'bodies' in George Douglas Brown's great novel are the degenerate epigones of those hardened and godly congregations whose duty as well as pleasure it was to correct and humiliate one another; and who welded themselves into an indissoluble body by those most binding and intimate ties, the ties of reciprocal envy and hatred.

It is symbolical that the Book opened with a command to persecute, and almost closed with a plea for the extension of the scope of capital punishment. Parliament was advertised 'that where idolatry is maintained or permitted where it may be suppressed, that there shall God's wrath reign, not only upon the blind and obstinate idolater, but also upon the negligent sufferers of the same; especially if God have armed their hands with power to suppress such abominations.' Parliament was admonished again at the end to 'give God His honour and glory' and punish adultery with death. To a priesthood set on gaining tyrannical power these two offences must necessarily have appeared the most heinous of all. The first denied their religion; the second denied in the most trenchant way possible the supremacy of spiritual rule. Idolatry and adultery had been from the beginning the two primary sins for Knox. As idolatry became feebler in Scotland, however, adultery rose in importance. In the next few years there is scarcely a remonstrance of the ministers which does not contain a despairing injunction to Parliament to punish adultery with death.

For clear reasons it was impossible for the Estates to pass the Book of Discipline. The nobles and lairds could not with their eyes open deliver themselves into the hands of such a powerful priesthood; but neither could they regard as anything but a 'devout imagination' Knox's grandiose scheme of education. For that scheme was to be supported out of the revenues of the Church, and a great part of those revenues were already in their pockets. The authors of the Book were forced to recognize this disagreeable fact. 'If ye will have God author and approver of your reformation,' they said, 'ye must not follow the Papists' footsteps;

but you must have compassion of your brethren. With the grief of our hearts we hear that some gentlemen are now as cruel to their tenants as ever were the Papists, requiring of them whatsoever before they paid to the Church; so that the Papistical tyranny shall only be changed in the tyranny of the lord or of the laird. We dare not flatter your honours, neither yet is it profitable for you that so we do; if you permit such cruelty to be used, neither shall ye, who by your authority ought to gainstand such oppression, neither they that use the same, escape God's heavy and fearful judgments.' But the nobles and lairds stuck to the Church lands and rents; they had become accustomed to threats of God's judgments.

Beaten for the time, the ministers returned to the attack in May, when Parliament met again. They presented a supplication demanding that provision should be made for their maintenance, and that those who took part in the Mass should be punished according to the Act already passed. Parliament met these demands with enthusiastic approval, but having ratified them thought that it had done its duty. The state of the ministers was no better; the Catholics were not being persecuted. By one measure, however, the Lords showed their devotion to the new religion. Arran, Argyll and Glencairn made an excursion into the West, burned the rich Abbey of Paisley, and wrecked the abbeys of a few other towns, and the Lord James and Maitland passed into the North, wrecking and looting. In these things their zeal for the time exhausted itself.

In his ministrations in Edinburgh, too, Knox was being tried. The majority of the citizens were Catholic still, it appeared, and the discipline of the Kirk was causing restiveness. Before the end of 1560 the ministers had made a regulation that adulterers should be carted through the town. One adulterer had been duly set on the cart, and was being driven piously through the streets, when the crowd, showing unexpected sympathy, made a rush and carried him off. Next year some of the younger men celebrated the traditional games of Robin Hood, which had been forbidden even by Mary of Guise on account of their licentiousness. One of them, a youth called Gillon, was arrested in May and condemned to death. A deputation went to Knox and asked him to use his influence to have the sentence postponed, but Knox refused, and the deputation told him that both he and the Bailies would repent it. He replied that he would not go against his conscience for fear of any man. The deputation went away and presently the mob broke into the Tolbooth prison and set Gillon free, along with a number of other prisoners.

While the authority of the new religion was so insecure the Lords were arranging to bring young Mary Stuart back to Scotland. The Lord James had been sent to France with a message from the nobility; he was to say that it would be advisable for Mary to return to Scotland as soon as possible; he was also to give her two pieces of advice: to let the new religion remain as established, and to choose for her advisers the nobles who were then in power. The more zealous had commanded him to refuse her the rites of her religion, even in private, as a condition of her return. He had declined, however, to go to such extremes, and Knox awaited the coming of the new queen with apprehension.

CHAPTER XIV

MARY STUART

On the 19th of August 1561 Mary Stuart's ships anchored in the Firth of Forth. 'The very face of heaven, the time of her coming,' wrote Knox, 'did manifestly speak what comfort was brought into this country with her; to wit, sorrow, dolour, darkness and all impiety; for in the memory of man, that day of the year, was never seen a more dolorous face of the heaven than was seen at her arrival, which two after did so continue; for besides the surface wet, and corruption of the air, the mist was so thick and so dark that scarce might any man espy another the length of two pair of butts. The sun was not seen to shine two days before, nor two days after. That forewarning gave God unto us; but alas, the most part were blind.'

In this wild shape the arrival of the young Queen appeared to the imagination of Knox. She was not so much a human portent as an enigma containing all unpredictable possibilities of danger and evil. She was the daughter of his old enemy and the fine flower of the most refined and subtle centre of Antichrist in Europe; she was the symbol of every peril which could strike the young and tender Kirk; she was all this and more; but she was not a girl of nineteen. This figure, moreover, possessed charms which, because they were strange, because they could never have been nurtured in a Calvinist community, had an occult and disturbing power. These charms he could not define, yet although for a time exercised harmlessly, he felt they were evil. 'We call her not a hoor,' he wrote doubtfully, after a few encounters, 'but she was brought up in the company of the wildest hoormongers (yea, of such as no more regarded incest than honest men regard the company of their lawful wives); in the company of such men (we say) was our Queen brought up.' This general and mystic fear which she awoke in his mind was intensified by his knowledge that she regarded him as her enemy. She had already written Elizabeth, he knew, inciting her against the author of *The First Blast*. She had said before she left France that she would punish him when she came to Scotland. For himself and for his religion he had everything to fear from her, if her power could not be curbed by the Protestant Lords; yet he did not know what to fear.

To Mary Knox was the man who had fought against her mother and had written against queens. He was also the friend, however, of her new counsellors, the Lord James and Lethington, and the chief representative of the new Church which she had promised to leave in power. She had agreed to reign with the advice of the powerful Protestant minority, she had no power except what they allowed, and she was in a country strange to her. She was resolved, therefore, to make herself popular, but it was necessary, above all, that she should be popular with the Protestants. Accordingly, she employed all her charm to that end, and she easily captivated a number of the nobles; but the very things which made her attractive to them, her beauty and gaiety, made her distrusted by the preachers. With the Lord James and Lethington she might have reigned wisely and prosperously; the preachers from the first were resolved to cast suspicion on everything she did.

Mary landed in Leith on the 20th of August. On the 24th Mass was celebrated in Holyrood Chapel for herself, her three uncles and the Duke of Montrose, and there was a riot. The faithful tried to force the door, but the Lord James and his brothers prevented them. 'The godly,' says Knox, 'departed with great grief of heart.' In a day or two Arran issued a protest whose style had a singular resemblance to that of Knox. The Mass, it was said, was more abominable to God than murder. Next Sunday Knox preached in St. Giles. One Mass, he said now, 'was more fearful to him than if ten thousand armed enemies were landed in any port of the realm of purpose to suppress the whole religion.' Later he regretted that he had expressed himself so mildly, 'for God had given unto me,' he said, 'credit with many, who would have put into execution God's judgments if I would only have consented thereto.' This was less than a fortnight after Mary's arrival. What were God's judgments at that time? Randolph, Cecil's agent, wrote to England: 'John Knox thundereth out of the pulpit, so that I fear nothing so much as

that one day he will mar all. He ruleth the roast, and
of him all men stand in fear.'

Mary's counsellors had probably listened to Knox
in St. Giles. They knew how difficult it was to silence
him, and now, so far as can be guessed, they advised
Mary to see him at Holyrood. At this interview the
Lord James was the sole auditor, but two of Mary's
maids stood in a window at the far end of the room.

Everything about the debate which followed makes
it extraordinary: the ability of both parties, their
difference in age and station, the subjects which were
discussed, and the tone of the controversy. Knox was
fifty-six; Mary was nineteen. He had helped to drive
her mother to defeat and death, she had sworn to use
her power against him. He had denied the right of
queens to reign, she was at the moment the queen to
whom he owed allegiance. He was one of the chief
heads of a sect which she half-scorned and half-feared;
she was the perfect representative of a society which
he disdained as much for its charm as he hated it for
its opinions. Yet their interview resolved itself into a
controversy about politics and theology, a controversy
which, because it took no account of all the things
implied by it, because it ignored Mary's rank, sex and
age, setting her aside completely, and assuming that
she had neither an individuality to be respected nor
feelings that might be insulted, had something night-
mare-like and unreal. Knox discussed queenship with
Mary as if she were not a queen and as if his opponent
were of the same sex and the same age as himself. It
was as if he were resolved to ignore not only her

rank, her beauty, and her talents, but her very nature.

Mary began by accusing Knox of exciting the people of Scotland against her mother and herself, of writing a book against the authority of queens, of once having caused bloodshed and sedition in England, and of using magical arts.

To the first charge Knox replied rhetorically that if to teach the Word of God and rebuke idolatry were to raise subjects against their princes, he was guilty, but if the true knowledge of God made subjects obey their princes, then he was innocent. He denied that he had raised sedition in England, and pointed to the change he had made in the manners of Berwick. He denied a little contemptuously that he was a necromancer. He admitted that he was the author of *The First Blast*. An Englishman, he understood, had written against it, but he had not read the book. If the author had refuted him he was willing to recant, but he was convinced that he could maintain his thesis against any ten men in Europe.

'You think, then, I have no just authority?' asked Mary.

Learned men, he replied, had in all ages been allowed freedom of judgment, yet they had borne patiently with errors they could not amend. Paul had lived content under Nero; he was prepared to live content under her. His book had been written particularly against the English Jezebel.

'But ye speak of women in general.'

It was true, but she would be wise not to raise

trouble over a thing which had never harmed her. 'Now, madam, if I had intended to trouble your estate, because ye are a woman, I would have chosen a time more convenient for that purpose than I can do now, when your presence is within the realm.' Neither Protestant nor Papist, however, could prove that he had done so, he said. Cecil could have proved it from Knox's own letters, but Mary, not knowing of those letters, could not. She changed her ground.

He had advised the people to embrace a religion different from that ordained by their princes, and God commanded subjects to obey their princes.

Religion derived its authority not from princes, he replied, but from God. If princes should always be obeyed in matters of faith then the Israelites should have embraced the religion of Pharaoh, and the early Christians that of the Roman emperors.

'But none of these men raised the sword against their princes.'

'Yet you cannot deny that they resisted; for those who obey not the commandment given to them do in some sort resist.'

'But they resisted not with the sword.'

'God, madam,' Knox replied surprisingly, 'had not given unto them the power and the means.'

'Think you that subjects, having the power, may resist their princes?'

'If princes exceed their bounds, madam, no doubt they may be resisted, even by power. For no greater power or greater obedience is to be given to kings and princes than God has commanded to be given to father and mother. But the father may be struck with a frenzy, in which he would slay his children. Now, madam, if the children arise, join together, apprehend the father, take the sword from him, bind his hands, and keep him in prison till the frenzy be over, think you, madam, that the children do any wrong? Even so, madam, is it with princes that would murder the children of God that are subject unto them. Their blind zeal is nothing but a mad frenzy; therefore, to take the sword from them, to bind their hands, and to cast them into prison till they be brought to a more sober mind is no disobedience against princes, but just obedience, because it agreeth with the will of God.'

This reply silenced Mary. The faults in the reasoning she could see; it was the monstrosity in her eyes of Knox's sentiments that dazed her mind. The Lord James tried to comfort her, and Knox stood looking on.

'Well, then,' she said at last, 'I perceive that my subjects shall obey you and not me, and will do what they please and not what I command; and so must I be subject to them, and not they to me.'

'God forbid that ever I take upon me to command any to obey me,' he exclaimed, 'or to set subjects at liberty to do whatever pleases them. But my travail is, that both princes and subjects may obey God. And think not, madam, that wrong is done you when you are required to be subject unto God; for it is He who subjects people under princes, and causes obedience to be given unto them. He craves of kings that they may be as foster-fathers to His Kirk, and commands queens to be nurses to His people.'

Mary grew impatient. 'You are not the Kirk that I will nourish,' she said. 'I will defend the Kirk of Rome, for, I think, it is the true Kirk of God.'

'Your will, madam,' Knox replied, becoming ruffled for the first time at the mention of Rome, 'is no reason, neither doth your thought make that Roman harlot to be the true and immaculate spouse of Jesus Christ. And wonder not, madam, that I call Rome a harlot; for that Church is altogether polluted with all kind of spiritual fornication.'

'My conscience is not so.'

'Conscience, madam, requires knowledge; and I fear that right knowledge ye have none.'

'But I have both heard and read.'

'So, madam, did the Jews who crucified Christ Jesus read the law and prophets, and heard the same interpreted after their manner. Have you heard any teach but such as the Pope and Cardinals have allowed? You may be assured that such will speak nothing to offend their own estate.'

'You interpret the Scriptures in one way, and they in another. Whom shall I believe, and who shall be judge?'

'You shall believe God, who plainly speaks in His Word, and farther than the Word teacheth you, you shall believe neither the one nor the other. The Word of God is plain in itself; and if there appear any obscurity in one place, the Holy Ghost, who is never contrary to Himself, explains the same more clearly in other places, so that there can remain no doubt, but unto such as are obstinately ignorant.' Warming to his work, he began a long refutation of the Mass. Mary impatiently cut him short. He took his leave with the hope that she might be as blessed in the commonwealth of Scotland as ever Deborah was in Israel.

Thus ended the first encounter between Knox and Mary. The debating honours went to the girl of nineteen, the last word to the prophet. Mary's questions, indeed, were such as only Bullinger or Calvin himself among the reformed could have answered. Knox gave the stereotyped replies which his experience and the clichés of his creed required; they could not have satisfied, they could, indeed, hardly have been understood by anyone who was not already a Calvinist. That he had not risen to the occasion, that Mary had mysteriously worsted him, seems, indeed, to have penetrated into his consciousness during the interview. His 'madam, madam,' became sharper as his arguments grew more mechanical. The hectoring admonitory style he could not have helped, perhaps – he had been preaching for fourteen years – but he lost something of the dignified superiority of the prophet under Mary's questions. He began by laying down God's law; he finished by arguing with a girl about points of doctrine. 'If there is not in her,' he reported to his friends, 'a proud mind, a crafty wit, and an indurate heart against God and His truth, my judgment faileth me.' He wrote to Cecil repeating his conviction. 'In communication with her,' he said, 'I espied such craft as I have not found in such age.'

His hostility to Mary must have been intensified,

however, by professional jealousy. The support of the Protestant nobles was as essential to Knox as to Mary, and to win that support he, no less than she, was restricted to methods from which compulsion was excluded. Their weapons, however, were completely different; she relied on her beauty, her intelligence, her charm; he exploited his great reputation and the spiritual terrors of the Church he represented. It was a battle, in his eyes, between the powers of the spirit and the flesh, between God and the devil; but it was also a battle between himself and Mary, a battle in which both had to marshal all their seductions and concentrate them on the flattered nobles.

In the beginning, though a newcomer, Mary had the best of it. The Lord James and Lethington were bound to her by interest perhaps rather than devotion; but others were genuinely seduced. 'As the Lords,' wrote Knox, 'called of the Congregation, repaired unto the town, at the first coming they showed themselves wondrously offended that the Mass was permitted; so that every man as he came accused them that were before him; but after that they had remained a certain space, they were as quiet as were the former.'

The humbler Protestants who did not share the coveted peril of coming under the Queen's immediate spell revenged themselves by tormenting her in every way they could. They greeted her public entry by burning in effigy a priest celebrating Mass. The Edinburgh magistrates issued a proclamation ordering all drunkards, adulterers, monks, priests and nuns to leave the town. The preachers thundered against her for keeping All Saints' Day. At Stirling her priests were driven from the choir with bloody heads while she wept helplessly. At Perth she had to witness an insulting pageant prepared in her honour, and broke down again. 'I hear she is troubled with such sudden passions,' wrote Randolph to England, 'after any great unkindness or grief of mind.' Her faintest attempts at gaiety were seized upon by the preachers as proofs of vice. Knox complained that her maids danced in the palace when they got it to themselves. Even Lethington could not but pity Mary. 'The Queen behaves herself as reasonably as we can require,' he wrote to Cecil; 'if anything be amiss the fault is rather in ourselves. You know the vehemency of Mr. Knox's spirit which cannot be bridled, and yet doth utter sometimes such sentences as cannot easily be digested by a weak stomach. I would wish he should deal with her more gently, being a young princess unpersuaded. Surely,' he added, 'in the comporting with him she declares a wisdom far exceeding her age.'

But in spite of public insult and the nagging of the preachers, Mary was winning over the more powerful of the nobles. The schism became clear to everybody at the next General Assembly of the Kirk. Previous Assemblies had seen the Lords, the gentry and the ministers gathered in one harmonious family. Now, four and a half months after Mary's arrival, the Lords stood aloof, and Lethington denied that the Kirk had any right to meet without the consent of the Queen. 'Take from us the liberty of assemblies,' replied Knox, 'and take from us the Evangel. If the liberty of the Church

MARY QUEEN OF SCOTS
Artist unknown. National Portrait Gallery, London.

Facing p. 241.

should stand upon the Queen's allowance or dis-
allowance, we are assured not only to lack assemblies
but also to lack the public preaching of the Evangel.'
The Lords compromised. The Assembly would be
allowed if the Queen's interests were represented.

The next business was the Book of Discipline, not
yet passed into law. The ministers asked that the
Queen should be desired to ratify it. Lethington was
openly ironical. 'How many of those that subscribed
the Book will be subject to it?' he asked. 'Will the
Duke?' To pass the Book, in fact, would have meant
for the Lords the loss of all the Church properties which
they had stolen. The ministers were defeated.

Their demand for maintenance came off little better.
In spite of the Acts of the first great Parliament they
were still living for the most part on charity. Some of
them, indeed, at this time, or later, had to keep public-
houses during the week in order to serve the Lord on
Sundays. The nobles found themselves once more in
a difficult position and another compromise was
reached. The ancient Church (and the Lords) should
retain two-thirds of the ecclesiastical revenues; the
other third should be halved between the Queen and
the ministers. 'Well,' exclaimed Knox, 'if the end of
this order, pretended to be taken for sustentation of
the ministers, be happy, my judgment faileth me. For
first I see two parts freely given to the devil, and the
third to be divided betwixt God and the devil. Well,
bear witness to me, that this day I say it, or it be long
the devil shall have three parts of the third; and judge
you then what God's portion shall be. O happy

servants of the devil, and miserable servants of Jesus Christ, if after this life there were not hell and heaven!' The nobles and the preachers parted in mutual dissatisfaction. Knox threw himself into his ministerial duties. He was at that time the only preacher in Edinburgh, and his audiences were huge. He preached twice on Sunday and three times during the rest of the week. He attended the Kirk Session weekly to chastise sinners, and every week he held a meeting for the reading and exposition of the Scriptures. There were the provincial synods and the General Assemblies as well demanding his attendance, and often he was asked to preach in distant parts of the country. He was at the same time keeping up a correspondence with Cecil, with the Protestants in France, and with Mrs. Locke. He was overworked, and at last, in April 1562, he was given an assistant.

But a little before that he had been a party to a very curious incident. The Hamiltons, naturally enough, had not been among those favoured by the Queen, and on Arran, therefore, the most promising as well as Protestant of them, Knox had more and more been building his hopes. One evening a rich burgess called Baron brought the Earl of Bothwell along to Knox's house. Bothwell had a feud with Arran, he was finding it very expensive, he begged Knox to bring about a reconciliation. Bothwell was an unscrupulous villain, Arran a simpleton, and Knox refused at first to have anything to do with the matter. 'But in the end,' he wrote Mrs. Locke, 'I was overcome, thinking that by their familiarity the Kirk of God within this realm should have received so small benefit.' His hopes were disappointed. At his request, it is true, these two noblemen from whom the Kirk had so much to hope embraced at the Hamiltons' mansion of Kirk-o'-Field. 'I was present,' he added, 'and spake as God gave utterance at the time.' Next day the reconciled enemies attended divine service together. But the day after, as Knox was settling down to his correspondence after his sermon in St. Giles, Arran, in a state of strange excitement, and accompanied by an advocate and the town clerk, burst in upon him.

Arran complained with tears that he had been betrayed. His friend Bothwell had suggested that they should kill the Lord James, Lethington and the other favourites at court, seize the Queen and put her in Dumbarton Castle, and both of them rule together. The whole thing was a plot of Bothwell's, he sobbed, to entangle him in treason and then accuse him to the Queen. But he intended to get his word in first, he would write to the Queen and the Lord James. Arran's behaviour was so strange that Knox did not know what to think, and he advised silence. If Arran had not consented to the plot he had nothing to fear. But, panic-stricken or in the early stages of insanity, Arran wrote to Mary and fled to his father's house at Kinneil, where he was locked up in a room. He escaped from his imprisonment and presently was handed over by the Lord James to the Queen at Falkland. Both he and Bothwell were put in ward. Thus ended the incident, and thus Knox lost the last of the greater nobles.

But he had still the lairds and ministers who were the

strength of the General Assembly, and the General Assembly met in June. It drew up an address to the Queen foretelling that if no remedy was found for the state of the realm God's hand could not spare the head and the tail, the disobedient prince and the sinful people. The Protestants asked once more that adultery should be punished with death and that the ministers and the poor should be provided for. They were grievously disappointed too that the Queen did not attend their sermons, and they threatened to take affairs into their own hands if the ministers were molested. This protest was read to the Assembly and though considered too mild by some was unanimously approved. The Lords were exasperated. 'Whoever saw it written to a prince,' asked Lethington in disgust, 'that God would strike the head and the tail; or that if Papists did what they list, men would begin where they left?' The most offensive assumption of all, however, was that the Queen would raise up Popery again. 'To put that in the people's head is no less than treason,' he exclaimed, 'for oaths have been given that she never meant such a thing.' Knox took Lethington up on the head and tail as the most important question; the prophet Ezra apparently had used the expression, and he had been well acquainted with courts. Lethington refused to lay the protest before the Queen in its present form, it was agreed that he should soften it; he softened it effectually. 'Here be many fair words,' Mary said in astonishment, 'I cannot tell what the hearts are.'

In autumn Mary set out for the North. Early in the year she had promised the Lord James the earldom of Moray. That earldom was claimed at present by Huntly, a Catholic, but a treacherous subject. He had been suspected of a plot to murder the Lord James and Lethington, and his son, imprisoned for wounding an enemy, had escaped and now refused to return to await Mary's sentence. Mary set out with an army, determined to assert her authority.

At the same time Knox left Edinburgh to animate the Kirk in Ayrshire and Galloway. Though Mary's expedition to the North was against a Catholic noble, it filled him with profound suspicion. Fearful rumours, disseminated, he thought, by the Catholics, came through to him in the West. The Queen was taken; the Earl of Moray and all his men were slain; the Queen had gone over to Huntly. Knox was convinced that in spite of appearances it was the destruction of her half-brother that she sought, for she hated him for 'his godliness and plain uprightness.' Old Huntly died fighting at Corrichie; his son, John Gordon, was executed at Aberdeen, and the Lord James became the possessor of the rich earldom of Moray. His plain uprightness, it was clear, had survived Mary's subtle plots. Knox, at Ayr, got the lairds to make another 'Band' pledging themselves to take common action against all enemies of their religion. Mary, of course, was one of these.

Mary returned to Edinburgh with the court on the 21st of November. That winter, accordingly, 'the preachers were wondrous vehement in reprehension of all manner of vice, which then began to abound; and especially avarice, oppression of the poor, excess, riotous cheer, banqueting, immoderate dancing, and whoredom that thereof ensues.' The Queen's presence, as ever, inspired and exasperated the preachers, but the court party were becoming weary of their abuse. Knox answered their complaints from the pulpit. 'Have ye not seen,' he exclaimed, recalling Huntly's recent doom — 'have ye not seen one greater than any of you sitting where presently ye sit, pick his nails, and pull down his bonnet over his eyes, when idolatry, witchcraft, murder, oppression, and such vices were rebuked? Was not his common talk: When the knaves have railed their full, then will they hold their peace? Have ye not heard it affirmed to his own face, that God would avenge that blasphemy, even in the eyes of such as were witnesses to his iniquity?' Yet, with this warning to guide them, had they amended? He prophesied, yet once more, that God's wrath would strike them.

This sermon was aimed at the Protestant nobles at court; the same winter he preached again against Mary. It was the old trouble; there had been great dancing at the palace, and Knox was certain it was in celebration of the sufferings of the Protestants in France. He was summoned to Holyrood a second time.

The Queen received him in her bed-chamber. Her maids were present, the Lord James, now Earl of Moray, the Earl of Morton, Lethington and a few more. Mary accused him passionately of exceeding the licence even of a preacher. He assured her that she had been misinformed of the purport of his sermon, and insisted on repeating it. He had only said, he

protested, that princes would not be taught as God
commanded them; that they despised God's law and
were more employed in fiddling and flinging than in
reading or listening to God's Word; and that flatterers
were more precious in their eyes than men of wisdom
and gravity, who by wholesome admonition might
tame their vanity. He did not altogether damn dancing
if it did not cause people to neglect their duties, and if
they did not dance, like the Philistines, for pleasure
in the tribulation of God's people. If they did that,
however, they should receive the reward of dancers,
which was to drink in hell. That, he assured her, was
all he had said.

The sermon, such as it was, had been reported to
Mary as still worse. She hoped now perhaps to
soften Knox's future tirades against her or to put a
stop to them.

'If you hear anything of myself that mislikes you,'
she said, 'come to me and tell me, and I shall hear you.'

To do that, however, would have been to lose his
right to rebuke her in public. Knox gave an
astonishing reply.

'I am called, madam, to a public function within
the Kirk of God, and am appointed by God to rebuke
the sins and vices of all. I am not appointed to come
to every man in particular to show him his offence; for
that labour were infinite. If your Grace please to
frequent the public sermons, then doubt I not but that
ye shall fully understand both what I like and mislike,
as well in your Majesty as in all others. Or if your
Grace will assign unto me a certain day and hour when

it will please you to hear the form and substance of doctrine, which is explained in public to the churches of this realm, I will most gladly wait upon your Grace's pleasure, time, and place. But to wait at your chamber door or elsewhere, and then to have no further liberty but to whisper my mind in your Grace's ear, or to tell you what others think and speak of you, neither will my conscience nor the vocation whereto God hath called me suffer it. For albeit at your Grace's command I am here now, yet cannot I tell what other men shall judge of me, that at this time of day am absent from my book and waiting upon the court.'

The same extraordinary tone which Knox had set in his first interview with Mary was maintained in this. He spoke now to a roomful of people, and no doubt he calculated the effect of his attitude. As before, he emphasised the dignity of his own vocation, and ignored that of the girl to whom he was speaking. Yet still more strongly than the first this interview leaves a curious sense of unreality. Knox's words reached the extreme of hardihood, as of insensibility, yet one feels that he did not mean what he said. As an instrument of the Kirk he claimed to make no distinction between his sovereign and 'any man in particular.' Yet he had everything to gain by securing Mary's sympathy for the Kirk, and it was his duty as an instrument to gain it if he could. He believed, it is true, that Mary was obstinately blind, but he wished to believe it. A few months before he had reconciled the fool Arran and the melodramatic ruffian Bothwell, and had hoped that through them the Kirk might be

strengthened. What was it that now, when confronted
with the Queen, made him behave in a manner dis-
advantageous to the religion which he served, and
inconsistent with his first duty towards it? Was it his
need to assert himself whenever he found himself in the
presence of an authority higher than his own? Was it
a need, still more profound, to prove his superiority
to a woman, whatever her position might be? Or was
there in his mind another fear, that if he allowed himself to meet Mary on any level save that of the prophet
there might be danger? In this second interview Mary
had made direct advances to him: he responded to
them by a humiliating refusal. He was not a courtier;
he had no knowledge of the arts by which an offer of
intimacy may be refused without insult. As a preacher
he felt on strong ground; as a man he probably felt
unequipped to encounter Mary's charm, as well as
deeply distrustful of a woman who so surprisingly
tried to meet him on a level of equality. His distrust
was indeed noted about this time. Knox distorted
everything Mary did or said, Randolph wrote, 'as if he
were of God's Privy Council, that knew how He had
determined of her in the beginning, or that he knew
the secrets of her heart so well that she neither did nor
could have one good thought of God or of His true
religion.' Mary was already, in fact, becoming an
obsession to him. He could not cease preaching
against her, writing about her and insulting her. His
distrust of her was turning to a fixed and pathological
aversion. Mary replied to his long harangue about
leaving his book by turning her back and saying: 'You

will not always be at your book!' Knox left the room
smiling. One of the courtiers said in surprise: 'He is
not afraid.' Knox retorted: 'Why should the pleasing
face of a gentlewoman affray me? I have looked in the
faces of many angry men, and yet have not been
affrayed above measure.'

He suspected, with the sickness of monomania, her
hand in everything. His second interview with her had
taken place in December 1562. In 1563, he wrote
in his *History*, 'There was an universal dearth in
Scotland. But in the North, where the harvest before
the Queen had travelled, there was an extreme famine,
in the which many died in that country. The dearth
was great over all, but the famine was principally there.
And so did God, according to the threatening of His
law, punish the idolatry of our wicked Queen, and our
ingratitude, that suffered her to defile the land with
that abomination, the Mass.'

In the beginning of that terrible year the preachers
were already praying that God might either convert
Mary or cut her off while she was young. In mid-April
Mary sent for Knox to come to Lochleven, where she
was hunting. At Easter several of the Catholic priests,
in defiance of the law, had celebrated the Mass. Mary
and her council had made no move, and the Protestants
had taken the liberty of carrying out the law themselves.
In Ayrshire several priests were seized and threatened
with the Biblical punishment for idolatry. Others were
in hiding, in the moors and woods. Mary sent for
Knox that she might intercede for them.

She pleaded with him for two hours on the evening

of his arrival. He replied that if she would execute the laws of the country he would vouch for the docility of the Protestants; if she would not, he was afraid the Papists would have to be taught a lesson. The argumentative demon which Knox always aroused in Mary sprang up again.

'Will ye allow,' she asked, 'that they shall take my sword in their hands?'

Knox replied that the sword of justice was God's. Samuel had slain Agag, Elijah had slaughtered the four hundred and fifty priests of Baal; obviously, therefore, the Ayrshire Protestants were entitled to persecute the Catholics. Mary could do nothing against such arguments. Knox next pointed out her duties. The chief of these was to punish offenders; if she neglected it could she expect to receive full obedience from her people? 'I fear, madam,' he said, 'ye shall not.' Mary went in to supper in a rage.

On reflection, however, she resolved to be gracious, and asked Knox to meet her early next morning near Kinross, where she was to be hawking. When they met she showed him a ring on her finger. Ruthven had given it to her as a charm against poison, but she did not trust him. Lethington, she ran on, had been responsible for getting Ruthven on the Council. Knox cut her short: 'That man is absent for this present, madam, and therefore I will speak nothing on that behalf.' Mary stomached the snub and changed the subject. He was going to Dumfries shortly, she understood, to elect an ecclesiastical superintendent. Yes. But the Bishop of Athens was to be superintendent?

Yes, he was one of the candidates. 'If you knew him as well as I do,' she said, 'you would not promote him.' The bishop was a great deceiver if that were so. 'Well, do as ye will,' she said, 'but that man is a dangerous man.'

Mary became still more confidential. She wanted his advice on one of the most important questions that had perplexed her since she had come to Scotland. The Earl of Argyll was not treating the Countess well. Knox was displeased to hear it; he had reconciled them some months before, he said, and the Countess had promised to apply to him first if she had any further complaints. 'Well,' said Mary, 'it is worse than you believe. But do this much for my sake, as once again to put them in unity, and if she behave not herself as she ought to do, she shall find no favour of me. But in any wise let not my Lord know that I have requested you in this matter.' Knox agreed, and Mary was elated at having wrung her first favour out of him. She mentioned their conversation the evening before. 'I promise to do as ye required,' she said. 'I shall cause summon all offenders, and ye shall know that I shall minister justice.' Knox was immensely flattered. 'I am assured then,' he replied, 'that ye shall please God, and enjoy rest and tranquillity within your realm, which to your Majesty is more profitable than all the Pope's power can be.'

They parted; Mary's flattery had done more in one short talk than all her admirable arguments; for Knox took her advice. He inquired into the character of the Bishop of Athens, and finding it very bad, postponed the election. He wrote to the Earl of Argyll in his most authoritative style: 'Your behaviour towards your wife is very offensive to many godly. Her complaint is grievous, that ye altogether withdraw the use of your body from her.' Even if the Earl had more repugnance to his wife 'than any flesh this day on earth,' yet he should do his duty, for if he did not it would kindle God's wrath. He must not abuse the long-suffering of the Deity, therefore, and continue in this impiety, 'for impiety,' the letter concluded, 'it is, that ye abstract your comfort and company from your lawful wife.' This letter 'was not well received of the said Earl.'

On the 19th of May Mary too redeemed her promise. The Archbishop of St. Andrews and forty-seven other Catholics were tried for celebrating Mass and committed to ward. The Protestants were delighted. 'The like of this,' they said, 'was never heard of within the realm; we will bear with the Queen; we doubt not but all shall be well.' 'In such ways,' Knox said, his distrust returning already, 'she obtained of the Protestants whatsoever she desired.'

A week later Parliament met. The opening cere-mony was of unprecedented splendour. 'Such stinking pride of women as was seen at that Parliament,' Knox wrote, 'was never seen before in Scotland. Three sundry days the Queen rode to the Tolbooth.' The preachers were outraged in particular by the tassels on the skirts of the court ladies. These were enough to provoke God's vengeance, they protested, not merely against their wearers but against the whole nation. All their warnings, however, Knox remarks despondently, were 'scripped at.'

This Parliament, moreover, like the others, would do nothing for religion. The Lords would not think of asking the Queen at present to pass the Book of Discipline. Soon she would be found a husband, and then when she would be asking favours from them they would insist in return on the ratification of the privileges of the Kirk. Knox had waited now for three years in the vain hope of seeing the Church of his desires established in power: it seemed to be as far away as ever. A handful of ministers, wretchedly underpaid, was all he could show in return for all his labours for a successful Protestant revolution, and in a country where the ruling power was on his side. His anger boiled over. He had an open quarrel with Moray, which was to keep them from speaking to each other for a year and a half. His anger, only half exhausted, was turned next, inevitably, on Mary.

After the dismissal of Parliament he preached before the nobility. He reminded them of the great things which they had done in 1559 and 1560. 'From the beginning of God's mighty working within this realm,' he said, 'I have been with you in your most desperate temptations. In your most extreme dangers I have been with you: Saint Johnstone, Cupar Moor, and the Crags of Edinburgh are yet recent in my heart; yea, the dark and dolorous night wherein all ye, my Lords, with shame and fear left this town is yet in my mind; and God forbid that ever I forget it.' He reproached them with their recent absence of zeal, which left the work of reformation half done. 'The Queen, say ye, will not agree with us. Ask ye of her that which by God's Word ye may justly require, and if she will not agree with you in God, ye are not bound to agree with her in the devil. Let her plainly understand so far of your minds, and steal not from your former stoutness in God, and He shall prosper you in your enterprises.' Once on the subject of Mary he could not leave it. There were rumours that Lethington was arranging a marriage between her and Don Carlos of Spain, a Catholic. The marriage would have been fatal to Protestantism in Scotland. He prophesied, as usual, that the vengeance of God would strike the nation if it were allowed.

Mary summoned him for a fourth and last time. A body of his friends escorted him to Holyrood, but only Erskine of Dun was allowed to go with him into the Queen's presence. At the sight of him Mary's long-curbed anger burst out. 'I have borne with you,' she cried, 'in all your rigorous manner of speaking, both against myself and my uncles; yea, I have sought your favours by all possible means. I offered unto you presence and audience whensoever it pleased you to admonish me; and yet I cannot be quit of you. I vow to God I shall be revenged!'

She burst into tears. Knox remained exasperatingly calm. 'Scarcely could Marnock, her secret chamber boy,' he wrote later, 'get napkins to hold her eyes dry for the tears; and the owling, besides womanly weeping, stayed her speech.'

He waited until the storm passed.

'When it shall please God,' he said, 'to deliver you from that bondage of darkness and error in which ye have been nourished for the lack of true doctrine, your Majesty will find the liberty of my tongue nothing offensive.'

'But what have you to do with my marriage?' Mary cried.

The nobles were so charmed by her graces, he replied, that they had no regard to God or the commonwealth. Consequently he was bound to point out their duty to them.

'What have you,' she repeated, 'to do with my marriage? Or what are you within this commonwealth?'

'A subject born within the same, madam,' Knox replied, achieving the most splendid rhetorical retort of his life, 'and albeit I neither be earl, lord, nor baron within it, yet has God made me (how abject that ever I be in your eyes) a profitable member within the same. Yea, madam, to me it appertains no less to forewarn of such things as may hurt it, if I foresee them, than it does to any of the nobility.' He warned her once more of the curses which should follow her marriage with an idolatrous husband.

Again Mary burst into helpless sobbing, and 'tears,' Knox wrote, 'might have been seen in greater abundance than the matter required.' Erskine tried to comfort her, but she could not stop. 'The said John stood still without any alteration of countenance for a long season, while that the Queen gave place to her inordinate passion.' At last he opened his lips: 'Madam, in God's presence I speak. I never delighted in the weeping of any of God's creatures; yea, I can scarcely well abide the tears of any of my own boys whom my own hand corrects, much less can I rejoice in your Majesty's weeping. But seeing that I have offered unto you no just occasion to be offended, but have spoken the truth, as my vocation craves of me, I must sustain (albeit unwillingly) your Majesty's tears, rather than I dare hurt my conscience, or betray my commonwealth through my silence.'

Mary started up and angrily asked him to leave the room. He should wait in the ante-chamber until she signified her pleasure. There he stood for over an hour 'as one,' he wrote, 'whom men had never seen (so were all afraid).' He was still pleased by the interview, and amused by his present situation. The ladies-in-waiting were sitting about 'in all their gorgeous apparel'; he could not resist the opportunity of teasing them. 'O fair ladies,' he said, 'how pleasing were this life of yours if it should ever abide, and then in the end that we might pass to heaven with all this gay gear. But fie upon that knave Death, that will come whether we will or not! And when he has laid on his arrest, the foul worms will be busy with this flesh, be it never so fair or so tender; and the silly soul, I fear, shall be so feeble that it can neither carry with it gold, garnishing, targeting, pearl nor precious stones.' In this way, he wrote later with naïve pleasure, he procured the interest of the ladies. His last interview with Mary had ended in a complete triumph for him. She could do nothing but dismiss him; she did so at last.

From now on the antipathy between them deepened; and before the end of the year it was to blaze up again and Mary was to be once more discomfited. In the summer she made a progress through the west country, and in her absence her servants celebrated Mass in Holyrood Chapel. The Protestants sent a deputation to the Chapel Royal to take the names of those who were present. The deputation burst into the holy precinct, the sight of the idolatrous images inflamed them, and a brawl ensued. Two of the ring-leaders were cited at Mary's command to await their trial on the 24th of October, on a charge of invading the royal palace.

Knox's religion was threatened again. He could not go to Moray, for Moray and he were not on speaking terms; he dared not intercede with the Queen after their last interview. But he was not to be beaten, and he sent out letters summoning all the faithful to meet in Edinburgh on the day of the trial. His excuse was that the fearful summons of the two brethren was the prelude to more comprehensive cruelties. The blood of some of their dearest ministers, moreover, had already been shed, for Captain Lauder had struck Mr. Robert Pont on the head with his sword, and no punishment had followed! What might they expect next?

One of the letters came into Mary's hands. Hoping that she had caught Knox at last, she laid it before the Privy Council. They agreed that it was treasonable, and on two counts: Knox had summoned her subjects without her permission, and he had declared that she intended to perpetrate cruelties. Knox was summoned to answer these charges on the 21st of December. Mary was exultant.

Moray and Lethington, however, had no wish to see their old colleague brought up for trial. To condemn him would compromise their relations with the Protestants, without whose support they were powerless; to set him free would anger the Queen. They did their best, therefore, to get him to confess his error. But he remained immovable; he believed that the power of the Kirk was at stake, and he knew, no doubt, the strength of his position. Yet at the time he was in despair over the prospects of religion in Scotland. Moray, in whom he had trusted, had failed him. The Kirk was still without money for its ministers. The Book of Discipline remained unratified. The rebukes of the preachers had only hardened the Queen in her vain opinions; and through her agency the Kirk was split in two. He longed for death, he wrote to England. The apprehension of the calamities that would be brought about by the inordinate affections of Mary was more fearful than ten deaths, he told Cecil. He even wrote to Lord Robert Dudley, Elizabeth's favourite. 'God hath placed you in favour, credit and in some authority,' he said hopefully, 'by which ye may greatly advance the purity of religion.' Leicester was less interested in the purity of religion than in that of Elizabeth, and good Protestant as he was, his god had few points of resemblance with Jehovah. The state of the Kirk was desperate indeed. Mary, too, had been strangely depressed for two months, bursting into tears without reason, and complaining of a pain in her side which often troubled her.

On the winter evening Knox went to Holyrood to stand his trial. An immense crowd accompanied him. The palace yard, the passages, the stairs were crammed, and the crowd surged to the very doors of the chamber where the trial was to take place.

Knox arrived about six o'clock. The Lords were sitting around talking, the Queen had retired to another room. At Knox's entrance the nobles took their places at the Council table, and presently the Queen came in and sat down beside Maitland. She looked across at Knox standing bareheaded at the foot of the table and laughed. 'This is a good beginning,' she cried. 'But know ye why I laugh? Yon man gart me greet, and grat never tear himself. I will see if I can gar him greet.'

The Lords looked uncomfortable at this outburst, and Maitland rose and stated in dignified terms the reasons why Knox had been summoned. But Mary could not restrain her eagerness. 'Let him acknowledge his own handwriting,' she cried, 'and then we shall judge of the contents of the letter.' The letter was handed to him; he glanced at it, and admitted it was his.

'You have done more than I would have done,' said Maitland.

'Charity is not suspicious.'

'Read your own letter.' Mary broke in again, 'and then answer to such things as shall be demanded of you.'

Knox read the letter in a clear voice.

'Heard you ever, my Lords, a more despiteful and treasonable letter?' Mary exclaimed.

Knox asked what his offence was.

'Offence!' replied Lethington, 'if there were nothing but the convocation of the Queen's lieges, the offence cannot be denied.'

'If I have been guilty in this, my Lord, I have offended oft since I came to Scotland; for what convocation of the brethren has ever been to this hour unto which my pen served not?'

'Then was then,' replied Lethington hurriedly, remembering his own part in the revolution, 'and now is now. We have no need of such convocations as sometimes we have had.'

'I see the poor flock now,' replied Knox, 'in no less danger than it has been at any time before, except that the devil has got a visor upon his face.' At one time Satan appeared openly, now he came under the cloak of justice. Mary listened in amazement.

'What is this?' she broke out at last. 'Methinks you trifle with him! Who gave him authority to make convocation of my lieges? Is not that treason?'

The accusation of trifling, being too like the truth, rankled in the Lords' minds. No, replied Ruthven morosely, it was not treason, for Knox convoked people daily to hear prayers and sermons.

'Hold your peace,' cried the Queen, 'and let him answer for himself.'

Knox replied that Lord Ruthven had given the instance.

'I will say nothing against your religion,' retorted

Mary, fatally drawn into argument for the last time, 'nor against your convening to your sermons, but what authority have you to convoke my subjects when you will, without my command?'

From that moment she was lost. With perfect mechanical precision Knox wove a maze of those sophistries in which he believed so implicitly; and in it her most searching questions were lost. At his own will he had never convened four people in Scotland; at the command of his brethren he had convened multitudes. His authority was the Church; if it could be proved that he had done wrong in acting upon it, he would acknowledge his error. He had never preached rebellion, he said mildly, forgetting his epistles from Dieppe and his admonitions a few years ago to the Scottish nobility. Mary knew him as one of the men who had driven her mother from the throne and as her own most inveterate persecutor; now she saw him slipping through her fingers. She turned impatiently to the next charge.

'You shall not escape so,' she cried. 'Is it not treason, my Lords, to accuse a prince of cruelty? I think there are Acts of Parliament against such whispers.'

'But wherein can I be accused of this?' Knox inquired ingenuously.

'Read this part of your own bill.'

The sentence was read in which Knox asserted that the summons of the two brethren was intended to lead to greater cruelties. It seemed conclusive.

'Well,' said the Queen, 'what do you say to that?'

The Lords sat gazing in anxious silence at the reformer.

'Is it lawful for me, madam,' Knox began coldly, 'to answer for myself? Or shall I be condemned unheard?'

'Say what you can; for I think you have enough to do.'

'I will first then desire of your Grace and of this most honourable audience, whether your Grace knows not that the obstinate Papists are deadly enemies to all such as profess the religion of Jesus Christ, and that they most earnestly desire the extermination of them, and of the true doctrine that is taught in this realm?'

Mary was silent, but several of the Lords devoutly agreed.

'I must proceed, then,' Knox went on. It would be a barbarous thing to destroy the multitude of the faithful in Scotland; this they had agreed; yet to this the Catholics were making the Queen an unwitting instrument under colour of law. He did not accuse the Queen, but only the Catholics of cruelty; therefore his words had not been treasonable. He began to paint the vices of the Catholics when Lethington sharply interrupted him.

'You forget yourself! You are not now in the pulpit.'

'I am in a place,' Knox replied, 'where I am demanded of conscience to speak the truth; and therefore the truth I speak, impugn it who list.'

The retort was magnificent, peculiar as was Knox's conception of the truth. It was magnificent because, though the Catholics were not persecuting the Protestants, but were themselves being persecuted, and though his main accusation had been against the Queen and not the Catholics at all, he no doubt had worked himself up, with his unexampled talent for sincere self-deception, to a state in which he believed these things. In any other man in the room the retort would have been a piece of magnificent effrontery; in Knox it was merely magnificent.

It made Mary completely lose what control she had put upon herself. She began helplessly to reproach him for his former behaviour; he spoke fair enough now, but he had made her weep, and said he 'set not by her weeping.' Knox routed her by giving a faithful account of their last interview. Maitland whispered with the Queen and told Knox he could return to his home.

'I thank God and the Queen's Majesty,' he replied, and went out.

When he had gone the Queen retired to her room and the Lords considered their verdict. All of them, except a few of the court party, found him innocent. Maitland had assured the Queen that Knox would be condemned, and he was in a rage. He brought her back into the room and ordered the vote to be taken a second time, but the nobles refused to be over-awed.

'What!' they cried, 'shall the laird of Lethington have power to control us, or the presence of a woman cause us to condemn an innocent man?' They voted as before.

Mary crowned her evening's display. It was the

Bishop of Ross who had given her the letter; he now voted with the majority.

'Trouble not the child!' she cried. 'I pray you trouble him not, for he is newly wakened out of his sleep. Why should not the old fool follow the footsteps of those that have passed before him?'

'That night,' wrote Knox in his *History*, 'was neither dancing nor fiddling in the court; for madam was disappointed of her purpose, which was to have had John Knox in her will by vote of her nobility.'

Nowhere, perhaps, are the intrepidity, the unflinching will and the intellectual subtlety of Knox more clearly revealed than in this astonishing triumph. Maitland might perhaps have been a better match for him if his plans had not been disconcerted by the Queen. Mary herself was undone by her imagined security and her eagerness to attain her revenge. The verdict, moreover, would have almost certainly been what it was in any case. Knox's victory was entirely the fruit of his pre-eminence, in character, in natural force, in will, in mind, in composure, and in the arts of debate. With the worst case he was never daunted, never once shaken. The argument from beginning to end was directed by him into the course which he had resolved upon and which suited his purposes. He was guilty by his own confession of an act which the Council considered treasonable; he was acquitted with enthusiasm.

This was his last personal combat with Mary, and it marked the beginning of a new royal policy which was to end disastrously. Her present counsellors could not protect her from insult; Moray had voted for Knox's acquittal; Lethington had been unable to prevent it. Where should she turn now? David Rizzio, a young Italian, had been a valet de chambre in the Palace during 1561 and 1562. He was ambitious, and he was not a Protestant; she began to think he might be of use. Rizzio rose rapidly, and at the end of 1564 she appointed him French Secretary. The Protestants had failed her and insulted her. She had come to the breaking-point.

CHAPTER XV

DOWNFALL OF MARY STUART

A FEW days after Knox's acquittal the General
Assembly met. Knox refused to take any part in it
until it decided whether his convocation of the
Protestants was lawful. Lethington tried to prevent
the discussion but failed. The Assembly approved,
Knox had won again.

Portents, caused by the licentiousness of the court,
ushered in the new year. 'Upon the 20th day of
January,' writes Knox, 'there fell wet in great abundance, which in falling froze so vehemently that the
earth was but a sheet of ice. The fowls, both great and
small, froze and might not fly; many died, and some
were taken and laid beside the fire that their feathers
might resolve. And in the same month the sea stood
still, as was clearly observed, and neither ebbed nor
flowed the space of twenty-four hours. In the month
of February, the 15th and 18th days thereof, was seen
in the firmament, battles arrayed, spears and other
weapons, and as it had been the joining of two armies.'
The threatenings of the preachers became fearful, but
the Queen continued her banqueting.

Soon afterwards these natural portents were followed
by one still more awful; the Protestants at the Court

began to deny that the Mass was idolatry. Knox prophesied from the pulpit yet once more that the plagues of God would descend upon them. Some of them broke into sobbing as they listened, but others mocked, saying they would have to recant now, for the preachers were angry. A little before this Lethington had quite lost his temper with the ministers. The devil take him, he shouted, if he paid any more attention to them, let them bark and blow as loud as they liked. Religion was in a bad way.

On Palm Sunday Knox married again. He was now fifty-nine; his bride was not yet sixteen. Mary went about denouncing him to everybody. The marriage was monstrous in itself, but the bride was also a daughter of Lord Ochiltree, a Stuart, and a remote relation of her own. But Knox's ardour in this as in more spiritual matters was not to be restrained. He rode out gaily to his sweetheart's house on a trim gelding, his jacket adorned with ribbons and gold. Three daughters were the fruit of this second alliance, even more extraordinary than the first. His household now consisted of old Mrs. Bowes, his two young sons, his new wife and himself. Of Margaret Stuart we know as little as we know of Marjory Bowes. After Knox's death, however, she married Ker of Faldonsyde, one of the most brutal actors in the murder of Rizzio and a visitor at Knox's house.

In June the General Assembly met again, and the court Protestants stayed away. On the second day, importuned by the preachers, they appeared, but held their deliberations in a separate room. Knox, with

ten other delegates from the Assembly, was asked to
confer with them.

The conference, as was inevitable, turned into a
duel between Lethington and Knox. Lethington
complained that Knox had modified his public prayers
for the Queen. He now used the words, 'Illuminate
her heart, if it be Thy pleasure.' This was bound, said
Lethington, to give the people the impression that she
was past praying for. He was not blaming Knox; but
others, he said ironically, might imitate him without
showing his moderation.

Knox replied that Christ had prayed, 'Thy will be
done.' He could not feel certain that God had singled
out Mary as one of the elect, and only prayers for the
elect were effectual.

In what way did the Queen rebel against God?
asked Lethington.

In all the actions of her life, but especially in not
listening to the Gospel.

She would gladly hear anyone. When had she ever
refused admonition?

Yes, but when had she ever obeyed it? And when
did she mean to attend the public sermons? It was a
sore point.

Never, probably, so long as she was treated as she
had been.

The stubborn, wearisome argument went on.
Lethington, who was unwell, had to lean on the Master
of Maxwell's shoulder to rest himself. His reasons
were sensible; his pleas were for humanity; but by
persistence and texts judiciously chosen Knox wore

him down. Could princes be withstood? Could princes be slain? Could they be slain by a minority of the people? The theme of the discussion was Mary. The debate, narrowing from stage to stage, was carried at last to the point where Knox desired it to stay; idolaters must be slain, no matter who they were.

Mary was now acting less on the advice of Moray and Lethington. The Earl of Lennox had been brought back from England, and in the February of next year Henry Darnley followed him. Darnley was young, handsome, vicious and empty-headed, but he was the nearest heir to the English throne after Mary herself, and he had the support of the English Catholics. Weary of her trials with Moray and Lethington, weary above all of the perpetual insults of the Protestants, Mary threw herself at him and married him in July 1565. Rizzio became her chief adviser, and soon the ambiguous Bothwell joined him. Maitland still hung round the court, his services neglected, but Moray and his followers fled after a brief resistance into England. The preachers who had been grudgingly paid while Moray was at court, were not paid now at all. Some of them, it was said, died of hunger in the streets.

Mary continued to acknowledge the Kirk without providing for it. She would worship now as she liked; the Protestants could do the same. Knox, supported by his large congregation, still preached in Edinburgh, and presently the new King, drawn perhaps by curiosity, came to hear him. He was unlucky that Sunday, for Knox preached one of his dreariest sermons.

The text was apt enough: 'O Lord our God, other lords than Thou have ruled over us.' Some of his observations, too, were to the point. God, he said, set on the throne boys and women. Ahab, he feared, had not kept order with that harlot Jezebel. This was excellent, but the sermon dragged on and on, for an hour, for another hour, for an hour longer than even Knox was accustomed to preach. Darnley left St. Giles' in a rage, he would not touch his dinner but jumped on his horse in a fury and went hawking. While he was resting in bed that afternoon, Knox was summoned by the Privy Council. New faces were there, but one old face he knew, Lethington's. Knox's supporters, as usual, were outside the Palace, but they had no terrors for the new Council. Knox was forbidden to preach in the town while the King and Queen were present, and Lethington had the pleasure of delivering the ultimatum. The old reformer sullenly replied that if the Kirk would command him to preach or abstain he would obey — so far as the Word of God would permit him.

He abstained for a while, but by autumn he was preaching again. The Kirk, however, was at a low ebb, and when the General Assembly met in December its ranks showed many notable gaps. The ministers accordingly decreed a public fast for the beginning of next year, to hold from the last Sunday of February to the first Sunday of March. It was to be a week of mourning for the toleration of idolatry, for the manifold sins of all estates, for the starvation and oppression of the poor, and the tribulations of the brethren in France, Flanders, Denmark and other places. God was angry, the framers of the fast affirmed, and He remained still the same God who had drowned the world in the Flood, consumed Sodom and Gomorrha with fire, plagued Pharaoh and destroyed Jerusalem. What might not be expected? Texts for the different days of the week were given out, all dreadful and all from the Old Testament. Knox was one of the four who arranged the conduct of the fast.

The fast was in due course observed, and a few days later Rizzio was murdered in Holyrood. Mary was sitting after supper in the little box-like cabinet which opened off her bedroom; Rizzio and the Countess of Argyll were with her. Presently Darnley came in by the secret stair which led from his bedroom to hers. As he was talking with her there was a sound of other footsteps on the stair, and Ruthven and Morton, armed and followed by a party of armed men, crushed into the little room. They asked Rizzio to come out with them; Rizzio hid behind the Queen and clutched the train of her dress. At that Ker of Faldonsyde levelled his revolver point blank at Mary's breast; she struck it down with her hand. There was scarcely room to move; the table was knocked over; as it fell the Countess of Argyll caught the single candlestick and held it up. Rizzio was screaming and clutching Mary's skirts; Ruthven, who had just risen from a sick-bed, had taken the Queen round the middle and was holding her; the others were frantically unloosening Rizzio's fingers. Rizzio was dragged into the bedroom and there, still screaming, was stabbed to death; fifty dagger wounds were found on his body. Mary was in the sixth month of her pregnancy at the time. The conspirators were her husband, who was jealous of Rizzio, and the Protestant nobles, who were out of favour and jealous for another reason. Mary was imprisoned in her room, and the Protestant nobles took possession of Holyrood. That night Moray with his men entered Edinburgh.

But in two days Mary had won Darnley over. On the night of the 11th, with the connivance of her husband, the Queen escaped to Dunbar on horseback. The plot had failed, and next day Knox was praying as he had not prayed since the days before he fled to France. In his first anguish he asked God to put an end to his life. His whole prayer breathed remorse and terror. Remorse for what? For having been elated by the murder of Rizzio? For having built hopes on it? Strangely enough, for neither of these. His mind again, as in England and Geneva, returned to offences more general, more ancient. 'Be merciful unto me, O Lord,' he prayed, 'and call not into judgment my manifold sins; and chiefly those, whereof the world is not able to accuse me. In youth, mid age, and now, after many battles, I find nothing in me but vanity and corruption. For in quietness I am negligent, in trouble impatient, tending to desperation, and in the mean state I am so carried away by vain fantasies that, alas, O Lord, they withdraw me from the presence of Thy Majesty. Pride and ambition assault me on the one part, covetousness and malice trouble me on the other.'

At that moment he saw himself in a flash, as

he had perhaps never seen himself before. But the revelation was unendurable; he sought for some palliation and, obedient as ever, his conviction that he could not have been wrong began to return. 'I take Thee, O Lord, Who only knows the secrets of hearts,' he went on. 'I take Thee to record that in none of the aforesaid I do delight; but that with them I am troubled, and that sore against the desire of my inward man, which sobs for my corruption, and would repose in Thy mercy alone. I doubt not myself to be elected to eternal salvation, whereof Thou hast given unto me (unto me, O Lord, most wretched and unthankful creature) most assured signs. For being drowned in ignorance,' he went on, confidence steadily growing stronger, 'Thou hast given unto me knowledge above the common sort of my brethren; my tongue hast Thou used to set forth Thy glory, to oppugn idolatry, errors, and false doctrine.' Then all his old arrogance came back in a clap. 'Thou hast compelled me to forespeak both deliverance to the afflicted and destruction to some disobedient; the performance whereof, not I alone, but the very blind world has already seen.' As always when his cry was from the depths, the prayer was an argument with God. The ejaculation of self-reproach quickly passed into the petition for comfort, and that as quickly unto the assurance of favour; but all three came from the heart, and in the almost apprehensive rapidity of the transition all Knox's complex and ambiguous nature was laid bare. As, when he became a Protestant, his life as a Catholic was at once forgotten, so here within the compass of a short prayer, the cry of sincere self-contempt was smothered behind the sound of a few pattered sentences of hurried justification. He had mentally annihilated his offence as he had mentally annihilated the Catholic, the man who fled from England, and the man who had hesitated at Dieppe. Yet, while he thus regained his belief in himself as a prophet of God, he could not annihilate the objective position, which was that the Protestants had failed and that Mary must soon return in anger. The realization of this, breaking through his triumphant argument with God, left him where he had begun. 'Lord,' he cried again, 'put an end to my misery.'

He had asked, after one of his most successful interviews, why the face of a pleasant gentlewoman should affray him. But that face was angry now, and he fled from it and from Edinburgh on the same day as the murderers of Rizzio. Mary returned in greater power than she had ever known before. Even the people, shocked by the murder of Rizzio, were on her side. Knox took refuge in the solitudes of Kyle and in great bitterness continued his *History*. The murder had already become for him an act pleasing to God. Looking over his manuscript he refreshed himself by reading his witty description of another murder, that of Cardinal Beaton. He recollected with relief that all the assassins, except one, had regained their liberty and were still alive; it was a proof of God's approbation. 'And to let the world understand in plain terms what we mean.' he wrote now, 'that great abuser of this commonwealth, that poltroon and vile knave Davie, was justly

punished for abusing of the commonwealth and for
his other villainy, which we list not to express, by the
counsel and hands of James Douglas, Earl of Morton,
Patrick, Lord Lindsay, and the Lord Ruthven, with
others assisters in their company, who all, for their
just act, and most worthy of all praise, are now un-
worthily left of their brethren, and suffer the bitterness
of banishment and exile.'

But against Mary, the third queen who had made
him flee, his hatred at last blazed up openly. 'And so,'
he said now, writing of the child of six, 'she was sold
to go to France, to the end that in her youth she should
drink of that liquor that should remain with her all her
lifetime, for a plague to this realm, and for her final
destruction. And, therefore, albeit that now a fire
comes out from her that consumes many, let no man
wonder, she is God's hand, in His displeasure punishing our former ingratitude. Let men patiently abide
and turn unto their God, and then shall He utterly
destroy that hoor in her hoordom, or else He shall
put it in the hearts of a multitude to take the same
vengeance upon her that has been taken of Jezebel
and Athaliah; for greater abomination was never in the
nature of any woman than is in her, whereof we have
seen only the buds; but we will after taste of the ripe
fruit of her impiety, if God cut not her days short.'

His hatred could not for the moment touch Mary,
however. He remained in Kyle while his assistant
Craig ministered to the poor flock in Edinburgh. By
the end of the year Mary had pardoned the murderers
of Rizzio. About the same time the General Assembly

gave Knox permission to visit England for a few months.

It was while he was there that Mary brought about her own destruction. Darnley was murdered in February 1567; in a few weeks Mary yielded herself to the murderer Bothwell, and married him; in a few weeks more she was seized by the enraged nobles at Carberry Hill and taken to Edinburgh amid cries of 'Burn the hoor!' Mary Seton, the last of the Maries to remain faithful, rode by her side. On the 16th of June the Queen was imprisoned in Lochleven Castle.

On the 25th the General Assembly met, and Knox had returned in time for it. But the nobility were torn in two by the recent events; the attendance was wretchedly small; and it was resolved to meet again on the 26th of July. Meanwhile appeals were sent out to the Protestant Lords who had remained away, and six delegates were given the task of talking them over. Knox was sent, as once before, to the west country.

He returned on the 17th of July; his mission had been but moderately successful, but his views about Mary were unchanged. Throgmorton, sent to Edinburgh by Elizabeth, made an appeal to him for clemency; Craig, Knox's assistant, was present at the interview. The ministers were amply prepared, and Throgmorton could make nothing of them. He wrote to Elizabeth: 'I have persuaded with them to preach and persuade lenity. I find them both very austere in this conference; what I shall do hereafter I know not. They are furnished with many arguments; some forth of the Scriptures, some forth of histories, some grounded, as they say, upon the laws of this realm, some upon practices used in this realm, and some upon the conditions and oath made by their prince at his coronation.' He had to listen to Knox thundering daily against the Queen, shouting that she must be executed as a murderess and adulteress if the wrath of God was to be averted. Apprehensive of the outcome, Throgmorton urged the nobles to stop the preachers' mouths; the people might be inflamed to such a pitch, he feared, that no reasonable measures could be taken. Lethington argued but the preachers would not be silenced. On the 26th the General Assembly met.

Once more only a few of the nobility attended. The extreme counsels of the preachers, however, were not listened to, Mary was not condemned to death, but she was deposed, and a new authority was set up in the name of her son. The handful of nobles and barons swore that they would defend the religion of Jesus Christ and punish the murder of Darnley. Among them were Lethington, who had signed the murder contract, Morton, who had known beforehand all about it, and Archibald Douglas, who had been present at the deed. Moray became Regent on the 22nd of August and in his first Parliament showed that he intended to see justice done at last to the suffering Kirk. The General Assembly wrote jubilantly to one of their preachers in England: 'Our enemies, praised be God, are dashed; religion established; sufficient provision made for ministers; order taken, and penalty appointed for all sort of transgression and transgressors; and above all, a godly magistrate, whom God, of His eternal and heavenly providence, hath reserved to this age, to put in execution whatsoever He by His law commandeth.'

Yet, with the eclipse of Mary, Knox's own light seemed for a time to be diminished. He had hated Mary in her period of tutelage under Moray and Lethington; he had hated her in her hour of triumph after Rizzio's murder; now that she was defeated and a prisoner his hatred followed her still. But the savour seemed to have gone out of the feud, and his furies, which he could not restrain, were becoming wearisome even to himself. The truth was that he was now an old man.

Sometimes his thoughts turned back to Geneva. He remembered his talks with Calvin, now in his grave; his busy and orderly days admonishing his flock; his hours of quiet study; his circle of adoring and pious women, so unlike Mary; his triumph over the Anabaptist. All the agonies and doubts; his agitated farewell to his congregation on that evening, long ago, when he had set out for Scotland and never reached it; his coldness with his master over *The First Blast;* his painful letters to the sisters in Edinburgh explaining why he had stayed in Dieppe; the death of Mrs. Locke's daughter; the daily domestic troubles; all now were softened by memory, and he wrote to a friend: 'God comfort that dispersed little flock, amongst whom I lived with quietness of conscience and contentment of heart; and amongst whom I would be content to end my days, if so it might stand with God's good pleasure. I can give you no reason that

I should so desire, other than that my heart so thirsteth.'

But he was not given the respite that from now on, with failing powers, he longed for ever more strongly. On the 2nd of May next year Mary escaped from Lochleven, and in a few days was joined by the greater part of her nobility. The terrified Kirk decreed a fast and Knox addressed a public letter to the Protestants. This, he wrote a little wearily, was what came of showing mercy to a murderess and idolatress. The terrors which God would presently let loose on the people would be a just punishment for their sinful remissness. The terrors, however, did not fall; Mary was defeated with strange ease at Langside; she fled into England and was imprisoned again. But she still lived, and Knox's hatred followed her there.

Absence and distance, indeed, nourished and strengthened his hatred. His powers and his interests were contracting, but the hate remained constant, feeding on his physical and mental dissolution. Had he been able to meet Mary face to face, the lineaments which he knew so well might have kept his hatred within human bounds. He had already a physical repulsion for her, it is true; her youth, her moods, angry or inviting, her laughter, her habit of bursting into tears, the very clothes she wore, aroused a sort of disgust in him, as his descriptions of their interviews showed. But now that, though a prisoner, she was beyond his reach, now that he could neither see nor know what she was doing, she became to him a malign creature which struck from the darkness, a wounded snake which lay in hiding, its fangs still charged with venom; Scotland and the Kirk would never be safe until it was sought out and stamped to death. He and his fellow preachers had insulted and humiliated Mary; but insult had not broken her, it had driven her to desperation, and now in England she was more dangerous than when she had been partaking of the abomination in Holyrood. For her misfortunes had raised defenders even among the Protestant nobles. A great number of the Lords, with the Hamiltons at their head, were openly or secretly on her side. An attempt had already been made to assassinate Moray. The Kirk itself, established in power at last, was torn in two; Christian was against Christian, brother against brother. Ever since his arrival in Scotland, Knox's whole energy had fastened itself upon the advancement and establishment of the Kirk, as upon an absolute and eternal value. Now he began to see that all he had striven for was contingent and unstable; that triumph, fully gained, as suddenly vanished; and that the fight must go on, forever uncertain, and forever demanding new energy. Deceived by his hopes, he turned more and more to the thought of that hope which he felt could not fail him. 'I live as a man already dead from all affairs civil,' he wrote to a friend in September 1568, 'and therefore I praise my God; for so I have some quietness in spirit, and time to meditate upon death, and upon the troubles I have long feared and foreseen.' Even the ties binding him to his contracting circle of friends became meaningless and burdensome. 'Albeit,' he wrote to the same correspondent, 'I have been tossed with many storms, yet might I have gratified you and others faithful, with some remembrance of my estate, if that this my churlish nature, for the most part oppressed with melancholy, had not stayed tongue and pen from doing of their duty. Yea, even now, when that I would somewhat satisfy your desire, I find within myself no small repugnance. For this I find objected to my wretched heart: "Foolish man! what seekest thou, in writing of missives in this corruptible age? Hast thou not a full satiety of all the vanities under the sun? Have not thy eldest and stoutest acquaintance barred thee in present oblivion; and art not thou in that estate, by age, that nature itself calleth thee from the pleasures of things temporal? Is it not then more than foolishness unto thee, to hunt for acquaintance on the earth, of what estate or condition soever the persons be?"'

Yet, in the same letter, he wrote as violently as ever against Mary. Of everything else in the world he was weary for the time; of his hatred, too, he was perhaps weary, but it remained in him as if it had a terrible objective existence of its own. 'I see England,' he wrote, 'become more foolish than foolish Scotland. For foolish Scotland would not obey the mouth of God when He had delivered that vile adulteress, and cruel murderer of her husband, into their hands, to have suffered as her iniquity deserved; and therefore now sob they for the foolish pity.' England, he complained, was as bad. In January 1570 he was still writing on the same theme. 'If ye strike not at the root,' he said in a letter to Cecil, 'the branches that appear to be broken will bud again.' He signed himself, 'John Knox with one foot in the grave.'

The Regent Moray was assassinated on the 23rd of the same month, and Knox was drawn back once more into the centre of the conflict of which he was so weary. The news reached him on Saturday, and next day he rose once more to his old heights of indignant eloquence. There was a new note in one passage, it was true: 'He is at rest, O Lord, and we are left in extreme misery.' But the old tones returned in full volume in his one reference to Mary. Having nobly praised Moray, he lamented 'that foolish pity did so far prevail with him, concerning execution and punishment which Thou commanded to have been executed upon her, and upon her complices, the mur-derers of her husband.' It was one of the Hamiltons who had assassinated Moray, and the Hamiltons were now on the Queen's side.

With Moray gone the country, indeed, presented a picture which must have appeared both strange and without hope to the old man. In different parts of it Protestant nobles upheld the cause of Mary against their old friends. Family was divided against family, parish against parish. Kirkcaldy of Grange, Knox's old comrade in the galleys and the victor over Mary at Langside, held Edinburgh Castle in the Queen's name. Lethington, a traitor over and over again, was his right hand. All hope of peace for Scotland and the Kirk was farther away than it had been at Perth eleven years before.

After the murder of Moray Knox still stayed on in

Edinburgh, but he had no peace there. The Castle
and the people were for Mary; the prosperous burgher
families and the ministers were for the infant King.
And now that the old reformer was failing his enemies
began to bait him. A skit appeared, purporting to
have been written by someone who had overheard a
secret council meeting held by Moray. The intonation
of Knox and the other characters was cleverly imitated,
and they were shown adducing ingenious arguments
why Moray should accept the crown. Worn out as he
was, Knox could not let the challenge pass. He took
the pasquinade seriously, attributed its authorship
to the Father of Lies, and prophesied that the tran-
scriber would die friendless in a foreign land.

That autumn fate played him an ironical trick; he
had a stroke which affected the use of his tongue. For
a few days that formidable weapon was powerless, and
a universal sigh of relief went up from the enemies of
God. Fantastic rumours went about, that the old man's
face 'was turned into his neck,' that he was dead, and,
most persistent of all, that he would never preach again.
But in a few days he was in the pulpit, and before the
year ended he was in the middle of a violent squabble
with his old friend, Kirkcaldy of Grange.

A relative of Kirkcaldy's had been assaulted in
Dunfermline by a neighbouring laird and his servant,
a man called Seaton. Shortly afterwards Seaton came
to Edinburgh. As he was leaving Kirkcaldy sent six
of his men to give him a beating. Seaton drew his
sword and wounded one of the six; the others also
drew, and Seaton was killed. One of the six was

arrested for murder and put in the Tolbooth. Kirkcaldy demanded that he should be released; the
magistrates refused. Kirkcaldy sent a force and broke
open the prison.

Next Sunday Knox preached a violent sermon
in which he talked of cut-throats. Kirkcaldy in a rage
wrote a letter and asked Craig, the other minister,
to read it from the pulpit. 'This day,' the letter ran,
'John Knox, in his sermon, openly called me a murderer and a throat-cutter! Wherein he has spoken
further than he is able to justify; for I take God to be
my damnation, if it was in my mind that that man's
blood should have been shed, whereof he has called me
the murderer. And the same God I desire, from the
bottom of my heart, to pour out His vengeance
suddenly upon him or me, which of us two has been
most desirous of innocent blood.' The reference was
to the Queen. 'This I desire you openly, in God's
name, to declare to the people.'

Craig refused to read the letter, but the news of it
spread, and Kirkcaldy addressed another letter to the
Session in Edinburgh, in which, ponderously and
formidably, he insisted that injustice had been done to
him. He asked that his good name should be restored
in the place where it had been taken away, and offered
to submit himself to the judgment of the Kirk. The
Session sent a copy of the letter to Knox. Knox replied
that he would answer it in writing next Thursday, but
as it contained manifest lies his conscience would not
permit him to pass it over in silence in his next sermon.
He preached, therefore, complaining of impudent and

manifest liars, denying that he had called Kirkcaldy a cut-throat, maintaining that the killing of Seaton was an unjust and cruel murder, and finishing by saying that Kirkcaldy's was the most terrible example that he had ever seen in Scotland.

But before he wrote his letter to the Session other arguments had occurred to him. To Kirkcaldy's indictment, he said now, 'I answer nothing, save only this; that his own confession convicts him to be a murderer in heart, before that his servants committed murder. For our Master Jesus Christ, and His apostle John, pronounced the hatred of the heart to be murder before God; yea, John affirms that "Whoso loveth not his brother is a manslayer." ' Did he himself love Mary? He did not say, but having called Kirkcaldy a murderer he protested again that he had never called him a cut-throat, and that his admonition had not violated the rule of Christian charity.

Being no longer a cut-throat but only a murderer, Kirkcaldy was content, and he wrote expressing his satisfaction. But Knox was not appeased, and leaning on his stick he tottered to the Session. He accepted the truce, but asked that his complaisance should not be taken as a precedent by other ministers, and that the Session should rebuke Kirkcaldy for his offence against God, the Kirk and the law. Next Sunday he preached on the true nature of repentance, which should be shown in the sincere humiliation of the sinner without exculpation. He went into the story of Elijah, and told how the prophet had rebuked Ahab for the murder of Naboth. Kirkcaldy flew into a fury again.

Next Sunday Kirkcaldy attended church and brought his offending servants with him. Knox preached against proud contemners and those who with knowledge proudly transgressed. Rumours presently began to fly about that the laird of Grange intended to murder the preacher, and the brethren of Ayrshire sent a letter proclaiming that they would defend Knox. The squabble died down.

But in March of the new year Knox rose once more to the bait. Anonymous charges were sent to the Session accusing him of seditiously railing against the Queen, of refusing to mention her in his public prayers, and of mingling political and religious matters in the pulpit. The Session asked his accusers to come forward; they boasted that they would appear at the next General Assembly if he would face the charge and not fly 'according to his accustomed manner.' They nailed their challenge to the door of his church. Knox might easily have ignored an attack so cowardly, but he could not.

The notice was brought to him in the morning of the last day of the General Assembly, as he was putting on his clothes. He told his servant, Richard Bannatyne, to run to the Assembly with it. Arrived at the Assembly, Richard made an indignant speech asking the ministers to approve his master's opinions and share the burden with him. They said they would share the burden. Richard asked them to put it in writing; they asked if Knox had required it. Richard confessed that he had not and went away in a huff.

The ministers next tried to persuade Knox to pass the

accusations over in silence. But he would not be ruled. 'The Kirk,' he replied, 'may forbid me preaching, but to stop my tongue being in the pulpit they may not.' The Kirk knew it and ceased to argue with him. He preached next day, a Sunday, and the burden of his sermon was Mary. 'That I have called her an obstinate idolatress,' he said, 'one that consented to the murder of her husband, and one that has committed whoredom and villainous adultery, I gladly grant, and never mind to deny; but railing and sedition they are never able to prove in me, till that first they compel Isaiah, Jeremiah, Ezekiel, Saint Paul and others to recant; of whom I have learned, plainly and boldly, to call wickedness by its own terms – a fig a fig, and a spade a spade. Now for the rest of my accusation – I pray not for her; I answer, I am not bound to pray for her in this place, for sovereign to me she is not; and I let them know that I am not a man of law, that has my tongue to sell for silver or favour of the world.' He admitted that he had called upon the Deity to confound her and her flatterers. 'I praise my God, He of His mercy has not disappointed me of my just prayer; let them call it imprecation or execration as pleases them. It has after that once stricken, and shall strike, in despite of man; maintain and defend her who list.'

His reply went on and on. His accusers had charged him skilfully with having 'arrogantly entered into God's secret counsel.' The accusation was most bitter and fearful to him, he said, for he had never gone beyond the bounds of God's revealed Word. Whether he should remain and meet their charge, he concluded wearily, 'I know not, for my days and ways are in the hands of Him upon whom I depend, and Who hath guided me through so many troubles, and has yet preserved me to this decrepit age, which now is not apt to fly far.'

He would have been better advised to remain silent, for his tormentors next brought out a second set of charges. *The First Blast* was raked up again. If he had spoken the truth in it, why did he pray for the Queen of England? Knox rose to the bait once more.

But his furies now were beginning to be feared even by himself. 'God grant me patience,' he began despairingly, 'that I may bear the opprobrium of the cross of Jesus Christ.' But the prayer was in vain; presently he was shouting that the framer of the charge was a manifest liar, and after a long and exhausting diatribe he concluded with that vehement protestation which afterwards became so famous: 'What I have been to my country, albeit this unthankful age will not know, yet the ages to come will be compelled to bear witness to the truth. And thus I cease, requiring of all men that have to charge me with anything, that he will do it so plainly as that I make myself and all my doings manifest to the world; for to me it seems a thing most unreasonable that, in this my decrepit age, I shall be compelled to fight against shadows and howlets that dare not abide the light.' After that his accusers left him alone.

But in Edinburgh there was no rest for him. The Hamiltons had joined Grange in the Castle, and the new Regent Lennox, for the time being a Protestant, was talking of a siege. With the people Knox was unpopular, and the streets were filled with Mary's supporters. One night a shot came through the window of his room; it would have hit him if he had been sitting in his accustomed place. His friends set a guard round his house and begged him to leave the town; but he refused. On the 30th of April Kirkcaldy of Grange issued a proclamation that all enemies of the Queen should leave within six hours. Knox still refused. But his friends this time were urgent and Kirkcaldy, who did not wish any harm to come to him, told him that his life was not safe; he must either leave Edinburgh or come into the Castle. Knox decided at last to leave. But before he left Grange and Lethington asked him to go to the Castle for a final interview. Craig and Wynram went with him; they anticipated that some composition of the conflict would be proposed; they were disappointed. They were taken to Lethington's bedroom; Châtelherault was there with Grange; Lethington, who was unwell, sat playing with a dog on his knee. As always, the conference became a duel between him and Knox. The coronation of the King, said Lethington, was only a fetch to save them from greater inconveniences; he had no further use for it. Men of upright and simple dealing, replied Knox, had not thought it a fetch. The old enemies enjoyed themselves and when Knox rose to leave everybody was laughing.

Knox left Edinburgh on the 5th of May for St. Andrews.

CHAPTER XVI

THE END

Not even in St. Andrews, however, did Knox find his needed rest. The town seemed to be full of Hamiltons and relatives of Kirkcaldy of Grange. Only one of the colleges, St. Leonards, was on the King's side. The old man rose to the challenge again. He went about now leaning on the arm of his servant Bannatyne and supporting himself on a stick, but he still preached on Sundays. Some of the Hamiltons were in his congregation; he denounced them as murderers.

The Hamiltons retaliated. Robert went about telling people that Knox himself had once given his hand to a plot to murder Darnley at Perth. Knox wrote asking him to withdraw the accusation, Robert denied that he had ever made it, Bannatyne ran about zealously fanning the flames. Next Archibald Hamilton refused to attend Knox's sermons; he did not like, apparently, to hear his family called murderers. He was summoned to appear and explain his absence before Knox and a committee drawn from the heads of the university. Archibald appeared and said he was grieved to see the pulpit abused so grossly. The university did not chastise him, and Knox issued a protest affirming that no minister, at St. Andrews or elsewhere, should be subject to the jurisdiction of universities. 'It is evident,' he said, 'that universities raised up to defend the Kirk of God have oppressed it; and the malice of Satan is always to be feared.'

During the fifteen months that he remained in St. Andrews the wrangling went on. All Scotland had once been his arena; he had fought with queens and broken them; now he squabbled with petty university authorities, and called down the wrath of God on scandal-mongers. One incident pushed him once more into the main current. Morton was bringing back bishops again, and pocketing the greater part of their benefices. St. Andrews as the old ecclesiastical centre of Scotland was assigned a bishop; Knox refused to inaugurate him, and preached against Morton, who was listening. But this did not satisfy him. The General Assembly was to meet at Perth in the beginning of August. He wrote protesting against the new bishops, and, remembering his feud with the Hamiltons, added a second warning: 'Above all things preserve the Kirk from the bondage of the universities.'

All this time he was scarcely able to move. Sometimes, leaning on Bannatyne's arm, he would walk in the courtyard of St. Leonards and converse with the students, exhorting them to stand by the good cause. On Sundays he had to be lifted up into the pulpit by Bannatyne and another servant. A young student, James Melville, attended his sermons and took notes. 'In the opening up of his text,' that charming diarist wrote, 'he was moderate for the space of a half-hour, but when he entered into the application, he made me so to grue and tremble that I could not hold a pen to write. He behoved to lean at his first entry, but or he had done with his sermon, he was so active and vigorous, that he was like to ding the pulpit in blads and fly out of it.'

In his few letters he mingled violent exhortation with complaints about his bodily weakness and prayers to be released. He denounced 'the traitors and murderers' in Edinburgh Castle, and signed himself 'lying in St. Andrews half-dead.' 'Out of bed, and from my book,' he wrote to Wishart of Pittaro, 'I come not but once in the week, and so few tidings come to me. I see no appearance of right conversion to God, but both the parties stand as it were fighting against God Himself in justification of their wickedness, the murderers assembled in the Castle of Edinburgh and their assisters justifying all they have done to be well and rightly done, and the contrary party as little repenting the troubling and oppressing of the poor Kirk of God as ever they did. Daily looking for an end of my battle,' the astonishing old man went on, 'I have set forth an Answer to a Jesuit, who long hath railed against our religion. Pray the faithful in my name to recommend me to God in their prayers; for my battle is strong, and yet without great corporal pain.'

At the end of July 1572 a truce was concluded between the two parties in Edinburgh, and Knox's old congregation sent for him to return. He was as weary of St. Andrews as it was of him, but he would agree to return only if he were not required to temper his admonitions, or asked to cease thundering against the murderers in the Castle. His congregation replied that he could speak his conscience as he had done so often before.

He travelled by slow and painful stages to Edinburgh, and preached in St. Giles on the last Sunday of August; but his voice was by now so feeble that he could scarcely be heard, and he was given a separate pulpit in a small bay of St. Giles, where, in a voice almost spent, he still called down the curses of God. The congregation looked round them for an assistant. They chose Lawson, sub-principal of Aberdeen University. Knox wrote to him to come that they might confer about heavenly things. 'Haste, lest ye come too late,' he added in a postscript.

About this time the news of the Massacre of St. Bartholomew reached Scotland. Du Croc, the French Ambassador, attended St. Giles the next Sunday. The opportunity could not be lost, and Knox, his voice still audible, asked Du Croc to tell the King of France that he was a murderer, and that God's vengeance would strike him and his descendants. The astonished Du Croc complained to the nobles, they replied that they could not keep the preachers from speaking even against themselves.

On the 9th of November Knox inducted Lawson in a voice that could scarcely be heard and left St. Giles for the last time, his congregation accompanying him from the church to his door. Two days later he had an attack of coughing which left him very weak. On the

Thursday he could not give his daily reading from the Bible, and feeling his end near asked his wife to pay the servants, and gave his own servant a present of twenty shillings. 'Thou wilt never get any more of me in this life,' he said.

On the same day Maitland of Lethington, lying sick in the Castle, sent a bitter complaint against Knox to the Session. Knox, he said, had called him an atheist and an enemy of religion, and had charged him with saying that there was neither a heaven nor a hell, for these were things devised to frighten children. Maitland denied those accusations with horror; he had, he praised God, been brought up from his youth in the fear of God. He begged the Session not to accept every word of Knox as an oracle. They should know, he ended, 'that he is but a man subject to vanity; and that many times does utter his own passions and other men's inordinate affections, in place of true doctrine. It is convenient that, according to the Scriptures, ye believe not every spirit, but try the spirits, whether they be of God or not.'

Coming from Maitland the appeal was extraordinary enough, and coming when it did Knox, hourly expecting his death, might well have ignored it. He could not speak now without great pain. His mind was wandering. On the Friday he got up and prepared to go to the Kirk to preach, thinking it was Sunday. On Sunday he stayed in bed and would not take food, imagining it was the beginning of a fast that had been appointed. Yet next day, at his earnest bidding, the elders and deacons came to see him, and he gave a

long address to them. He had never taught any but
true and sound doctrine; he had menaced the stubborn
with God's judgments, and comforted the troubled
with promises of God's mercy; he had never hated
men, but only their vices and rebellion against God;
he had never made merchandise of the Word. And so,
although he was unworthy and by nature fearful, he
had not feared the faces of men. Then, with an
astonishing change of tone, he took up Lethington's
charge; it seemed that he was not yet able to resist a
stimulus. He pointed to Lethington's works and asked
if these were not a sufficient proof that he denied God
and a heaven and hell where virtue should be rewarded
and vice punished. The reply was in his best casuistical
style, for the question was not whether Lethington
believed these things, but whether he had said them.
The refutation went on. Lethington boasted he had
been piously brought up; so had Julian the Apostate.
Lethington had said that John Knox was subject to
vanity; perhaps he was; yet the things he had said would
be found as true as any of the oracles spoken by the
servants of God before his day, for he knew with
certainty that God would destroy the wicked and cast
them into hell, as might be seen from the ninth Psalm.
The ninth Psalm was read, and he commended the
elders and deacons to God. They went away in tears.

The long effort made him worse. Every day now his
wife and Bannatyne between them read the seventeenth
chapter of St. John to him, the fifty-third of Isaiah,
and a chapter from the Epistle to the Ephesians.
Sometimes as well he asked for Calvin's sermons in

French and the Psalms. He was so feeble that they did not know whether he heard them; and sometimes they imagined he was asleep. 'I hear,' he would say, 'and understand far better.'

His will was still unbroken. While he could speak he continued to denounce 'that damnable house of the Castle of Edinburgh.' The most powerful of the nobles, Morton, soon to be Regent, Lindsay, Ruthven, Glencairn, came to see him, and women came too. On the Friday of the second week he ordered his coffin to be made; he had underestimated his persistence of will. On Sunday afternoon, when everybody was at the sermon, he called to his attendants, 'If any be present, let them come and see the work of God!' He thought he was dying. 'I have been fighting against Satan,' he said, 'who is ever ready to assault; yea, I have fought against spiritual wickedness in heavenly things and have prevailed. I have been in heaven and have possession, and I have tasted of these heavenly joys, where presently I am.' He repeated the Lord's Prayer and added, 'Who can pronounce such holy words?'

Someone asked him if he had any pain. He could not understand for a little. 'I am content, if God please,' he said at last, 'to lie here for seven years.'

Sometimes as he lay, apparently asleep, he would mutter broken sentences, 'Live in Christ!' 'The Kirk!' 'Now, Lord, make an end of the trouble!' His last sermon had been on the death of Christ; while he lay powerless he was meditating on a second one on the resurrection, which was to follow it. He was tempted

297

by the thought that he had prevailed by his own strength, but he conquered the temptation.

Next morning, the 24th, he got up from his bed and put on his hose and doublet, but he was unable to stand, and after sitting for half an hour had to be helped back again. In the middle of the day he asked his wife to read the fifteenth chapter of the First Epistle to the Corinthians, which treats of the resurrection. 'Is not that a comfortable chapter?' he said. A little later he suddenly began: 'Now for the last time I commend my soul, my spirit and body,' counting then on his fingers, 'into Thy hands, O Lord.' But death had not yet come. About four in the afternoon he said to his wife, 'Go read where I cast my first anchor.' She read the seventeenth chapter of St. John, then he asked for Calvin's sermons. At seven they ceased reading, for he seemed to be asleep. The time for evening prayers came, but everybody sat still, thinking he was still sleeping. At half-past ten they knelt down at last. When they rose up someone asked, 'Sir, heard ye the prayers?' He answered, 'I would to God that ye and all men heard them as I have heard them; and I praise God for that heavenly sound.' Then he cried suddenly, 'Now it is come!' and gave a shuddering sigh. Bannatyne sat down by his bed and urged him to remember the comforting promises given in the New Testament. 'And that we may know that ye hear us,' he ended, 'make us some sign.' Knox's will gathered itself together for the last time; he lifted one hand and immediately passed away. It was eleven o'clock at night on the 24th November 1572.

Knox left only a few pounds behind him. His debts were all settled; he had spoken the truth when he said that he had not made merchandise of the Word of God. On the 26th he was buried in St. Giles churchyard. All the nobility in Edinburgh attended the funeral, and Morton, now Regent, pronounced the epitaph. 'Here lies,' he said, 'one who neither flattered nor feared any flesh.' It was a splendid tribute, worthy of the theme, though only half-true.

Thus passed from Scottish history a man who, for almost a generation, had amazed everybody, princes, statesmen, divines, burghers, students and common people alike, by three magnificent qualities: his vehemence, his persistence, and his incorruptibility. The first of these was his distinguishing quality; the others only served to emphasise it. Other great men of action have been vehement and placable, capable of both devouring ardour and repose; what distinguished Knox was the uniformity of his vehemence, his perpetual possession of an extreme ardour. To him the excessive was the normal. He was not, even to his contemporaries, so much a great natural force, like Luther, as a terrible and inexplicable natural portent. It was this that gave his denunciations, drawn appropriately from the terrible arsenal of the Hebrew prophets, their overwhelming force. It was this that made even the hardened Scottish nobles look upon him as an almost supernatural figure. Yet he had not been designed by nature, it seemed, to make peoples tremble. He was of insignificant stature; his health was delicate; his temper at the beginning timid and apprehensive. One-half of his equipment was in keeping with this: his extraordinary adroitness in changing his opinions when it suited him, his almost feminine skill in personal debate, his employment of threatenings, his instinct for and delight in damaging gossip about his enemies, his indefatigable capacity for twisting and turning. The man who in England proclaimed that subjects were bound to obey their prince; who in Dieppe incited subjects to murder their prince; who in Geneva exhorted the faithful in Scotland to depose their prince; who in Dieppe once more declared that the Anabaptists certainly, but the faithful never, would harm their prince; who in Scotland helped to drive one prince after another from the throne while loudly proclaiming his loyalty; who maintained that two brutal murders were admirable in the sight of God, and that a third, less brutal, must be wiped out by the execution of an unfortunate woman who had no direct part in it, and whose guilt could not be proved; who pursued that woman to disgrace and destruction, and yet called another man a murderer because he did not love his enemy: this man was clearly not that model of consistency and strength which history and his biographers have set before us. He was rather a man who, when his object required it, was always ready to contradict himself, and used any means which suited him.

This was one element in Knox, the substratum of weakness from which developed all the qualities which made him unassailable. What was it that transformed a man so timid and apprehensive into a heroic figure? So far as one can tell it was a theory now completely outworn; a belief that before the beginning of the world God had ordained that mankind should be separated into two hosts, the reprobate and the elect; that the elect should prevail, and that after death they should enjoy everlasting bliss; and finally, that it was alike fated that they should fight and that they should win. To embrace this creed was to enrol in an invincible army; to remain outside was destruction. At a crisis in his life Knox found himself a soldier in it. From that time forward his fear and his thirst for power alike made him work to make that army supreme. As its power increased, however, so did his, and it was the Church Triumphant in Geneva that finally turned him into the marvellous instrument which changed the fate of Scotland.

It is easy to point out Knox's faults, and it is impossible to deny their seriousness. He had no sense of justice; what he praised in his friends he condemned in his enemies. He was not sagacious; his wild epistles to England, and his treatment of the young Scottish Queen intensified the calamities which they were intended to avert. He was disingenuous, as all his writings prove. He was vindictive in his unrelenting pursuit of Mary Stuart, he was ruthless towards the Catholics, repeatedly clamouring for their extermination. Normally he was altogether without self-control; he could, however, assume it in an emergency. He was incapable of living in peace; he quarrelled in succession with almost all his friends, with Cranmer, the English at Frankfort, Calvin, Moray, Kirkcaldy, Lethington; he fought in his maturity with queens, and in his dotage with the nonentities of St. Andrews.

His greatness lay in two qualities: the inexhaustible vehemence of his powers, and the constancy of his aim. The effect he had on men less unrelenting was like that of a wind, which blows with a steadfast violence, and by its persistence bends everything and keeps it bent. His will, like the *mistral,* had something in it unnatural and mechanical. It never relaxed, because it could not. It went on, as if independent of him, when his body was powerless, and he was lying on his deathbed; it lived in his last gesture, the hand stubbornly upraised as he gave up his spirit. It had goaded the Scottish nobles to revolt and Mary to shame and destruction: it had not given its possessor a respite for thirteen years. It was cruel and terrible, but it is perhaps the most heroic and astonishing spectacle in all Scottish history.

APPENDIX A

KNOX AND SCOTLAND

'Dost thou ever think to bring thine ears or stomach to the patience of a dry grace as long as thy table-cloth; and droned out, till all the meat on thy board has forgot it was that day in the kitchen? Or to brook the noise made in a question of predestination, by the good labourers and painful eaters assembled together, put to them by the matron your spouse, who moderates with a cup of wine, ever and anon, and a sentence out of Knox between?'

BARTHOLOMEW FAIR.

OF the effect which Knox had upon the destiny of Scotland, as it is past human computation, I have not till now thought of saying anything. But the confidence with which practised and venerated historians have pronounced on it has led me to see that I have been wrong. No historical study is complete, it is evident, without the appropriate concluding generalities. I have thought it wise, however, to transfer them to the comparative obscurity of an appendix.

On this question of the influence of Knox on Scottish history and life I shall first quote a few pronouncements from historians of standing. Carlyle's is perhaps the most noteworthy. According to him the collaborator in the Book of Discipline was the man who set Scotland free. Had he not done his work, the authors of the Essay on Miracles and 'Holy Willie's Prayer' would never have adorned Scottish literature.

My next authority happens to be the author of the Essay on Miracles, and he does not agree with Carlyle. Indeed, writing of Knox's letter to the Catholics from Perth, he observes: 'With these outrageous symptoms commenced in Scotland that hypocrisy and fanaticism which long infected that kingdom, and which, though now mollified by the lenity of the civil power, is still ready to break out on all occasions.' David Hume, then, was quite ungrateful for what Knox had done for him; but he lived in an age when Kirk Sessions were still formidable. Burns' hatred of the Calvinism of his time shows that his judgment was Hume's, not Carlyle's.

I come now to Froude. 'Good reason,' he exclaims, 'has Scotland to be proud of Knox. He only saved the Kirk which he had founded, and saved with it Scottish and English freedom. The Covenanters fought the fight and won the victory, and then, and not till then, came the David Humes with their essays on miracles, and the Adam Smiths with their political economies, and steam-engines, and railroads, and philosophical institutions, and all the other blessed or unblessed fruits of liberty.' All because of Knox and the Covenanters.

Professor Hume Brown, with that generous readiness to attribute everything to everybody which makes him such a likeable writer, gives the total credit for the Reformation to the nobles and then gives it to Knox as well. 'It is clear,' he says, 'that had Knox never left Geneva the revolution with which his name will be forever associated must inevitably have come.' 'Thinkers as wide as the poles apart from him,' he says again, 'have seen in Knox one of the great emancipators of humanity, whose work left undone would irremediably have injured the highest interests not only of his own country but of the community of civilized nations.' Professor Hume Brown, it will be seen, is more vague, if more impressive, than the others; Knox is not credited with Hume, Adam Smith, Burns and the steam-engine, he is not even credited completely with the Reformation, but only with advancing certain 'highest interests,' which remain unspecified.

In learning and historic method I make no pretence of rivalry with these great authorities. But applying ordinary critical tests it seems to me that the testimony of Hume is more valuable than the rest, seeing, to begin with, that he lived most of his life in Scotland, and secondly, that he lived at a period when Calvinism was still powerful. Again, without going into the recondite question of the steam-engine, there seem to be certain developments and phases of Scottish life which may not unreasonably be traced to Knox. Among these are his tradition of denunciation and his habit of prophecy. The first, I am convinced from experience, is still a feature of Scottish life; the second was carried on and developed richly by the Covenanters. The Covenanters, their work done, are now, thank God, dead and buried. But I shall resuscitate one of them for a moment and show two of the results of the Knoxian tradition of eloquence. The first is from a sermon of Sandy Peden, the prophet. 'There are four or five things I have to tell you this night. First, a bloody sword, a bloody sword, a bloody sword for thee, O Scotland, that shall pierce the hearts of many. Secondly, many miles shall ye travel, and see nothing but desolation and ruinous wastes in thee, O Scotland. Thirdly, the most fertile places in thee shall be as waste as the mountains. Fourthly, the women with child shall be ript up and dashed to pieces.' And so on. The second is from a particular prophecy by the same ornament of the Covenant. Sandy would be buried, he himself foretold, and dug up again; and the man who first touched his corpse would suffer the following mishaps: 'First, he would get a great fall from a house. Secondly, he would fall into adultery. Thirdly, in theft, and for that he should leave the land. Fourthly, make a melancholy end abroad for murder.' 'All which came to pass,' the pious biographer adds. It seems to me that in both these prophecies the note of Knox may be heard, amplified and richened, it is true, by the hand of an artist.

Another thing which may be reasonably attributed to Knox is the Kirk Session. To describe the sordid and general tyranny which this fearful institution wielded for over two hundred years would be wearisome and would take too long. It is only necessary to say that the time-honoured Scottish tradition of fornication triumphantly survived all its terrors.

As for the more general effects of Calvinism in Scotland, who can compute them? Knox's religion, it is probable, stiffened the independent political spirit of the people, if with the other hand it imposed a spiritual and moral tyranny.

But here I shall accept the almost unanimous opinion of the historians, for it is unlikely that they should all be wrong. Their opinion briefly is that Knox, the reformers, and the Covenanters have made Scotland what it is; and they give the chief credit to Knox himself. Now if this is true, Knox's influence would be most clearly seen in the hundred years or so after his death. What did Calvinist Scotland produce during that time? In politics a long and wearisome series of civil conflicts; in theology 'The Causes of the Lord's Wrath,' 'The Poor Man's Cup of Cold Water ministered to the Saints and Sufferers for Christ in Scotland,' and 'Lex, Rex'; in literature the charming diary of James Melville, the letters of Samuel Rutherford with their queer mixture of religious feeling and Freudian symbolism, and the Scottish version of the psalms; in philosophy, profane poetry, the drama, music, painting, architecture, nothing. Whatever was done in literature during this time came from the opponents of Calvinism or from men out of sympathy with it; Drummond of Hawthornden's poetry and his still nobler prose work, *A Cypress Grove*, some fine verses by Montrose, and Sir Thomas Urquhart's great translation of Rabelais. Yet, during the same hundred years the nearest-lying country could show Shakespeare, Spenser, Jonson, Marlowe, Donne, Milton, in poetry and the drama; Bacon, Hooker, Browne, Taylor, Clarendon, in prose; the beginnings of modern science; and music, architecture, philosophy, theology, oratory in abundance. Was it the influence of Calvinism which preserved Scotland from that infection? There are reasonable grounds, I think, for believing so. Calvinism, in the first place, was a faith which insisted with exclusive force on certain human interests, and banned all the rest. It lopped off from religion music, painting and sculpture, and pruned architecture to a minimum; it frowned on all prose and poetry which was not sacred. For its imaginative literature it was confined more and more to the Old Testament, and though the Old Testament contains some splendid poetry, it has at all times been over-praised at the expense of greater works. Calvinism, in short, was a narrowly specialized kind of religion, but it was also a peculiar religion – a religion which outraged the imagination, and no doubt helped, therefore, to produce that captivity of the imagination in Scotland which was only broken in the eighteenth century. For this religion laid down that God had elected certain men for His approval from the beginning of time, and it was impossible to believe that His choice showed discrimination. Looking down on the island of Great Britain in the century which followed Knox's death, the Almighty, it seemed, had rejected Shakespeare, Spenser, and Donne, and chosen Andrew Melville, Donald Cargill and Sandy Peden. And if

His choice was restricted to the godly, it was equally
strange, for He liked the translators of the Scots
version of the Psalms, and rejected Herbert, Vaughan,
and Crashaw. Passing over the cacophonous:

> I saw Eternity the other night,
> Like a great ring of pure and endless light,
> All calm, as it was bright,

He listened with rapture to the more truly Calvinistic
music of

> But loved be God which doth us safely keep,
> From bloody teeth and their most cruel voice,
> Which as a prey to eat us would rejoice.

This, then, was the strange belief which prevailed
in Scotland for so long as a consequence, if the
historians are right, of Knox's labours. How could
the country have avoided its fate of becoming for over
a century an object-lesson in savage provincialism?
Hume, Burns, and men like them, it is true, lifted it
from its isolation for a time during the next hundred
years.

What Knox really did was to rob Scotland of all the
benefits of the Renaissance. Scotland never enjoyed
these as England did, and no doubt the lack of that
immense advantage has had a permanent effect. It
can be felt, I imagine, even at the present day.

APPENDIX B

BIOGRAPHICAL

As in this biography I have had sometimes to choose between conflicting accounts of Knox's life, the alternatives I have rejected may as well be indicated here, and my reasons for their rejection. Knox's birth year was for a long time taken to be 1505, on the rather belated authority of Spottiswoode's *History of the Church in Scotland*. In 1895, however, Professor Hume Brown gave in his Life a letter from Peter Brown, later a tutor of James VI, in which it was stated that Knox died in his fifty-ninth year. For some reason Professor Hume Brown did not draw the consequences, but Dr. Hay Fleming repaired the omission and pointed out that, if Young was right, the birth year must have been approximately 1513-15. Andrew Lang in his *John Knox and the Reformation* tacitly accepted the new date; it appeared 'to fit in better with the deeds of the reformer.' With all deference to the historical learning of Dr. Hay Fleming and Lang, which is much greater than I can pretend to, I find it difficult to believe this. The justification for the alternative date is one letter, the justification for the original one is a tradition, and there is little to choose between them. But the tone of Knox's letters to Mrs.

Bowes during his stay in England (1549-54) seems to me credible enough in a man of 44 to 49, but quite unlike that of a man of 34 to 39, or alternately 36 to 41. Again, the letters of his last two years, complaining of his decrepit age, must surely sound very strange, coming from a man of 57. There is another faint hint which supports my argument, I think. Knox married his second wife in 1564; if he was born in 1513-15, he was then somewhere between 48 and 51, yet he is called by a Catholic writer 'an old decrepit priest.' But it is not these isolated facts merely, it is the whole tone of Knox's utterances at different stages of his life which has determined me to remain by the original date.

If Dr. Hay Fleming's date were accepted, however, an alternative version of Knox's problematical early life would follow. He would probably have gone straight to St. Andrews, not to Glasgow and then St. Andrews. His bondage to the Roman Catholic Church would have been shorter, he would have embraced the reformed faith earlier, and so on.

Certain stories about Knox's early life I have rejected altogether. They come mostly from Archibald Hamilton, the Archibald with whom the old reformer had such a savage feud in St. Andrews. Hamilton later became a Catholic, and his evidence is to be discounted for theological as well as personal reasons. His story briefly was that Knox was distinguished as a young man by his licentiousness; that he had always three whores at his heels; and that, moreover, he committed adultery with his step-mother. Knox's faults were grievous enough, but these do not fit in with them.

There is finally the question whether or not Knox had any hand in the Rizzio murder. The evidence that he had is once more contained in one letter from Randolph to Cecil. In this letter Randolph gives a list of the accomplices of the murderers, and another marked 'all at the death of Davy and privy thereunto.' At the bottom of this is written 'John Knox, John Craig, preachers.' It has been adduced as a confirmation of Knox's guilt that he fled from Edinburgh on the same day as the murderers. But then why did Craig remain behind, as he did? The natural explanation is that Knox had reason to fear Mary and that Craig had none. Moreover, among the seventy odd names of people summoned for the murder, neither that of Knox nor that of Craig appears. Knox approved of the murder, as we have seen, but the balance of probabilities is against his having taken part, even indirectly, in it.

INDEX

INDEX

314

INDEX

315

INDEX